# Crisis Management by Apology

## Corporate Response to Allegations of Wrongdoing

## LEA's COMMUNICATION SERIES
*Jennings Bryant/Dolf Zillmann, General Editors*

For a complete list of titles in LEA's Communication Series, please contact Lawrence Erlbaum Associates, Publishers at www.erlbaum.com.

# Crisis Management by Apology

## Corporate Response to Allegations of Wrongdoing

Keith Michael Hearit
*Western Michigan University*

LAWRENCE ERLBAUM ASSOCIATES, PUBLISHERS
2006    Mahwah, New Jersey                    London

Lawrence Erlbaum Associates, Inc., Publishers
10 Industrial Avenue
Mahwah, New Jersey 07430
www.erlbaum.com

Cover design by Kathryn Houghtaling Lacey

**Library of Congress Cataloging-in-Publication Data**

Hearit, Keith Michael.
  Crisis management by apology: corporate response to allegations of
  wrongdoing / Keith Michael Hearit.
      p.  cm—(LEA's communication series)
  Includes bibliographical references and index.
ISBN 0-8058-3788-4 (c: alk. paper)—ISBN 0-8058-3789-2 (alk. paper)
1. Corporate image.  2. Crisis management.  3. Apologizing.  4. Cor-
  porations—Public relations.  5. Business communication.  I. Title.
  II. Series.
HD59.2.H43 2005
659.2—dc22                                              20050740114
                                                              CIP

Books published by Lawrence Erlbaum Associates are printed on acid-
free paper, and their bindings are chosen for strength and durability.

Printed in the United States of America
10  9  8  7  6  5  4  3  2  1

# Contents

# Preface

Whether it is a president who must apologize to the nation, a company that has developed a product that has caused a grievous harm, or a celebrity trying to repair a damaged image, apologia and apologies are frequently in the news.

The study of apologetic crisis management, particularly from the perspective taken here, is one that views most crises to be self-generated. This book has grown out of a desire to account for the many ways individuals, organizations, and institutions try to "save face" as they seek to extricate themselves from difficult straights. Although this text tries not to feature only corporations and their crisis management, it does note that the hegemonic effect of for-profit corporations on crisis discourse is nothing short of dramatic.

The guiding assumption taken here is that crisis researchers are wise to pay particularly close attention to the language used by those who would extricate themselves from their wrongdoing—to try to uncover the lexicon of the lie. As a result, this book takes an unabashedly rhetorical approach to the study of crisis management, and specifically examines that genre of crises whereby individuals and organizations are believed to be guilty of an offense and have to enter into the public confessional in order to repair their damaged reputations.

The need for close attention to the nature of language used by apologists is evident even in the two major terms of this study: *apologia* and *apology*. *Apologia* refers to the act of giving a defense, whereas *apology* typically means the offering of a mea culpa. Yet, even here, the confusion as to the difference between apologiae and apologies has tremendous rhetorical benefit for an apologist. Discerning parties that face criticism often capitalize on this ambiguity by offering an apologia that sounds like an apology: Auditors are then placated by the rhetor's apparent act of contrition.

Two other comments are needed. First, the references at the beginning of each chapter to Scripture are by design, and are rooted in Kenneth Burke's writings, especially his book *The Rhetoric of Religion* (1970), in that religious terminology offers a helpful entrance into the common language and scripts that human actors use as a vehicle to situate their actions. Second, when possible, this book uses *The New York Times* as a primary source for public statements on the part of apologists. This is intentional for two reasons. First, the *Times* is the United States' "newspaper of record." As such, it is viewed as a highly credible if not authoritative source (although one not without imperfections). Second, the *Times* also has been shown to have a significant effect on subsequent broadcast and newspaper coverage (Batulis, 1976; Beniger & Westney, 1981; Charles, Shore, & Todd, 1979). As such, this book has emphasized the public statements of apologists in the *Times* with the idea that they are the statements likely to be mediated by journalists throughout the nation.

## ACKNOWLEDGMENTS

I would be remiss if I did not thank the many people who played a role in the publication of this book. In particular, I wish to thank those who helped in the collection of data and research materials: Jennifer Brown, Candace Dixon, and especially Lauren Teal. To my colleague Sandra Borden, I especially thank you for your help in developing the role of ethics in the apologetic exchange as well as your participation in writing chapter 4. To my department chair, Steve Rhodes, thanks for all your support and encouragement. Finally, I would like to say a note of thanks to a number of friends for their encouragement at critical times in the writing of this book: Dan Darnley, for your confident assurance that this project would be completed; Joe and Rudy, for a quiet place to write; and Matt Seeger, whose interest and encouragement in this project were immeasurable. Finally, I wish to thank my editor, Linda Bathgate, for her indefatigable support, copyeditor Gale Miller, as well as senior production editor Providence Rao and the entire LEA staff for their work in bringing this book to publication.

Last, I would like to thank my family, to whom I dedicate this work. Without your support, this project would never have reached completion. You are the reason why I go to work and come home every day.

—*Keith Hearit*
*November 2004*

# About the Author

Keith Michael Hearit is an associate professor of communication and director of undergraduate studies at Western Michigan University. Professor Hearit teaches courses in organizational communication, public relations, corporate advocacy, and crisis management. His research focuses on noncommercial forms of external organizational communication by corporations, particularly in those instances when companies are accused of wrongdoing. He has published articles in the *Handbook of Public Relations, Communication Studies*, and *Public Relations Review*, as well as contributed chapters in a number of edited books. Hearit is active in the National Communication Association, Association for Journalism and Mass Communication Education, and the Central States Communication Association. He received his doctoral degree in Public Affairs and Issue Management from Purdue University.

# About the Contributor

Sandra L. Borden is an associate professor of communication at Western Michigan University, where she also is codirector of the Center for the Study of Ethics in Society. Borden's research in media ethics has been published in *Communication Monographs, The Journal of Mass Media Ethics, the Journal of Communication Inquiry, The International Journal of Applied Philosophy*, and *Southern Communication Journal*. She also is a contributor to two edited books on journalism and professional ethics. Borden is active in the Association for Education in Journalism and Mass Communication and the Association for Practical and Professional Ethics. Borden, a former newspaper journalist, has a PhD in mass communications from Indiana University and a MA in journalism from The Ohio State University.

# 1

# Introduction

But the LORD God called to the man, "Where are you?"

He answered, "I heard you in the garden, and I was afraid because I was naked; so I hid."

And he said, "Who told you that you were naked? Have you eaten from the tree that I commanded you not to eat from?"

The man said, "The woman *you* put here with me—*she* gave me some fruit from the tree, and I ate it."

Then the LORD God said to the woman, "What is this that you have done?"

The woman said, "The *serpent* deceived me, and I ate."

Genesis 3:9–13 (*The Holy Bible*, 1973/1984; emphasis added)

## INTRODUCTION: A TALE OF TWO CRISES

The propensity to justify one's behavior is a compulsion that has roots in humanity's earliest days. Contemporary times appear to be no different. Individuals, organizations, and institutions act and react, and use communication in order to present themselves in a favorable light. This impulse is particularly true when people are facing crisis management situations—situations that often occur because of people's own misdeeds.

Subsequently, a central theme of much crisis management research is that organizations are wise to monitor their environments for the emergence of triggering events that may plunge them into a crisis (Barton, 1993; Mitroff & Kilmann, 1984; Seeger, Sellnow, & Ulmer, 1998). Certainly, the most oft-cited incident to illustrate this point is the case of Johnson & Johnson's Tylenol, the victim of a psychopath who laced the popular pain reliever with cyanide. Indeed, the case is so familiar and frequently intimated that it alternately has been labeled the "paradigm case" (Berg & Robb, 1992) and the "gold standard" (Murray & Shohen, 1992). Yet, if Tylenol is the standard by which crisis management efforts are measured, the Exxon Corporation, after its accidental discharge of oil into Prince William Sound, has become the paradigm case of what *not* to do in a crisis (Hearit, 1995; Murray & Shohen, 1992; Sellnow, 1993; Small, 1991; Williams & Treadaway, 1992). From the bumbling CEO who did not go to the scene of the accident to the misguided attempts to scapegoat a captain by leaking the story of his alcohol problems to *The New York Times* (Egan, 1989), critics have excoriated and pilloried the company. Yet, what at root differentiates these two cases is not that Johnson & Johnson was led by an astute crisis management team and that Exxon was not (although an arguable case may be made); rather, the primary difference between the two cases is that Exxon was the guilty *agent* responsible for despoiling the environment whereas Johnson & Johnson was the *victim* of a consumer terrorist.

Contrary to popular belief, most crises are not the result of an external psychopath but instead are *self*-generated, the result of internal screwups on the part of companies. Whether it be a product that is defective and causes egregious harm to people, an illegal scheme concocted on the part of the senior officers of an organization, or an accident that results in the loss of life, organizations are more often than not the victims of their own misdeeds. Undeniably, given the complex nature of organizations as well as the difficulty of locating responsibility for managerial decisions, crises of a company's own making, rather than being random and sporadic, are an inevitable and "normal" part of organizational life (Jackall, 1997; Perrow, 1984). This chapter seeks to introduce the concepts of apologia and apology; chart the concomitant rise of the modern organization, with its discursive status; and account for the proliferation of corporate apologiae.

## APOLOGIA AND APOLOGY

The necessity to extricate oneself from an unfavorable circumstance is one of the oldest compulsions of the human condition. Rooted in the problem of guilt (real or perceived; Burke, 1984), the speech of defense, or *apologia*, has always been a response to this predicament, whether the defense was by the aforementioned Adam and Eve, who shifted the blame for their rebellious acts; President Bill Clinton, who insisted that he had no "improper" relationship with a White House intern; or the juicemaker Odwalla, which in 1996 acknowledged "responsibility" for the presence of *E. coli* in its juice (Rawson & Thomsen, 1998). Simply put, these corporate advocates, most often due to the obdurate nature of their own actions, faced criticism that almost required them to offer a verbal or written defense in order to clean up their tarnished images (Bitzer, 1968). The need to engage in facework is central to human nature; indeed, it is not a large leap to define human beings as a *Homo Apologist/Confessor* (Foucault, 1980, p. 59).

When responding to criticism, these corporate advocates have at their disposal a wide variety of potential responses. Some apologists deny charges and, while doing so, claim that they have been made a target by media. Others attempt to explain away their guilt by scapegoating or blaming another party. Still others, in a turn of honesty, acknowledge their responsibility and seek forgiveness. Whatever the response, these individuals and organizations use their communication strategically and have as their motive the desire to rebut the criticisms leveled against them and purify their damaged images (Benoit, 1995; Fisher, 1970).

Historically, the study of apologia has primarily been concerned with individuals accused of wrongdoing who seek to clear their names (Ware & Linkugel, 1973). Early analyses focused on political figures (Harrell, Ware, & Linkugel, 1975; Rosenfield, 1968), leaders of religious and social movements (Ryan, 1982; Ware & Linkugel, 1973), and other orators who used a speech to defend their integrity (Downey, 1993; Hoover, 1989). Yet, with the advent and rise of the modern organization, the nature and source of apologetic discourse has changed (Crable, 1986, 1990; Dionisopoulos & Vibbert, 1983; Sproule, 1988). Rather than just emanating from individuals caught in a wrong, parties as diverse as politicians, sports figures, entertainers, businesses, not-for-profit organizations, institutions, and governments now face daily criticism to which they must defend their actions or face damage to their carefully constructed images and the loss of consumer confidence and patronage.

It is my position that all of these individuals and institutions are examples of corporate advocacy. By *corporate advocacy* I do not mean the "persuasion of corporations"; rather, I use the term to mean "organized groups of people who act in concert." In this way, an apologia delivered by a star athlete is a form of corporate apologia in the same way as that crafted by a company—both are organized attempts at persuasion that constitute a form of a dramatic production, because both the individual and the corporate official are likely to follow a script written for them by a team of agents, lawyers, and media handlers. Although this book does feature corporations as a primary focus of theory and analysis (e.g., in terms of the role of liability), I consider individuals, organizations, and institutions as part of the scope of corporate apologetic studies, in that all three forms of agents represent attempts at organized persuasion in response to vocal criticism. It is the substance of these responses that serve as the focus of this book.

Some might respond that good public relations takes a proactive approach to problems and that a book on the topic of apologia has an undue emphasis on a reactive form of public relations—strategies for "getting the horse back in the barn" after it has escaped. In response to such a position, I would make a number of observations. First, such a criticism is not unique to apologia but can also be leveled against crisis management theory as a whole, an area that has witnessed a considerable amount of scholarly in-quiry of late (Albrecht, 1996; Coombs, 1999; Rouland & Jerome, 2004; Seeger et al., 1998, 2003). Apologia studies represent a critical subset of crisis management and, as such, warrant critical exploration on its own. Second is the point that public relations officers admonish corporate man-agers to consider the ethical dimensions of their decisions and behaviors, yet said managers do not always comply with this counsel. This book fo-cuses on those times in which organizations do not follow public relations' counsel and, as a result, face messes of their own making. Finally, given that organizations operate in a polyarchic context (Zald, 1978)—a com-plex economic and political system within a multifaceted mediated envi-ronment—no matter how ethically pure the motives, there is an inevitability that an individual or an organization's actions are likely to of-fend someone or some group. Hence, a knowledge of how to respond apol-ogetically is both reasonable and necessary.

## Key Terms

When one considers the term *apologia*, the first inclination may be to con-fuse it with *apology*; yet, the two terms could not be more different in their implications. *Apologia*, taken from the Greek word *apologia* (Gk. *apo*, away off, absolve; *logia*, speech), means "defense" or "speech in defense" (Moulton, 1978, pp. 40, 45; Simpson & Weiner, 1989, p. 533; Tavuchis, 1991, p. 14; Thayer, 1889, p. 65); similarly, the verb *apologeomai* means to "speak so as to absolve one's self" (Thayer, 1889, p. 65). *Apology* is a newer term that, conversely, has just the opposite connotation. In common us-age, to apologize is "[t]o acknowledge and express regret for a fault *without defence* ..." (Simpson & Weiner, 1989, p. 533, emphasis added). In other words, apologies acknowledge guilt and present the accused as defense-less; apologiae may express concern yet more typically offer a vigorous counteroffensive.

Such a distinction is not to suggest that *apology* is the antonym of *apologia*; their roots are similar enough to allow for considerable overlap. Rather, as I use the terms here, *apologia* is a broad term that means to respond to organi-zational criticism by offering a vigorous and compelling defense. This re-sponse may be a defense that denies the validity of charges, such as when General Motors responded to criticisms that its C/K trucks were unsafe in side-impact collisions; it may feature an acknowledgment of some responsi-bility while attempting to scapegoat its employees, such as the Toshiba Cor-poration did after it was revealed one of its subsidiaries had sold top-secret technologies to the then-Soviet Union; or it may include a response that is primarily an apology, such as American Airlines did after its pilots staged a "sickout" and the company was forced to cancel an unusually large number of flights (Hearit, 1994, 1995b, 1996, 2001). All of these have as their motive the same outcome: the restoration of the corporations' damaged images. In some instances, that may warrant a forceful defense; in others, a prostrate apology. Hence, "[a]n 'apologia' is not an apology (although it *may* contain one), but a defense that seeks to present a compelling, counter description of organizational actions" (Hearit, 1994, p. 115).

Central to this "counter description" of an apologetic response is the use of a persuasive narrative that attempts to alter the interpretation of the alleged act. This understanding is consistent with the etymological origins of *apologia,* which include the idea of a "story," in much the same manner in which lawyers for a defendant construct a narrative that accounts for the evidence (Partridge, 1958). As such, apologiae are persuasive stories that encompass and make use of excuses, which according to Snyder, Higgins, and Stucky (1983) are explanations that try to palliate behavior; and accounts, which, from Scott and Lyman (1968), are explanations that attempt to situate behavior. "Successful" apologiae, then, are primarily good stories that auditors find believable due to their plausible accounting of the "facts" (Benoit, 1995; Hearit, 1994, 2001).

Apologiae are responses to public criticism—criticism that most frequently, although not always, has an ethical dimension. These accusations often are described as a *kategoria,* a transliteration of the Greek word that means "to charge" (Ryan, 1982). Although Ware and Linkugel (1973) defined an apologia as a speech made in defense of character, Ryan argued that the historical usage of apologia includes both ethical and policy defenses. For my purposes, to draw a distinction between character and policy as it relates to corporations is of little critical value. Organizational policies are an expression of character, and character is but a reflection of policy: Both have an effect on the public image of organizations. Kruse (1981a) observed that the key in any apologetic analysis is that charges have been made that warrant a response.

## A Communicative Approach to Behavioral Misdeeds

Although some individuals and companies are victims of disgruntled consumers or employees, or face unjustified criticism, it is important to recognize that most public relations problems that individuals and organizations face are due to organizational *misbehavior.* For example, an aging oil tanker is caught in a terrible storm and breaks up, causing an egregious spill. A chain restaurant fails to cook ground beef thoroughly enough to destroy *E. coli* bacteria, resulting in the deaths of a number of children (Ulmer & Sellnow, 2000). Or a corrupt executive lives a lavish lifestyle at a not-for-profit's expense. Indeed, organizations are considered legitimate when their *behaviors* are congruent with the values of the social system in which they operate

(Dowling & Pfeffer, 1975). Yet, the achievement of legitimacy, rooted in corporate behavior, nonetheless has a fundamentally communicative dimension to it. Dowling and Pfeffer (1975) acknowledged the point when they asserted that a key component of legitimacy occurs when organizations use "communication to become identified with symbols, values, or institutions which have a strong base of social legitimacy" (p. 127).

As a result, this book takes as a guiding assumption that organizational *discourse* is a corporate resource—just like "men, money, and machines"—that can be marshaled to "resolve" organizational problems. Such a proposition has two important implications: one communicative and another managerial. Communicatively, this proposition argues that the use of communication in public relations is not just "spin control" on individual or company acts; rather, it means that social reality is constructed primarily through language (Berger & Luckmann, 1967; Orr, 1978), and the names and terms proffered to describe organizational actions can and do have a tangible effect on how they are experienced by consumers and how issues and crises are resolved.

Public relations problems come into a mediated existence when someone "makes an issue" of the difficulty. In this way, issues are distinctively communicative creations, borne out through the media, and the primary resolution to these issues is communicative in nature (Crable & Vibbert, 1985). Once these actions are committed, they become public relations issues when media workers report on them and they subsequently function as a "currency" of discussion. Hence, what this communication approach argues is that the behaviors and activities of organizations, once committed, enter into a symbolic world in which public comment is made, and hence the ongoing process becomes one of arguing over definitions, evidence, proof, and what such an act "means" (Schiappa, 2003). Was such an organizational act, for example, a "mistake," an "accident," an "egregious error," or an "example of a systematic desire to despoil the environment?"

Even the aforementioned case of Tylenol bears this out; early in the crisis, corporate officer James Burke justified the decision to withdraw capsules from the market with the statement, "[W]e cannot control random tampering with capsules after they leave our plant" (McFadden, 1986, p. A1), and offered a $100,000 reward for information about the source of the crime (Murray & Shohen, 1992). These symbolic statements positioned the company as the victim of "consumer terrorism," which created a reality that sought an external villain (Benson, 1988). Does not the later introduction of "tamper-proof packaging" tacitly admit that the company is responsible to provide for the safety of its consumers and that the previous packaging was less than safe? This example shows that rather than just being a deceptive mask for harsh organizational acts (e.g., when a company uses the term *rightsizing* when in reality it is firing or laying off employees), the use of language does affect how actions are interpreted and experienced. As it relates to this study, attention to the symbolic, ritual, and temporal factors can and does have a tangible impact on the quality of the corporate response to criticism.

Such a primary emphasis on the role of corporate discourse has important managerial implications as well. In referencing the oft-quoted cliché of organizational resources being "men, money, and machines," this book recognizes the critical role of the management of organizational resources in guiding the strategic decision making of an organization. Yet, in asserting that organizational discourse is an organizational resource, it argues for an elevation of the public relations function, for, in so doing, it argues that a fixation on capital, technological, and human resources overlooks a critical component in an organization's strategic mix—the ability to utilize the public relations function in order to bring about strategic/marketplace advantage (Cutlip, Center, & Broom, 2002).

An organization can marshal its discourse as a vehicle by which to gain strategic, political, or marketplace advantage in order to bring gain to a company. This can be seen in the communication efforts in support of President George W. Bush's proposal to allow workers to invest a portion of their social security tax in a stock market account, or in recent efforts by the Insurance Information Institute to argue for a "lawsuit crisis" to which they recommended a number of policy "reforms" that should be enacted (Vibbert & Bostdorff, 1992). The elevation of the public relations function should not be thought of only in a positive, market-expanding context; the opposite is true as well. When organizations make crucial missteps, such as when they face a crisis, it is the role of public relations—particularly in the form of external organizational communication, acting as a management function—that allows an organization to extricate itself from a crisis. Other ways, for example, that demonstrate the public relations role in this approach include the frequent decisions to offer compensation in institutional apologies, the attempts to navigate the liability issues that organizations face in a crisis, as well as the emphasis on ethical decision making during a crisis.

Perhaps Grunig and Hunt (1984) put it best when teasing out the relationship between communication and behavior:

> Communication is a behavior of individuals, groups, or organizations. People communicate when they move messages to or from other people. Public relations professionals communicate not just for themselves, however. They manage, plan, and execute communication for the organization as a whole. They manage the movement of messages into the organization, for example, when conducting research on the knowledge, attitudes, and behaviors of publics and then using that information to counsel mangers on organizational policies or actions. They may manage the movement of a

message out of the organization when they help management decide how to explain a policy or action to the public and then write a news story or fact sheet to explain the policy or action. (p. 6)

Following Austin (1979), this book takes as its central purpose the examination of the "common stock of words [that] embodies all the distinctions men have found worth drawing, and the connexions they have found worth making, in the lifetimes of many generations ..." (Austin, 1979, p. 182), in order to arrive at an understanding of how corporate apologists frame their communicative responses to criticism. In particular, this book seeks to examine the many variations that characterize this form of speech, and to address the options and choices available to apologists in their attempt to deal with the problem of their guilt. (For more on the linguistic approaches to the study of apology championed by Austin, see Scher & Darley, 1997; Sugimoto, 1999; Tannen, 1996, 1998.)

## THE RISE OF THE MODERN ORGANIZATION

### Congregation

The 20th century witnessed an (r)evolution in terms of the speech making of its citizenry; in particular, although there are still legions of individuals who use discourse to persuade—be they politicians or social agitators—more and more persuasion has become a corporate act (Crable, 1986, 1990; Sproule, 1988). Although there always has been congregation of some sort or another (Burke, 1973), American culture has entered an organizational age best characterized by William Whyte's eponymous "organizational man" (Whyte, 1956). Not just congregation, but "hyper-congregation," characterizes this organization-driven society, one in which individuals' identity results from an amalgam of their memberships (Cheney, 1991). Would-be "organizational men and women" do not hesitate in the least to trade part of their own personal identity for the benefits they receive from membership in the modern organization (Burke, 1984). This affiliative identification is not just sought after by (potential) employees; consumers readily purchase brands because of the status a company's name confers on them. In short, contemporary society has become an "organizational society" (Boulding, 1978), defined by its memberships in ever-more (perceived to be) exclusive clubs. Even the aforementioned politicians have teams of speech writers, and the social agitators of note exist because they lead large-scale organizations and movements. In short, Western culture has created an eponymous society, one in which social identity is composed of the many organizations to which its residents belong.

## The Modern Organization as Social Actor

Concurrent with the evolution of Western culture to an organizational one, the modern organization has become a social actor, and is, by extension, a fictive creature. On a de facto, day-to-day level, society tends to treat corporations as individuals, and although they are recognized to consist of large numbers of people, their acts nonetheless are viewed to have a *singular* quality to them. This creates a situation analogous to the book of Genesis (6:1–2) in which the author noted that "giants" roamed the earth; although they had anthropomorphic characteristics their nature appears to have transcended the station of mere humanity.

*Political and Economic Status.*    A number of factors contribute to this conclusion. For one, corporations have considerable political and economic resources that individuals do not possess. Through a favorable tax code, the freedom to lobby Congress, and regulatory agencies such as the FCC that come to promote corporate interests over consumers, corporations accrue large amounts of political and economic clout and become important players in these arenas. Concomitantly, many *Forbes* 500 companies have balance sheets larger than the gross domestic product (GDP) of many developing and *developed* countries. General Electric, for example—the largest corporation in the world in 2003, with 312,500 employees—reported net profits of $15,133 million ($15 billion) and overall company assets at $575,244 million ($575 billion); Citigroup, second on the list, reported profits of $14,606 million ($14.6 billion) and assets of $1,097,190 million ($1 trillion; "The *Forbes* 500s," 2003).

*Legal Status.*    Attendant with this political and economic status, corporations also have a legal status that although different than the traditional conception of a "natural person" (Coleman, 1974; Heath, 1997) nonetheless has the effect of treating organizations as having a distinct social persona. Before the law, corporations are "juristic persons" (as are churches, trade associations, and labor unions), nonpersonal entities that nevertheless have many of the same legal rights as individuals (Coleman, 1974). Like individuals, corporations can own property and sue. Although they lack some of the protections that individuals have (such as the Fifth Amendment and a right to privacy), corporations do have legal protections that natural persons do not, because juristic persons cannot be put in jail; neither can a single corporation be charged with conspiracy, because a juristic person cannot conspire within itself (Middleton & Chamberlin, 1988). Indeed, the tendency of the law is to treat organizations as singularly distinct in that legal thought has a historical tendency to treat a corporation as an individual (Millon, 2001).

*Discursive Status.*    In analyzing organizations as social actors it is important to recognize that organizations "speak" in much the same way as individuals (Cheney, 1992). Newspapers regularly use synecdoche in a singular tense that furthers this extraordinary quality; they report, for example, that "Toyota denied ..." or "DaimlerChrysler announced ...." This organizational voice, which reflects the persona that emanates from the cultural identity of the corporation, is distinct from that of the individual members (Black, 1970). Opinions that organizations take on issues are *not* solely those of upper-level management or public relations officers; rather, the positions are those of the organization as an entity in itself (Namenwith, Miller, & Weber, 1981).

Most germane to the point of this book, and highly suggestive of the individual rights of persons, is the fact that the modern organization also has free speech rights. In the case *First National Bank of Boston, et al. v. Bellotti, Attorney General of Massachusetts* (1978), the U.S. Supreme Court ruled that speech that is otherwise protected (i.e., political speech) does *not* lose its protection because it emanates from a corporate source (Vibbert, 1990). This ruling, more than any other, extended to corporations free speech rights similar to those of individuals (Vibbert, 1990). Although Justice Marshall wrote in 1819 that a corporation is a "mere creature of law" and possesses "only those properties which the charter of creation confers upon it" (*Trustees of Dartmouth College v. Woodward*, 1819, p. 636), there seems to be little desire on the part of the courts to limit their free speech rights. As such, corporations, with their considerable resources, not only have the right to advertise products but enjoy the right to speak out when they believe it to be in their best interests, such as when they are criticized, be it rightly or wrongly. It is in these cases that they can marshal their considerable resources in the defense of their organizational image.

## Personae, Masks, and Social Drama

The fact that organizations have an identifiable image is the final point that needs to be made in locating organizations as social actors (Boorstin, 1961; Boulding, 1956; Cheney & Vibbert, 1987, Fisher, 1970). Following Grunig (1992b) and Williams and Moffitt (1997), this book asserts that *image* is an umbrella term used to describe a receiver-based interpretation that people make about organizations based on individuals' intermittent past experiences with an organization (Boorstin, 1961; Boulding, 1956; Cheney & Vibbert, 1987, Fisher, 1970). This interpretation is composed of both what organizations communicate about themselves as well as how individuals experience companies physically and behaviorally. At root, images are constructed through the many messages about an organization (Baskin & Aronoff, 1988) and are valuative in nature (Crable & Vibbert, 1986).

As social actors, organizations spend considerable resources on institutional advertising, which constructs images or, better (in fitting with the primary metaphor used in the book), "social personae"—social personalities that they present to the world (Simpson & Weiner, 1989, p. 598). Like Bostdorff and Vibbert (1994), this book uses the terms *image* and *persona* largely interchangeably, although the use of *social personae* is intentional in that it focuses more precisely on the aspect of the fact that organizations attempt to create social personalities, which function as a means of exchange, through their use of discursive and visual images. In the same manner in which an organization is legally a juristic person before the law, it also is a distinct social persona before the public. In this way, a company may seek to anthropomorphize its form in order to make it more accessibly experienced in a precise way.

For most companies, their social personae is their currency, their stock in trade. Damage to their carefully constructed personae conceivably will have a tangible effect on their bottom lines. With public criticism, a previously unadulterated persona has become soiled and the organization's persona has become *the* issue.

Although personae are synthetic creations, they in effect become a "real fiction" (Fisher, 1970, p. 132), because they develop into the vehicle by which individuals experience an organization. Dionisopoulos and Vibbert (1983) reported the results of a J. Walter Thompson study that bears this out. In answering the question "What is a company?" respondents asserted:

- Chase Manhattan Bank always wears a vest. "I think he has a vest with his pajamas ... and probably sleeps right in the bank so he can be close to the money" appraised one man.
- Hallmark Cards "is a wonderful man," smiled another. "Yes, I'd like him. He's just like Santa Claus."
- Mrs. Campbell (she makes soups) is also very nice—like Grandma. "You'd certainly accept her invitation to Sunday dinner."
- Exxon Corp., though, isn't so nice; "chubby and not terribly charming." Although one interviewee judged Exxon to be adventurous, "like Errol Flynn," she didn't think she'd like him. (p. 8)

The net effect of these efforts is that organizations come to be recognizable as individual entities; in each of these instances, a complex and diverse organization is described as if it were a person. This reveals the success of organizations in creating a distinctive social persona.

It is commonly known that the origin of the term *persona* is that of a "mask"; the Latin root suggests an instrument of disguise and alchemy through which actors would project their voices on the stage (Hopcke,

1995). As such, the term *persona* is suggestive of a drama metaphor—a powerful metaphor used by symbolic interactionists to explain symbolic human and, in this case, organizational behavior (Rueckert, 1982). Social actors don a mask in order to conceal some aspects of their personality and, in so doing, *transform* an audience's perception of their image. Application to this study is no difficult task: Corporations are actors in a social masquerade who don masks and then seek to deliver a compelling performance (Snyder et al., 1983), such as Phillips Petroleum's image campaign about how its use of a fuel additive made possible the life-saving helicopter rescue of young Becky Sharp from the side of a snowy mountain (Bostdorff & Vibbert, 1994), or the spirited denial by the Mobil Corporation to charges by CBS News that the company had engaged in "creative bookkeeping" in order to mask obscene profits (Dionisopoulos & Vibbert, 1988). Audiences (e.g., consumers) and critics (e.g., social activists) then judge the caliber of the performance with observations about how real, dramatic, or believable the performance was, with normative behaviors specified based on the judgment.

Of course, only when organizations make a "bad performance" in the form of wrongdoing does the need to repair a mask arise—a situation that requires a communicative response. Snyder et al. (1983) noted, "Excuses occur when our carefully crafted masks slip a bit, showing something unsavory underneath. They then become part of the masks we wear. Not only do we deny the masks but deny it's a mask we're repairing" (p. X). The motive for such image repair is to receive a favorable review by the critics of organizational actions. Such a fact is demonstrated by the common appearance of newspaper analyses of corporate decision making that typically appears after a corporate crisis.

This is not to say that the use of a social persona is inherently deceptive or unethical; in addition to drama, other cultural uses of masks, such as when coupled with a religious ceremony, help people to become or invent a venerable persona. The point is, however, that the images and masks of organizations are designed to personify, anthropomorphize, and give a face to an otherwise faceless entity—to create a *persona grata*. These images then, of course, become reified and treated as real by their auditors.

## Legitimation Needs of the Modern Organization

These "masks" that organizations use are critical to the organizations because the masks help to legitimate them. Given their considerable economic, political, and social resources, corporations as a whole have substantial problems in the establishment and maintenance of their social legitimacy (Boulding, 1978; Epstein & Votaw, 1978). Legitimacy, according to Dowling and Pfeffer (1975), concerns the degree to which corporate activities are congruent with the values of the social system in which they operate. The actions of an organization are legitimate, for example, to the degree that they can be shown to reflect public values such as telling the truth, not following the flow of capital, and not damaging the environment. A legitimation crisis, then, occurs when stakeholders perceive an incongruity to exist between a corporation's values, as evidenced in its acts, and those of the social system (Boyd, 2000).

As social actors, organizations are comparably large. Consequently, given the inequities of size, they find criticism to be a routine part of their existence. This occurs because individuals find their only response to this size is to challenge the social legitimacy of corporations by criticizing their actions. Sennett (1980) asserted, "[T]he fear of dependence [on corporations] is counteracted by doing something more complicated than debating the masters. It is accomplished by calling the integrity of their very person into question" (p. 48). The fact that challenges to social legitimacy can be brought through actual or potential disparities highlights the communicative nature of both the maintenance and loss of legitimacy. Corporations establish their social legitimacy through discourse. Conversely, it is through charges that purport to represent the "public interest" that legitimacy is challenged; at this juncture, organizations find it necessary to respond to criticism through the issuance of an apologia (Dionisopoulos & Vibbert, 1988).

## THE RISE OF THE CORPORATE APOLOGIA

### Proliferation of Corporate Apologia

As mentioned earlier in this chapter, the concept of apologia first focused on individuals, be they athletes who did not work for the good of the team (Kruse, 1981b), church leaders or heretics (Ryan, 1982), or politicians caught in a wrong (Ware & Linkugel, 1973). In recent times, however, organizations have become the source of more and more apologiae: General Motors, Odwalla, Sears, AT&T, and Firestone (not to mention the Swiss and Japanese governments, and the Vatican) are just a few of the organizations in contemporary times that have found the need to defend themselves from criticism.

A number of factors account for the rise of this phenomenon. First, through the success of various social movements in the 1960s (among them were the consumer, ecology, civil rights, women's rights, and the antiwar movements), big business learned that it was no longer the goose that laid the proverbial golden egg in the form of postwar prosperity. Instead, in this era of growing mistrust of institutions, business increasingly was challenged—in the areas of product safety, equal opportunity, and, most visibly, its environmental record (Heath & Nelson, 1986). It was against this backdrop that business learned the importance of responding to criticism in order to counterinfluence public opinion.

More recently, technology has spawned a number of developments that account for the proliferation of corporate apologiae. First is the multiplication of media outlets. The so-called 500 channel media universe is almost upon us. With this comes increased specialization in terms of business reporting, with CNBC, Bloomberg, and various other business networks and programs; their productions serve as a vehicle for questions to be raised about corporate decision making and provide a forum for corporate responses to criticism. Also contributing to the upsurge in apologiae is the rise and popularity of news broadcasts that make use of the newsmagazine format—shows that are relatively inexpensive for networks to produce. These programs are always on the lookout for some harm done to an innocent person by a faceless corporation; they can then frame the harm as a good versus evil morality drama in which David triumphs over Goliath.

Indeed, as the efforts to take RJR Nabisco private proved in the 1980s, corporate exchanges make great spectacle. In fact, that case was the first business story to transcend the business section and be viewed in more mythical terms, as is evidenced by the book (and movie of the same title) *Barbarians at the Gate* (Burrough & Helyar, 1990). Social drama is inherent to an apologetic exchange, because with an apologia there is a huge corporation charged with an egregious wrong, which is being tried in the court of public opinion via the television news. With this there is a wonderful cast of characters—reticent patrician CEOs humbled and brought to their knees, media reporters who act for the public good, attractive and compelling victims, human or otherwise, tragically harmed. All of these facts together—the drama of business actions coupled with the confessional and voyeuristic nature of television—serve as grist to fill the growing number of media outlets. Witness the legal saga of Martha Stewart, for instance; it was the ultimate in reality programming.

Another factor that contributes to the proliferation of apologiae is the triumph of consumerism. The consumer has become the final arbiter of corporate behavior, and organizations often find that they have no other choice but to acquiesce to customer demands. For example, when Intel faced criticism for a potential error in its much-ballyhooed Pentium chip, it initially resisted offering to replace the chips due to the incredible costs of doing so, only to be forced to comply by the demands of consumers (Hearit, 1999). In its announcement of its decision to replace the chip the company claimed, "What Intel continues to believe is technically an extremely minor problem has taken on a life of its own. Although Intel firmly stands behind the quality of the current version of the Pentium processor, we recognize that many users have concerns. We want to resolve these concerns" (Grove, Barrett, & Moore, 1994, p. A7). Note the company's phrasing. Intel essentially said, "There's nothing really wrong with our product, but our customers continue to think there is, so we have no other choice but to fix it." With customers as the final judge, companies have found that they have no choice but to respond vigorously to customer complaints before they lose control of an issue or problem.

Another factor involves corporations' need to recoup their investments. As organizations spend billions of dollars to develop, tool, launch, market, and distribute products (e.g., Windows 2000 cost $2 billion to develop; Kahney, 2000), they become increasingly less likely to be willing to allow public criticism to tarnish the record of such a product. Consequently, a subtrend in the phenomenon may be the emergence of much more "aggressive" response to criticism, such as what occurred when McDonald's sued a couple of harmless British hippies for libel because the pair challenged the integrity of McDonald's operations and environmental record (Lyall, 1997).

Finally, the puncturing of an economic bubble and concomitant economic recession tends to result in more apologiae. Simply put, with the loss of considerable sums of money, people look closely for fraud and find that scapegoats are plentiful. To account for this phenomenon, in a book about the great stock market crash of 1929 John Kenneth Galbraith (1997) coined the term *bezzle*. *Bezzle* is rooted in the term *embezzle*, and is used to mean that when economic times are good, people do not watch questionable economic practices too closely and, as a result, bezzle (the undiscovered inventory of illegal behavior) increases. Yet, when economic news turns bad, money and audits are watched more closely—and, as a result, unlawful corporate activity is uncovered and legal action is taken, resulting in the need for apologiae.

## Prototypical Apologia

But what constitutes the communicative nature of the response? At root, there are five distinct prototypical stances that company officials make use of to defend their actions: denial, counterattack, differentiation, apology, and legal. The choice as to the communicative nature of the response is driven by the question of guilt and responsibility. In other words, the type of reply is dictated by the degree to which the organization as an agent is seen to be responsible for the act or as a victim of some misfortune.

***We Didn't Do It.***    The first type of apologia this book addresses is that of a denial stance. In this situation, an organization is accused of impropriety and, in effect, responds to the criticism with a denial that it is guilty of any wrongdoing. The use of denial is limited to those organizations for which no public evidence exists that they are guilty of committing any offense—or to those that have decided that, although they are guilty, for liability reasons they had better choose to continue to deny any wrongdoing. This response deals with the problem of guilt by denying that there is any. Such was the approach used by Chrysler when it was accused of unhooking odometers as part of an executive perk program; it responded to the criticism by denying that any such program was in place and instead argued that the company simply had a valid test program that suffered some minor abuses (Hearit, 1994). Within this stance, organizations do vary in the degree to which they forcefully deny; some take the denial further and counterattack the credibility of the accuser.

*Counterattack.*    In this second type of apologia, corporate officials combine the denial with a counterattack by which they not only deny that they are guilty of any wrongdoing but also concomitantly point the finger at their accuser, claiming that their accuser is the party that is *really* at fault in the whole drama. Media organizations present useful counterattack targets for companies caught in a wrong. Regardless of whether a company is guilty or not, there are three built-in criticisms that can be leveled against any media organization: the reporter/producer unfairly edited the story, the reporter "hunched" the story by keeping a preconceived storyline in mind the whole time, and the story was an attempt to garner ratings rather than to get at the "truth" (Hearit, 1996). When using this stance against nonmediated corporate actors, apologists take one or a combination of two approaches: They seek to increase the perceived responsibility for the act or attempt to amplify the opinion of the offensiveness of the act (Benoit & Dorries, 1996).

*It's Not Really Our Fault.*    For organizations that do not have the luxury of denying that they are guilty of the criticisms leveled against them, some choose to enact a differentiation strategy to distance themselves from their guilt. They acknowledge that they are in some degree responsible for the act, but argue that mitigating factors limit their culpability. Here, for example, an organization might admit that an act occurred but claim that it was the result of an accident, or that a disgruntled employee who acted without organizational authorization was responsible. If an organization can successfully locate responsibility in one of its employees, *corporate* culpability will be more limited. Such was the case with Domino's Pizza, which responded with a carefully crafted apologia to allegations that its 30-minute delivery guarantee created conditions that forced its drivers to speed. The company suggested that because delivery drivers have 18 minutes in which to drive an average of 2 miles, any unsafe driving is the result of reckless drivers, not a negligent policy (Hearit, 1995a). Interestingly, Domino's later abandoned its promise of "delivery in 30 minutes or the pizza is free."

*We Promise Not to Do It Again.*    Some organizations face criticisms that clearly are valid to all and consequently find that they have no other choice but to admit guilt and deliver an apology. The use of an apology allows an organization to do remedial work in order to repair the tear in the social fabric its actions have brought about (Goffman, 1971). This is accomplished by splitting the self or, in this case, the persona of the organization in two, and by drawing a distinction between the good self and the bad self. For example, Texaco—after an embarrassing tape of an executive meeting surfaced, which led to allegations of discrimination and racism—asked that it not be judged by this one situation as representative of how it typically does business (Brinson & Benoit, 1999).

*Talk to Our Lawyers.* Finally, some companies choose not to take a public relations stance to the charges of criticism due to the fact that significant legal issues inhere in the criticism—and thus avoid participating in the public drama that surrounds the allegations of their wrongdoing (Fitzpatrick & Rubin, 1995). In such instances, these organizations follow the counsel of their legal departments in formulating their response. As a result, the major issuances of communication occur in conjunction with legal developments of the issue, be they the filing of a lawsuit, the onset or close of a trial, or the reading of a trial verdict. The fact that organizations take a legal strategy in responding to the criticism, due to the potential for significant jury awards, does not mean that they are insensitive to the public opinion that surrounds the case. Such was the tact taken by General Motors to legal charges, brought by the family of Shannon Moseley, that its C/K trucks were prone to catch fire in side-impact collisions. In this instance, it was company lawyers who fashioned the substance of the critical response (Hearit, 1996).

## CONCLUSION

This book seeks to examine how organizations accused of wrongdoing manage their guilt. Accordingly, it supports two theses. First, because the offense is in the territory of the social persona of an individual or organization, apologetic exchanges are dramas that constitute secular remediation rituals that attempt to alter the terms of the discourse. They have as their goal the repair of an image-based social relationship, not through forgiveness but instead through public acknowledgment.

Second, although apologia have as their goal the repair of a social relationship, they are a remarkably ineffectual vehicle by which to accomplish such a purpose. Indeed, it is the position of this book that they are best characterized as a rhetoric of failure. At root, their primary virtue is that they complete the typical wrongdoing, guilt, and restoration drama; by doing so, they deny media a continual story. As such, apologia constitute a ritualistic form of communication, one in which an organization enters into a public confessional, taps into well-established themes of guilt and restoration, and, in so doing, completes the story and gets the individual or organization off the front page.

To develop these positions further, chapter 2 locates and develops the problem of guilt and responsibility, as well as advances the understanding of the ritualistic, temporal, and symbolic dimensions of apologia. Chapters 3 and 4 address the legal and ethical ramifications of corporate response to criticism. Chapters 5, 6, and 7 address the substantive and stylistic nature of corporate response to criticism, examining in more detail the contexts of individual, corporate, and institutional forms of apologia and apology. Chapter 8, the final chapter, draws a number of conclusions, among them the problem of the growing corporate nature of apologetic discourse as well as the critical role of ritual in completing a "successful" apologia.

# 2

# Apologia, Social Drama, and Public Ritual

Now the LORD God had planted a garden in the east, in Eden; and there he put the man he had formed.

And the LORD God made all kinds of trees grow out of the ground—trees that were pleasing to the eye and good for food.

In the middle of the garden were the tree of life and the tree of the knowledge of good and evil.

Genesis 2: 8–9 (*The Holy Bible*, 1973/1984)

So opens one of humanity's oldest archetypal stories. Set in an idyllic and lush garden that teemed with life, it begins with humanity's parents living a life of matchless harmony surrounded by abundant food and perfect beauty. In a phrase, they lived in paradise—a place of order. Yet, the purpose of this ancient text was not to revel in the perfect social harmony that was, but no doubt to account for the disorder and death that ancient readers no doubt saw about them, for the narrative ends with the Lord casting Adam and Eve out of the garden. The rest of the Hebrew Scriptures and the Christian Bible, then, serve as an attempt to restore social order through the offering of a perfect victim (Burke, 1984).

The manner in which ancient Israelites sought to restore order was through a complex system of rite and ritual, led by a high priest (Leviticus 16) who would offer animal sacrifices in order to atone for the sins of the congregation of Israel. The need for sacrifice in order to restore order was one that sought to deal with the problem of "guilt" (Burke, 1984), the symbolic fracture of the identifications held in common that allows society to maintain social order. When public order is at stake, individuals and institutions seek to propitiate their guilt through public ritual. In one sense, the entrance into the public confessional is more important that what is said once one gets there; that is, the act of the confession signifies the reacceptance of the current order—in this way, a declaration of guilt is

19

both *conformative* and *transformative*. Absolution is able to occur, then, through the presentation of a victim on whom the guilt is centered and absolved (Burke, 1984), a ritual played out numerous times on both religious and secular levels.

Communicatively, this restoration is accomplished through apologetic address that utilizes strategies of denial, mortification, or scapegoating discourse, which individuals and institutions use to purge themselves of guilt. After an apologist reaffirms adherence to the values it was reputed to have broken, the fracture in the social order is able to be healed and restored; in this way, the deliverance of an apologia functions to complete the order/guilt/redemption cycle. In so doing, an apologia performs a social action; it conforms to and reaffirms the mystery of the current order (Miller, 1984).

Having introduced the ritualistic cycle of order, guilt, apology, and absolution, now let us examine some of the particulars of the apologetic situation in more detail. To accomplish this purpose, this chapter first surveys the role of guilt and the subsequent role of apology and absolution, then seeks to locate the study of apologia within a ritualistic context, and finally concludes with a discussion of problems related to apologies.

## GUILT

Referencing Coleridge's *Aids to Reflexion,* Burke (1984) argued that the ideas of original sin and redemption are the two points that, in many ways, form the basis of his notion of a drama of human relations, because what *motivates* human behavior is rooted in the idea of where we locate our tribal guilt and from whence we seek redemption and deliverance, deliverance that can only occur through offering up a perfect victim. This offering up a ritual victim appears both "normal" and "natural" and has the requisite effect of promoting "social cohesion" (p. 285). Although Burke's oeuvre is tantalizing in laying out some of the particulars of the sociological problems that our guilt brings, it is by no means exhaustive in its explanation of how guilt functions rhetorically in apologetic situations, because the problem of guilt is more complex than simply an offender/offended relationship. Relating to apologia, Burke's notions raise a number of critical issues that must be negotiated when ascertaining the level of guilt.

### Determinism Versus Free Will

The first issue to be addressed in the determination and location of guilt is the role of responsibility. Stated simply, a bedrock principle of Western culture is that people are individually responsible for their actions. However, such a statement is deceptive in its simplicity, because it fails to address the problem as to whether our behavior is determined or freely chosen (Kane, 1996). Although a complex discussion of this point is well beyond the scope of this book, there are a number of germane issues worth considering as it relates to the "public" determination of whether individuals are responsible for their actions. Determinism, of course, is the philosophical position that our actions are constrained, or predetermined by outside forces. Accident of birth, social and economic status, technology, and geography, for instance, all function to limit and constrain if not determine our daily choices (Honderich, 1988). Conversely, the position of free will holds that we are not the product of our environment but rather make countless decisions in the conduct of each day (Kane, 1996). To many it is inconceivable that each and every one of these choices is preordained by fate, biology, nature, or some divine presence.

## Responsibility for Choices

Practically speaking, we tend to act and make determinations of responsibility as if our choices are at once both determined *and* free. We do have certain physical, economic, and social limitations, to name but a few. A low income, for instance, limits significantly the choice of where to live. Yet, within these limitations there certainly appear examples of when we are free to choose and do so—such as when we decide between two choices of where to go out for dinner. As we make countless decisions throughout a day, although our choices may be limited, there is considerable freedom within these limitations. Furthermore, as evidenced in theology and jurisprudence, Western society is rooted in the understanding that we are both free to choose and capable of choice. Yet not only are we free to choose but with that choice comes a certain degree of responsibility. Such responsibility for each and every one of our choices is "inextricably woven into the concrete reality of our legal and moral institutions throughout history" (Snyder et al., 1983, p. 14).

When determining responsibility, not only are judgments made as to how one *did* act but responsibility also implies how one *could* have acted, *should* have acted, and in the future, how one *ought* to act (Goffman, 1971). In this way there is a moral dimension to our understanding of responsibility. Perhaps a cultural understanding of the multifaceted and difficult ways responsibility functions is best seen in reference to the law.

## Evidenced in Law

The law regularly makes distinctions as to the responsibility of individuals as well as suggests a requisite relationship to guilt (Darley & Zanna, 1982). Interestingly enough, adjudicators of the law are not concerned merely with the end result of an action but also seek to ascertain the motive in determining the level of responsibility and guilt of the accused (Goffman, 1971). A charge of first-degree murder, for instance, alleges that the premeditation and commitment of an act was so serious that the wrongdoing bears the full weight of responsibility and should be punished as such. A second-degree charge, concomitantly, shows that although an act was not premeditated, the level of guilt is still high because the intent to harm another was still present. A charge of third-degree murder, more typically called "manslaughter," represents the taking of a life but under circumstances in which it was most likely an accident—with a significant lessening of punishment due to the fact that there was no intent to harm.

Indeed, it is only when people are seen to act under duress do judges and juries make decisions that reduce the level of responsibility. This, however, only occurs when people are considered to suffer from insanity or some other form of "mental defect." In such cases, guilt is not assigned because such individuals acted in ignorance or without their full faculties, and, as a result, are not held responsible for their acts.

## Difficulty in Determining Responsibility

The problem of guilt is closely related to the concept of motive or intent when considering individual behavior; indeed, individual guilt is relatively clear-cut when compared with the problem of guilt as it relates to group and organizational behavior. Here, the problem becomes much more complex, because analysis reveals that it is difficult if not impossible to locate the guilt and responsibility of a single actor in complex organizational decisions (Ermann & Lundman, 1992; Jackall, 1988, 1997). In the infamous Kitty Genovese murder, 38 otherwise moral and upright neighbors refused to take action—not even making a phone call to police—as they watched the woman be stabbed to death in New York City in the spring of 1964. Some of her neighbors claimed it was not their responsibility to get involved, whereas others believed it was a "lover's quarrel" (Snyder et al., 1983). In response to instances such as this, Latané and Darley (1970) posited the existence of a "diffusion of responsibility" hypothesis, which noted that individuals feel less responsible when they act as a member of a group as contrasted to when they act alone.

Yet, determination of responsibility is even more complicated in organizations. Said succinctly, organizations are structurally evasive when confronted with the question of their guilt. Take the case of the Ford Pinto. As a result of the success of small import automobiles in the 1960s, the Ford Motor Company, led by then-vice president Lee Iacocca, embarked on a crash program to build a car to compete with the imports—the Pinto. The decision to build the small automobile was accompanied by the injunction that came to be known as the "Rule of 2,000": the automobile had to weigh less than 2,000 pounds and cost fewer than $2,000 dollars (Ermann & Lundman, 1992). This, of course, led to the tragic choices that resulted in the death and maiming of numerous Pinto owners (Dowie, 1977). Subsequent to the determination that the gas tank location was unsafe and would explode if hit directly, a fix for the tanks was considered but rejected on grounds of both cost ($11 per vehicle) and weight (Ermann & Lundman, 1992).

In this tragic Pinto case, who is responsible and where does guilt lie? Clearly, Lee Iacocca and his "Rule of 2,000" must bear some responsibility. Yet, in his defense, the rule certainly did not include orders to injure and kill. Similarly, the engineers who considered and rejected the metal support between the gas tank and rear axle that would have prevented many of the deaths also bear some responsibility, because the decision likely was made by a committee. Correspondingly, those in the executive suite who approved the design as well as those in manufacturing who built the car and those who marketed the automobile also can be shown to share in the blame. However, in adding these multiple groups to the mix, the problem becomes clear: Because guilt is located in more than one actor, it becomes diffused through the entire organization. Said another way, the "information and acts are distributed among many different employees engaged in various functional groups with the corporation" (Stone, 1975, p. 51–52).

The difficulty in locating wrongdoing within an organization is due to the fact that organizations are systems, and "systems are structurally evasive when it comes to responsibility taking" (Snyder et al., 1983, p. 301). Consequently, decisions are not and cannot be located in individuals. As a result, there is a sense that no one person is responsible. This thinking leads to the type of chilling cost/benefit analyses such as the one made at Ford whereby the company compared the cost of fixing the car with that of settling legal claims with the victims, and concluded it would be less expensive to pay the injury claims.

The fact that no one person is responsible is evidenced in the converse, because those who are "in control" often feel powerless to effect change and believe that their power is grossly overstated. All of the actors in the Pinto case based their decisions on limited information at different levels; that information seemed to be "rational" and based on sound business principles, and although some actors may have raised questions, they felt powerless to object too strenuously. Perhaps Robert Jackall (1997) described best the impact of organization on ethical decision making:

> [B]ecause moral choices are inextricably tied to personal fates, bureaucracy erodes internal and even external standards of morality, not only in matters of individual success and failure but also in all the issues that managers face in their daily work. Bureaucracy makes its own internal rules and social con-

text the principal moral gauges for action. Men and women in bureaucracies turn to each other for moral cues for behavior and come to fashion specific situational moralities for specific significant people in their worlds. (p. 121)

The organization qua organization, then, leads inevitably to even more diffusion of responsibility and creates situations in which if all actors are culpable then it is difficult for any actors to be culpable.

Part of the modern Western solution in such a situation is to punish subordinates for the wrongdoing of managers. Organizations and their officers tend to take credit for good outcomes but to externalize blame for bad outcomes. As a result, there is a propensity to blame the person who happens to be at the switch at the time of the accident, rather than managers who created the double-binds that led to an accident. In this way, blame is pushed downward while credit is moved upward. Indeed, it appears that as power rises, managers are able to divert more responsibility for misdeeds onto their subordinates (Jackall, 1997).

The difficulties of locating guilt when considering corporate acts are even more pronounced when one contemplates the case of the residential development known as Love Canal. In this case, Hooker Chemical (now Occidental Chemical Company) owned a waste site in the 1940s, which it administered in a manner that was consistent with EPA standards (Tabris, 1984). In 1952, the city of Niagara Falls wanted to purchase the property for construction of a school. When Hooker appeared reluctant to sell, the school board threatened legal action. The company relented and donated the land to the school board with the understanding that it would be used for no more than a park. Against the company's warnings the land was later developed and, as expected, hazardous wastes leached into the adjoining property. By 1978, the New York State Health Commissioner ordered the school closed, and a week later the governor announced that the 236 families who lived in the area would have to be moved. Again, to whom would responsibility be assessed? Hooker, although it tried to do the right thing, donated the property rather than face legal action. The school board also shares much of the guilt, due to its insistence in acquiring the land in spite of environmental concerns. Finally, guilt also has to be shared with city and corporate officials who stood to gain economically from development of the site. Examples such as this show the considerable difficulty in locating responsibility when dealing with organizational and institutional misdeeds.

## Difficulty in Punishing Wrongdoing

The diffusion of responsibility and the subsequent difficulty in locating guilt is evidenced further by an analysis of how societal, governmental, and legal institutions seek to punish corporate misbehavior. Indeed, such an analysis shows the historic difficulty that public institutions have had in dealing with the problem of wrongdoing by organizations. In treating individuals who work in organizations as instruments of wrongdoing, the courts have been highly reluctant to punish these agents as individuals, even when they are precisely identifiable. Such was the case of the elaborate check-kiting overdraft scheme that gave E.F. Hutton up to $250 million a day interest-free. Not one corporate executive was punished, in spite of the fact that those who instigated the wrongdoing were precisely identified (Coombs, 1999; Thackaberry, 1996). The case also illustrates the difficulty of punishing companies qua companies. The penalty leveled against E.F. Hutton as a company was a $2 million fine and the requirement to set up an $8 million fund for the banks it had defrauded. When measured against the free use of $250 million a *day* (Ermann & Lundman, 1992; Thackaberry, 1996) it becomes quite evident that the law is an ineffective vehicle by which to constrain corporate wrongdoing.

## Factors That Increase Level of Guilt

Although the determination of where guilt specifically lies within a corporate context is difficult and complex, given the hypermediated environment in which we live, paradoxically a number of factors function to increase the level of guilt for which corporate apologists are publicly held responsible as an institution. This next section attempts to articulate and explain a number of these factors.

The more clear a standard of morality or social norm, the greater the condemnation that is likely to be faced by those whose behavior falls below the standard (Snyder et al., 1983). Whereas in Western culture there are fewer and fewer actions that almost everyone agrees are immoral, in the event individuals or institutions engage in one of these vitiated behaviors, they are likely to suffer more guilt. This occurs due to the weight that accompanies the consensus that such an act was indeed ignoble. One such example is the idea of not despoiling the environment. Organizations found guilty of such an act face considerable social sanction, especially those in businesses and industries that are close to the customer (Hearit, 1995a).

Intentionality is inextricably linked to level of guilt that social actors face. In such cases, observers judge that the negative consequences were the ones the author intended to bring about due to ill will (Goffman, 1971). The more social critics view a maleficent act to be purposive, the more negatively they are likely to view it. This occurs because the "perception [of the act's meaning] is dependent on an assessment of intent and is necessarily subject to reappraisal" (Goffman, 1971, p. 110). As noted earlier, the law regularly distinguishes guilt and subsequent punishment based on intention. Consequently, those unable to deny committing an act are nonetheless likely to argue that they did not deliberately commit the wrongdoing—and by doing so they lessen their guilt and responsibility (Ware & Linkugel, 1973).

Concomitantly, if the execution of one act of wrongdoing is seen disapprovingly, repeated acts of wrongdoing are judged even more harshly. Although an individual can inadvertently be caught in a singular wrong, repeated offenses suggest a higher level of purposefulness—that an individual has given him- or herself over to the misconduct.

A third dimension that speaks to the extent to which individuals and institutions are held accountable for their transgressions is the degree to which they acted knowingly (Goffman, 1971; Snyder et al., 1983). Here, their guilt is measured by the extent to which they, as social actors, were able to predict how bad the outcome would be. An accident, for example, is a case in which the outcome was unanticipated and hence culpability is limited. Conversely, to the degree that foreseeability is predictable, social actors are held accountable to a higher standard. This is especially true in the legal profession, where foreseeability is critical to proving negligence: establishing that the results and outcome were well known and yet the party chose to engage in such actions (Snyder et al., 1983).

A fourth dimension that impacts the degree to which critics hold people culpable is actuarial rarity (Snyder et al., 1983). Said another way, if an act of malfeasance is particularly unusual or rare, the level of culpability is viewed to be even higher. The culpability of those who planned and carried out the September 11th terrorist attacks was compounded by how rarely the United States has been a victim of terrorist attacks on its own soil.

A fifth component that functions to increase the level of guilt is the degree to which a crisis is mediated. This comes to pass in three ways. First, the presence of a video "smoking gun"—the appearance of compelling media images and the attendant degree to which they make actors appear guilty—functions to amplify culpability. The case of the Exxon *Valdez* most clearly illustrates this point. The pictures were powerful—oil-stained birds and anthropomorphic-looking otters, caught in the harm wrought by humanity. Damage was serious, permanent, and driven by the presence of irrepressible images of a guilty actor and tremendous destruction left in its wake. Contrast the spill with a similar environmental crisis, the damage done in the nuclear power plant accident that occurred in Japan in 2004 (Brooke, 2004). There were four deaths, but no dramatic images, no one glowing in the dark, no picture of a fission-creating nuclear chain reaction, except for the pictures of a few people fleeing a building. Subsequently, although the damage was possibly just as severe as the oil spill in Prince William Sound, the pictures were less compelling and hence the story fell from public consciousness much more quickly.

Relatedly, a second manner in which media affects the assigning of guilt is how simplistically a crisis script can be communicated. Boorstin (1961) noted, "It is less the artificial simplification than the artificial complication of experience that confuses us" (p. 39). Scandals that can be explained cogently in a short news story are much more likely to increase the level of guilt that wrongdoers face than are stories that media consumers do not understand.

Finally, a third way in which media affects the level of guilt is through the use of third-party experts (Hearit, 1996). The media's employment of third-party experts is one of criticism, by which these experts offer judgments and assessments of behavior (Snyder et al., 1983). The high status and privileged position of the experts functions to increase the level of guilt that apologists face (Fearn-Banks, 1996). Furthermore, the degree to which there is unanimity across media sources and to which they all agree adds to the amount of culpability that is formed.

A final dimension that impacts the level of guilt ascribed to malefactors has to do with the characteristics of the harm perpetrated; that is, the nature and type of victims that the wrongdoing leaves in its trail. Surprisingly, the literature surrounding victims is particularly undeveloped, especially given the persuasive power that victims have when sharing their stories. This discussion draws from and expands on the work of Perrow (1984).

The case of Chrysler, which was accused of unhooking odometers in 1987, is illustrative of this first kind of victim, who really is not a victim in the conventional sense (Hearit, 1994). There were allegations of wrongdoing, along with images and insinuations of corporate bigwigs abusing the perks of their jobs—abuses for which a few executives eventually were found guilty of fraud. Although there was considerable press coverage, in reality there was no corporeal damage done to a person; this is evidenced by the penalty faced by Chrysler: a conviction on 15 counts of mail fraud and a fine of $7.6 million, but no jail time for its executives (Stodghill, 1990).

Contrast this type of damage with physical harm to individuals who Perrow (1984) called "first-order victims." First-party victims are "operators." They are the people who actually run a system or an organization—those who have the misfortune of being "at the switch" when something goes wrong. Included in the category are others who work alongside operators—in Perrow's words, "first-level supervisors, maintenance personnel, low-level engineering personnel, and laborers and assisting personnel" (p. 67). Most industrial accidents fall into this category. Rhetorically, this form of victim does not resonate culturally; in fact, most often the opposite response occurs: When looking for causes of wrongdoing, attributions of causality are often located in the term *human error*, and it is the person who is at the switch who receives the most blame (and, because they often die in the accident, are usually unable to offer a competing account). At best, first-order victims are seen as an unfortunate consequence of someone doing a job—but the fact that they knew the risks and were compensated for their work keeps spectators in the human drama we call apologia from experiencing compelling emotion toward them.

Second-party victims are those who are party to or participants in a complex system or organization, but with no real responsibility or control over it (Perrow, 1984). Perhaps the best example of this type of victim is passengers in an airline crash. Said passengers recognize the risks inherent in flight and still chose to fly, yet they are not in charge of flying or maintaining the plane. Other groups of people who exemplify these types of victims are women who received faulty silicone breast implants that manufacturers had reason to believe were in danger of leaking. Rhetorically, observers feel more sorrow for these victims and their families than for first-order victims: Observers find the victims' stories compelling and moving, yet all the while acknowledge that they did choose to assume certain risks by getting on that plane or electing to have medically unnecessary cosmetic surgery (Vanderford & Smith, 1996). Most corporate crises concern second-order victims, in that this form encompasses product safety concerns, fraud, and other forms of corporate crime.

Contrast such individuals with third-party victims who, according to Perrow (1984), are innocent bystanders who have no involvement whatsoever in the system as it is constructed but are nonetheless victimized by it. Using the aforementioned example of a plane crash, third-party victims are those who are asleep in their bedrooms and killed when wreckage from the plane careens into their house, killing them. In this way, those with no involvement in the system are nevertheless impacted by it. Similarly, victims who suffer death due to a tragic gas leak—such as occurred in Bhopal, India, when a Union Carbide facility experienced a leakage—are examples of third-order victims (Sen & Egelhoff, 1991). Harm to people is serious, although, as made clear in compensatory and punitive jury verdicts, the value placed on life does not neatly fall into the categories as one would expect. The value of an adult male with a lucrative career, for instance, is much greater than is the value of a child, just as the value of a hand is greater than that of a foot. Put another way, corporeal damage is very real and its victims resonate loudly with audiences and constituencies (Belkin, 2002).

Finally, fourth-order victims are much more long term in consequence. Perrow (1984) asserted that most fourth-order victims are victimized by "radiation and toxic chemicals" and are most typically "fetuses and future generations" (p. 67). Coupled with harm to humans is injury to environment. Perhaps this is due to the fact that a harm to the environment has long-term elements; it is generational, with implications that extend long beyond the normal life span of people. Incidents affecting fourth-order victims also encompass the potential for incurring large numbers of victims who might suffer as a result of problems with complex technologies, such as nuclear power accidents. Perrow argued:

> Fourth-party victims potentially constitute the most serious class of victims. Chemical or radioactive contamination of land areas could have far-reaching effects upon the health of future generations. Genetic defects harm future generations in other ways, including adding the burden of lifetime care and treatment of victims. Future generations carry the burden; the present generation reaps whatever rewards there may be from the activity. (pp. 70–71)

In conclusion, the more innocent the party of victims, the more compelling they come across rhetorically. This resonance functions to increase the culpability of individuals and organizations for their failures.

## APOLOGY AND ABSOLUTION

The nature of symbolic guilt is such that it requires a ritualistic absolution—the separation of the guilt from the midst of the congregation. The character of such rituals is that they are a form of spectacle in which participants are able to "visualize the complete and final purgation of the offender" (Gronbeck, 1978, p. 165). One such image of how this occurs, according to Burke (1984), is that of "the satisfying of a debtor by the paying of a ransom" (p. 292). In noting how this purification functions, the punishment of the offenders is sacramental in nature, producing a purification by which a congregation of people is cleansed (Duncan, 1968). Such an act "has a salutary effect" in that it reaffirms institutional principles as well as serves to preserve social order (Gronbeck, 1978, p. 171).

The form of these rituals, and the fundamental presumption of this book, is that the purging of guilt happens through a ritualistic communication vehicle known as an *apologia*. Goffman (1971) wrote that when one is alleged to have committed wrongdoing, there are available "a very limited set of ritual enactments … for contrite offenders" (p. 117). The variations are limited indeed: "I didn't do it," "someone else did," or "I did it." Prototypically, an apologia, then, takes one of three tacks in dealing with the problem of guilt: assert that the guilt does not exist through a posture of denial of responsibility, transfer it to another through a process based on the ancient Hebrew ritual of scapegoating, or accept it through a process of mortification (Hearit, 1994). Let us now examine in more detail each of the three ways that rhetors respond.

The first way that apologists deal with the problem of guilt is through an apologia in which they deny ever having committed the act that has led to public criticism of their actions. In such cases, they reject that guilt is present in the first place, or that, at the least, the alleged party is ultimately not the responsible party. According to Ware and Linkugel (1973) such an approach is at best reformative, in that there is no transformative way to deal with the charges.

A strategy of denial detaches an individual or institution from the guilt through an appearance/reality dissociation (Hearit, 1994). Dissociations, according to Perelman and Olbrechts-Tyteca (1969), are a rhetorical strategy by which communicators take a unitary concept or idea and bifurcate it into two separate or distinct entities—in this case, the guilty apologist. An appearance/reality dissociation in apologetic discourse occurs when an institution argues that there "appears" to be a perception that it is guilty of the alleged transgression. The dissociation occurs when, on closer examination, the "true facts" reveal that in reality the organization is a law-abiding company that is not guilty of the alleged wrongdoing. Such was the strategy used by the Suzuki Corporation in 1988 when it was charged by *Consumer Reports* that its Samurai was prone to rollover when maneuvered quickly (Hearit, 1995b). The company argued that the charges were but an untrue appearance of the reality that the vehicle was actually quite safe. Furthermore, Suzuki maintained that the company was being victimized by an organization in search of federal rollover standards for sport utility vehicles.

A second way to address the problem of guilt is to achieve absolution by transferring it to another. In a central Hebrew myth, this is a process of scapegoating—the object of which was to transfer the guilt to an animal (Lindsey, 1985). This complex rite must be understood in terms of its accompanying myth—the rite of atonement (Koesten & Rowland, 2004). To achieve forgiveness, the ancient Israelites would engage in two rituals. First, they would slaughter an animal that then would be sacrificed to Yahweh God. This would give them forgiveness for their sins. Second, they would then take a goat and, rather than slaughter it, have the high priest, through ritual, transfer the guilt of the people onto the goat. The goat would then be driven into the wilderness to die. The purpose of the scapegoating image was to symbolically and concretely remove the sin from the camp—that is, the congregation was purified by separation—but it also served a secondary purpose to inoculate the congregation from future violations (because the guilty party had been cast out; Perera, 1986). In the Christian counterpart to this ritual, Christ was crucified *outside* of the gate of the city—thus presenting a way for forgiveness and separation from sin (Hebrews 13:12).

In terms of apologetic speech, individuals and organizations guilty of wrongdoing often find scapegoating to be a compelling vehicle by which to deal with the problem of their guilt (Sellnow & Seeger, 1989). However, although in central religious belief guilt is transferred to a chosen one to make a sacrifice for the community (e.g., a goat or lamb), in this incarnation the guilt is transferred to a fellow social actor, a much less ethical move. It is probably for this reason that Burke described victimage as a ritual form of "killing" or "murder" (1970, p. 248). In this way, "purity" is achieved or restored and the party to whom the guilt has been transferred, which has become the "essence" of evil, is able to be cut off from the rest of the congregation (Burke, 1969).

Apologists rhetorically use scapegoating through individual/group dissociations. In such instances, a division is made by which guilt is transferred from the many to the one. Organizationally, individual/group dissociations occur when the single concept of a company is bifurcated into multiple divisions by virtue of a reference to its subsidiaries or simply the large numbers of people who work there. The dissociation occurs, then, when the company is able to locate guilt, not in the company as a company, but instead in the actions of a few individuals, thus repairing the company's social persona. Such was the strategy taken by the Toshiba Corporation when news broke in 1987 that the company had sold top-secret milling equipment to the then Soviet Union (Hearit, 1994). To deal with the problem of its guilt, the company bifurcated itself, claiming that it was not the Toshiba Corporation that had sold the milling equipment but rather its subsidiary, the Toshiba Machine Company, that made the illegal sale (Hearit, 1994). In this way, the company distanced itself from its wrongdoing by scapegoating an individual subsidiary whose actions were distinct from and unknown to the larger group.

The final way in which apologists handle their guilt prototypically is through acceptance of the guilt by engaging in a process of self-mortification—what Burke described as "suicide" (1970, p. 248) or a form of self-punishment (Burkholder, 1990; Tavuchis, 1991). In such situations the guilt is, in effect, accepted rather than denied or transferred, and the guilty party deals with its guilt by seeking forgiveness from the wronged party. In such an instance, the apologist admits guilt, often couples it with a statement of regret, and asks for forgiveness (Hearit, 1994). In this way, apologies seek to rehabilitate (Tavuchis, 1991). At root, the idea behind mortification is that redemption can only occur from and by the grace of another—that the wrongdoer stands naked and guilty before the offended party.

Communicatively, this form of guilt is handled dissociationally through an act/essence dissociation. In this way, the apologist must admit the commission of an act—such a move is, of course, reputation damaging. But in order to salvage its reputation the guilty party must prove that such an act is not emblematic of its persona as a whole, by splitting the self and transferring the guilt to the bad self (Goffman, 1971). Companies engage in an act/essence dissociation by arguing that although the act was committed, it was in no way representative of the essential quality of the company's nature. Hence, the dissociation occurs by, in effect, the company scapegoating part of itself. Such was the path chosen by Volvo in 1990 after charges of deceptive advertising, in which the company showed a mon-ster-truck driving over a row of automobiles, and the only vehicle not de-stroyed was a structurally reinforced Volvo wagon. The company could not deny committing the act of false advertising, so its approach to its guilt was to deny that the act was in any way representative of the essence of the company (Hearit, 1995b).

## RITUAL

### The Case for Apologetic Ritual

The success of this absolution is judged on two different levels. First is the understanding that the apologist has to justify his or her behavior; in other words, articulate his or her association to the alleged offense and deliver an apologia. Second is the recognition that the apologia is more than words: The apologist must show "proper regard for the process of correction" (Goffman, 1971, p. 100). By doing so, critics are able to judge the emotional identification of the apologist or the degree to which the apologist respects and pays attention to the *symbolic and ritualistic* dimensions of justificatory discourse. Perhaps Tavuchis (1991) was even more cogent in identifying the connection between ritual and justificatory speech; he defined an apology as a "secular ritual whose essential medium is speech" (p. viii).

Ritual "is the voluntary performance of appropriately patterned behavior to symbolically effect or participate in the serious life" (Rothenbuhler, 1998, p. 27). This next section draws heavily from the work of Rothenbuhler, who has developed the role of ritual in communication. He crafted 15 terms that define ritual communicatively. Although all 15 relate to this study, I focus on the half-dozen that most closely inform the conceptualization of apologia as a public ritual.

*Action.* First, a ritualistic form is a cogent vehicle for accomplishing ac-tion. A ritual has an identifiable external appearance, and it is close to im-possible to separate this external structure from the action it performs (Douglas, 1982). In one act, an apologia both delivers content (i.e., an apol-ogy) and performs a speech act (i.e., apologizing; Austin, 1979; Tavuchis, 1991). Said another way, the *act* of confession is as important as what is *said* in the confession. Just as an inaugural address functions to commence a presidency, an apologia functions to expiate guilt; although the discourse of each is important, the focus of auditors in both forms of address is on the ac-tion that the discourse performs. Furthermore, within this ritualistic re-sponse apologists seldom present new information; instead, organizations accused of wrongdoing enter the public confessional and reassemble previously known facts and arguments (Rosenfield, 1968).

*Performance.* Closely related is the fact that the action is, at root, a performance. Bauman (1989) noted that a ritual is performed as "an aesthetically marked and heightened mode of communication, framed in a special way and put on display for an audience" (p. 262). As a social actor, an apologist is in many ways subject to criticism as to the quality of his or her performance; in communication terms, this means the degree to which communication competence was demonstrated (Rothenbuhler, 1998). Said another way, although the guilt is in many ways substantive, the repair to reputation is done in a thoroughly expressive manner (Goffman, 1971).

In apologetic speech, for instance, commentators regularly opine on the physical characteristics and mannerisms of the performer, and to whether generic expectations were met, in an attempt to judge to what degree he or she really "meant it." Such was the case with President Clinton's first apology: Many observers did not believe that he demonstrated enough contrition. Apologists seldom reveal any new information (Rosenfield, 1968); this follows in that apologiae as ritual are not self-authored but are, in reality, the public performance of a script. To look as if one is "going through the motions" subverts the message of an apologia.

Another dimension that relates to the discussion of an apologia as performance is the role of timing. It is critical that the apology be delivered at just the "right" time, a determination that Tavuchis (1991) labeled as "structural rather than chronological" (p. 88). If, for instance, an apology comes too early or too easily, doubts are then raised about the apologist's motives; that it, the apology is seen as being self-serving or condescending (Tavuchis, 1991). The idea here is that a "meaningful" apology comes only after reflection on the wrong that was perpetrated. If the apology happens immediately, then it is clear that the apologist may not have fully considered the harmful impact of his or her actions. Conversely, if the apology comes not too early but too late, another less than desirable conclusion is drawn: The apologist is uncaring and unsympathetic, and lacks the basic human and communication competence to recognize that an apology needed to be made much earlier. Time does not heal old wounds; it makes new ones (Tavuchis, 1991).

*Voluntary.* Important to the successful performance of a ritual is that it be voluntary (Rothenbuhler, 1998). By this it is meant that a third characteristic of a ritual is that it is conducted in such a way that its participants enter into it freely. Voluntary participation is important in that it communicates acceptance of the meaning of the ritual. Rothenbuhler described this as an acceptance of a social compulsion (e.g., "Christ is in the blood")—and it is in the ritual that the acceptance is made formal. For an apologist, it is critical that a choice is made to issue an apologia, and that it is delivered freely rather than compelled, because only by doing so does the apologia offer a formal reacceptance of the social order that the apologist is reputed to have violated. Formal acceptance of the current social order is ritualistically reestablished in an apologia when an apologist claims to seek not a recasting of the rules as it relates to his or her negligence but instead a willingness on the part of the offended to treat the transgression as exceptional—that is, "to treat as out of frame an otherwise unsupportable occurrence" (Goffman, 1971, p. 165).

*Noninstrumental.* Rituals are not seen to rely on any form of a technical rationality. The idea that a wrong can be assuaged by an apology, for instance, is a non sequitur—it does not follow; it is irrational. Yet, that is exactly what happens once an apology is offered and guilt is expunged: The performers then act as if the wrong is forgiven or better, it never happened. The fourth characteristic, then, is that rituals are noninstrumental, cogent vehicles for accomplishing complex communicative acts (Rothenbuhler, 1998).

*Socially Structured.* Fifth, rituals are socially structured (Rothenbuhler, 1998). They are drawn from the language, traditions, and moralities of a given culture, and subsequently this cultural group imbues rituals with social meanings. Inherent in ritual is the social structure in which it is situated. Hence, in their public performance apologiae reproduce the prevailing social structure and reveal the contemporary hierarchy and social position (Burke, 1984; Leach, 1968). Each ritual, then, has a social group reference to it.

*Sacred.* Finally, rituals are serious if not sacred (Rothenbuhler, 1998). Social actors in their performance do not treat them lightly, but instead conduct them with all seriousness and sincerity. Apologetic rituals, even those that engage in counterattack, are characterized by their gravity and lack of levity.

## The Role of Media in Ritual

Although the two succeeding points discussed at the beginning of this section are not central to the definition of apologia as a social ritual, they are nonetheless critical to the development of ritual as it is used in this book. First is the fact that rituals have become significantly mediated, attaching an important dimension to their performance. This does not mean merely that rituals are televised, but rather that they are mediated. That is, observers increasingly become participants as they *experience* or participate in rituals through media. The presence of media, for instance, transforms the Olympic Games into a public spectacle in which participants engage in a ritualistic viewing and consumption of the proceedings (Rothenbuhler, 1988). Although it is on a smaller scale, in much the same way apologetic address is a mediated form of ritual that is constructed into a public spectacle by the news media (Edelman, 1988). This occurs because "television presents the content of myth, most significantly in its reporting of major collectively focused and focusing events, like coronations, weddings, or ball games" (Silverstone, 1988, p. 29).

*Rely on Social Myth and Moral Drama.*     Because rituals are socially structured, then it follows that they are rooted in social myth and moral drama (Turner, 1982). This moral drama can take numerous forms, but its primary appearance is related to the social construction of news, or what Edelman (1988) called the "political spectacle." "News stories," according to Bird and Dardenne (1988), "like myth, do not tell it like it is, but rather tell it like it means" (p. 71). In doing so the news functions to tell the same story over and over again, relying on standard forms and conventions, most notably good versus evil (Campbell, 1991; Edelman, 1988). Watching an apologetic address, then, is to be translated from sitting passively in one's living room to viewing an adjudicator judging good versus evil in a high moral drama. In this way, viewers become not audience members but rather participants in the social drama of ritual.

*Place on Public Record.*     The role of media, then, has critically transformed a central human exchange. Historically, the notion of an apology was considered a private matter. However, with the advent of television, what was once a personal discussion has become increasingly public. No longer is a wrong a private matter between two participants. This change is evident in two ways. First, there is a greater emphasis on the performance. Although appearing contrite was always important, now it is critical. Second, whereas apologiae historically were dyadic, no longer do the two parities handle the issue on their own (Kruse, 1981a; Tavuchis, 1991). Instead, apologists must deal with third parties who claim that they were also wronged, in addition to the victim. These third-party participants also seek to play a part in the resolution of the conflict or, at minimum, its ongoing perpetuation. In sum: Apologiae are public and secular remediation rituals that seek to put matters of wrongdoing on the public record. In this way, the purpose is no longer one of forgiveness or understanding but rather to exact some form of a proportional humiliation.

*Goal Is Not Effectiveness But Meaning.*     Second, the emphasis on such a public exchange is no longer on the "forgiveness" that results from an apologia—or, in a phrase, the effectiveness of the speech— but instead on the meaning that is created. When considered in terms of the success of the discourse, apologiae tend to be relatively ineffective (Hearit, 1992). Socrates was still forced to drink the hemlock; political outcasts were still hung and martyrs were still burned at the stake (Kruse, 1977). Rather, the emphasis on apologetic address, particularly a ritualistic conception of it, is on the speech act performed by the communication and the social meaning that is subsequently created. In this way, apologetic discourse offers a ritual that purges guilt and restores the guilty back into the congregation. To think about it in another way, although some people may not "forgive" someone for causing a social harm, it is nevertheless important for the perpetrator to *perform* an apologia: By doing so, an apologist, through the demonstration of contrition, reaffirms the very values that he or she was reputed to have broken. Socially, the community then can move forward with the recognition that said broken values have been redemonstrated to be vital (Hearit, 1995a).

*Ritual Act of the Apologetic Exchange*    In addition to the ritual dimensions of the apologia itself—that is, the voluntary, conscious, serious, performance of an apology that seeks a repair of the relationship—the association of the apology to the larger exchange of charge and countercharge also exhibits a ritual form. In an investigation into the rhetoric of public corruption, an idea very closely related to this study, Gronbeck (1978) diagrammed the ritualistic dimensions of this form of speech; he described it as "a ceremonial process—a public dancing of charges and countercharges, investigations, trials, and real or symbolic executions, which allow a public (a culture) to participate in the ritualistic purification of a country" (p. 157).

When an individual or institution faces ethical criticism, an entire social drama or ritual is set into motion. In this way, an apologetic exchange is really a play in three acts: the act, the charge, and the defense. The first act is the commission of an accident, scandal, or product safety incident by the organization as a social actor: a bad performance. This act is taken to have symbolic dimensions, because it exposes a crack in the carefully crafted mask of the performer through which is revealed a less than genteel form. To this act there is a mediated response from the offended, be they interest groups, media, or consumers. The primary nature of this second act is the performance of an accuser who alleges that the individual's or organization's act violates some cherished social value. Here guilt is established, guilt that requires some form of absolution. The third act of the drama is the response—the apologia. The rhetor enters the public (not private) confessional, and attempts to clear its name and seek restoration into the community. A compelling performance completes the dramatic cycle. If the apologia is "successful," it gets the organization off the front page. The story, at this point, has nowhere else to go. When considered in this way, Goffman's (1971) observation that remedial interchanges (i.e., apologiae) are in many ways quickly performed microcosms of the "entire judicial process" (p. 107)—allegation, indictment, testimony, and adjudication—becomes quite clear.

Summing up the ritual nature of confession, Foucault (1980) wrote:

> The confession is a ritual of discourse in which the speaking subject is also the subject of the statement; it is also a ritual that unfolds within a power relationship, for one does not confess without the presence (or virtual presence) of a partner who is not simply the interlocutor but the authority who requires the confession, prescribes and appreciates it, and intervenes in order to judge, punish, forgive, console, and reconcile; a ritual in which the truth is corroborated by the obstacles and resistances it has had to surmount in order to be formulated; and finally, a ritual in which the expression alone, independently of its external consequences, produces intrinsic modifications in the person who articulates it: it exonerates, redeems, and purifies him; it unburdens him of his wrongs, liberates him, and promises him salvation. (pp. 61–62)

Once the apologist has delivered his or her reply, there is evidence that there is no need to wait for an "official" reply. Indeed, when one examines many apologetic exchanges there one finds that often there is no final response; that is, the speaker assumes that the apologia is acceptable and then moves on. Goffman (1971), for instance, suggested that many apologists, in tune with their performance, take it for "granted that this relief has been provided" (p. 151). This occurs for a number of reasons. First, the crescendo of the exchange is the apologia, not the act of forgiveness. Hence, any subsequent response is at best a denouement to the exchange. Second, it demonstrates that a public wrong is more of an offense against a social order and less against the offended individual; thus, it seeks not the repair of a relationship but a restoration of social order. Finally, in many instances there is the question as to whom would "accept" the apology. By way of illustration, after President Clinton's apologia, who present could speak on behalf of the American people to whom he apologized? To follow through with the performance metaphor, critics judge the success of a performance, but they are not part of the drama.

## PROBLEMS IN APOLOGIES

### Rejected Apologies

The case of President Clinton's apology does raise some interesting questions: Are there not some apologiae that are rejected? The answer is in the affirmative. Three potential factors are at work. First, the offended party, after watching the performance, may judge it to be less than compelling, and as a result, reject the apology or have it in his or her interest to seek a form of proportional public humiliation (Tavuchis, 1991). This appears to be the case more and more, given the increasingly public and hostile nature of apologetic exchanges.

## No Agent Capable of Forgiveness

Second, and more critically, there are some acts that, from the perspective of humanity, really are unforgivable. The Holocaust, which witnessed the extermination of over six million Jews, is one example. It is a legitimate question as to whether an apology on the part of the perpetrators could be efficacious in the eyes of the victims, survivors, and their families. This point is in many ways akin to what Farrell and Goodnight (1981) concluded in their analysis of the root metaphors surrounding events at Three Mile Island: There exist certain situations in which, unlike the Bitzerian (1968) ideal, rhetoric can never be sufficient enough to account for the wrong; there can be no fitting response.

Third, there are victims of wrongdoing who cannot speak; therefore, who can accept an apology on their behalf? This especially is true in terms of environmental damage, such as in the case of the aforementioned spill of oil by the Exxon *Valdez;* miles of coastline were despoiled; countless otters, birds, and other waterfowl were killed; and considerable damage occurred to the ecosystem of Prince William Sound. Although Exxon chose to apologize to the people of Alaska, in many ways it was the environment that suffered the most damage and bore the greatest harm. Who, then, could speak for the damaged otters, birds, or ecosystem? Similarly, if exposure by companies of their workers to harmful substances causes children to be born damaged or carry radiation harms that will be generational, it is difficult to see how an apology could bring about forgiveness.

## CONCLUSION

This chapter has argued that social relations are constrained by the problem of guilt and disorder—the misconduct caused by the offender has resulted in a breach that must be socially repaired. Although it is often difficult to locate guilt when multiple actors are involved, there are nonetheless a wide variety of ways by which accusers are able to turn up the rhetorical heat on wrongdoers, particularly if compelling victims are readily available. It is against this backdrop that apologia emerge as socially and culturally important, in that they are a ritually structured communication exchange, one in which participants must be "in the dock" in order to deal with the problem of their offense. Observers of this ritual become participants in it and vicariously experience the transcendent guilt-and-forgiveness morality play. It is only through such a symbolic exchange that social communities are able to deal with the problem of guilt and restore social order.

It is important to note although wrongdoing and guilt result in a compelling social need for an apologia to repair, they do not occur in a social vacuum but rather in a complex social and mediated environment, particularly one in which there is a multiplicity of legal and liability problems. This next chapter introduces and explains how apologists seek to negotiate this dynamic environment.

# 3

# Legality and Liability

If men quarrel and one hits the other with a stone or with his fist and he does not die but is confined to bed, the one who struck the blow will not be held responsible if the other gets up and walks around outside with his staff; however, he must pay the injured man for the loss of his time and see that he is completely healed.

Exodus 21: 18–19 (*The Holy Bible,* 1973/1984)

Although apologiae and apologies are ritualized vehicles for restoring social relations, such restoration does not occur in a social vacuum in which it is self-evident to apologists how to "do the right thing," such as in the attempt to offer compensatory damages described in the chapter-opening epigraph (Hearit, 2001; Rothenbuhler, 1998). Indeed, the contemporary social and media environment is such that said apologists face a contested landscape in which they must cope with real and tangible costs if they negotiate the apologetic exchange incorrectly. One small misstatement can be a major detriment to an organization, not just in that it may damage a carefully crafted image, but it also may result in a negative legal judgment.

Hence, when one surveys the warp and woof of discourse proffered by those caught in a wrongdoing, it is no surprise that apologists tend to take one of two stances when they defend their actions: a public relations stance or a legal one. Neither is it a surprise that by far the preferred strategy in crisis management is a legal approach (Fitzpatrick & Rubin, 1995). By following a legal approach rather than a public relations stance, an organization acts as if the only court about which it must be concerned is a court of law. By giving preference to their legal counsel, an organization's public statements, when offered, tend to be of the "no comment" variety, or say little and cite the effect of privacy laws on company policy as the reason for doing so. When wrongdoers do speak explicitly, the chosen strategies used to defend themselves are denial (whether they are guilty or not) or blame shifting (Benoit, 1995; Fitzpatrick & Rubin, 1995). The motivation for such an approach, of course, is concern for the legal and liability complications that accompany the misconduct.

A legal strategy, although of use in limiting liability exposure, is ineffective at best, especially when one considers the dynamic social milieu in which organizations operate. Although damage to a bottom line is a bona fide concern, so too is damage to a company's reputation, which also has bottom-line implications. A more effective approach to a crisis is a public relations strategy, in which an organization voluntarily admits that a problem exists, aims to be candid as possible, releases all the bad news (at once, if possible), and articulates the measures that are being taken to correct the problem (Coombs, 1999; Fitzpatrick & Rubin, 1995). In so doing, organizational officials seek out ways to demonstrate to the community at large that they are socially responsible to public concerns (Hearit, 1995a).

Yet, despite the public relations counsel available to them, organizations and institutions nonetheless seem to be very willing to suffer great damage to their public persona in order to win—or at least not lose—in a legal environment in which actual and punitive damages can reach into the millions and even hundreds of millions of dollars. Indeed, given the critical effect that liability concerns seem to have on corporate discourse, it is remarkable that the concept is almost completely undeveloped in the research on apologia; to date, only Hearit (1994, 1995a, 2001), Kauffman, Kesner, and Hazen (1994), Patel and Reinsch (2003), and Tyler (1997) have attempted to account for its consequence on corporate speech choices. This chapter, then, attempts to remedy the problem by laying out the role and impact that legal and liability concerns have on organizational communication in a crisis. To accomplish this task, it first discusses the central tension of all apologetic speech; second, surveys the turbulent legal environment in which organizations operate; third, examines the arguments with regard as to whether to disclose information and offer an apology; and, finally, offers guidelines for how organizations and institutions caught in a crisis should communicate.

## COMPETING CONSTITUENCIES
## IN APOLOGETIC SITUATIONS

The question of whether to fully disclose information during a crisis is, at root, a question of which public an organization chooses to feature in its decision making (Ice, 1991). Organizations have multiple classes of publics: enabling (e.g., governmental), functional (e.g., employees, suppliers, and customers), normative (e.g., trade associations and professional organizations), and diffused (e.g., media and communities). These multiple publics or constituencies have competing informational needs, and in pleasing one an organization risks offending another (Cheney, 1991). Consequently, determining what to say in an apologetic crisis is embedded in a series of critical choices.

## Consumers

Although organizations have four classes of publics to consider, once a crisis hits, the critical choice has to be made between which of two core constituencies to privilege: its consumers or its stockholders. Functional publics such as consumers and diffused publics such as angry communities, as well as members of the media, tend to get agitated during a crisis and put organizational activities under a microscope, daily subjecting an organization to criticism, hostility, and negative media coverage. Customers make purchasing decisions in response to what they perceive to be immoral or unethical organizational actions. Critical media review daily organizational statements and find them lacking. All of this constant barrage of criticism results in significant and ongoing damage to an organization's image. These publics tend to clamor for some form of accommodative response from an organization. It is no surprise, then, that it is the impulse of organizational officials to follow the counsel of their public relations departments to come forth with a conciliatory response that features some form of an apology.

## Stockholders

Contrasted with the consumer-oriented publics, an organization during a crisis must also keep in perspective its financial interests as well as those of its enabling publics. For this reason, it is unlikely that a company will assume any responsibility for the wrongdoing, for to do so would be to invite legal action. Marcus and Goodman (1991), for instance, showed that, during a crisis, what investor communities most desire from organizations are strong statements of denial. Marcus and Goodman's study concluded that organizations that issue denial statements in crises find that their stock price holds firm; conversely, those organizations that issue more accommodative statements witness a negative effect on the valuation of their stock, because the market reads an accommodative statement as evidence that the organization is giving in to liability concerns. These accommodative statements, then, are seen to preview a future financial payout on the part of an organization. Cooper (1992) made the same point, but in a more direct manner; he noted, "Every word used to persuade the public is a word which may be used to persuade a judge" (p. 40). Hence, although it might be the impulse of corporate officials to issue an apology, that impulse is tempered with the realization, and reinforced by legal counsel, that to do so is likely to incur considerable liability costs.

## Conflicting Choices

In effect, organizational officers face a Hobson's choice. They have to choose between two impulses (to "do the right thing" or to protect the organization's stability and survival), two constituencies (victims, media, communities, and activists to whom they have an ethical obligation; or stockholders, to whom they have a legal responsibility), two kinds of damages (financial or image), and two kinds of advice from two competing departments (public relations, which says to apologize and fix the problem; or legal, which says to say nothing). As a result, no matter which choice an organization makes, it will offend and damage its relationships with a pivotal constituency group. Tyler (1997) summarized the problem this way:

> Corporate executives are thus trapped, because much as they might like to apologize, they cannot do so without violating their fiduciary responsibility to stockholders. Yet the media and the public are clamoring for an apology. This situation constitutes what conflict theorists term a communicative avoidance-avoidance conflict, in which both alternatives are equally untenable. Apologizing incurs legal liability; not apologizing incurs pubic anger and distrust. (p. 59)

Thus, the central tension in all apologetic discourse is that although it may be the personal inclination of corporate officers to admit and own up to their wrongdoing, matters of liability prevent them from doing so due to legally recognized shareholder obligations (Epstein, 1972).

## THE TURBULENT CONTEMPORARY LEGAL ENVIRONMENT

The contemporary legal environment is a difficult one indeed. Consider the following example. In 2002, a suit filed in federal court in Manhattan by attorney Samuel Hirsch, on behalf of two children, alleged that the ubiquitous fast-food restaurant McDonald's had committed consumer fraud. The charge was that the super-sized portions of McDonald's menus as well as the company's marketing efforts are designed to mislead consumers into thinking that Big Macs, French fries, and shakes are healthy. Consequently, the suit alleged, people who eat at McDonald's, particularly children, are more prone to develop diabetes and high blood pressure, and to suffer from obesity. On January 24, 2003, Judge Robert Sweet dismissed the lawsuit. He argued, "If a person knows or should know that eating copious orders of supersized McDonald's products is unhealthy and may result in weight gain, it's not the place of the law to protect them from their own successes …" ("Judge Throws Out," 2003, n.p.).

This is not the only outrageous lawsuit filed against the company. In April 2001, a woman sued an individual McDonald's franchisee, alleging that a hot pickle had given her a second-degree burn on her lip. She sued, asking for $110,000 and for an additional $15,000 for her husband, who lost her help and "consortium" due to her injury (Brabant, 2001). Yet, perhaps the most famous case involving McDonald's was the successful lawsuit of a New Mexico grandmother who was awarded $2.7 million for burns she received after spilling hot coffee on herself in a McDonald's drive-through. The award was later reduced to $500,000 (Brabant, 2001).

Although reaction to large jury awards is in many ways a political Rorschach test, when one considers the developments of recent years even the most casual observer is left with the point of view that the legal system in the United States, if not broken, is difficult, chaotic, and in a constant state of change. This is precisely the opposite environment needed by corporate advocates in which to engage in a process of strategic planning and calculated risk taking.

## The Rise of the Super-Lawyer

Indeed, the last 20 years has witnessed the emergence of the so-called "super-lawyer," an individual who is rich beyond belief due to his or her successful efforts in taking legal action against corporations with deep pockets. One such individual is Joe Jamail, who won a $10.5 billion judgment on behalf of Pennzoil against Texaco. His law firm's take in the matter: $3 billion (McGraw, 1996). Indeed, Texas appears to be a virtual hotbed of successful Robin Hood-types of firms; according to *Forbes*, the area around Houston is home to five of the seven highest-paid trial lawyers in the country. Fees for class-action suits typically are paid on a contingency basis, and awards based on these fees often result in payouts that average between $5,000 and $25,000 an hour, according to Lester Brickman, a professor at Yeshiva University (Seglin, 2002). The area also is home to John O'Quinn and Richard Mithoff, who successfully sued the makers of silicone breast implants for over $60 million. The irony of the judgments against silicone breast implant manufacturers: to date, medical evidence does not conclusively define a link between silicone breast implants and autoimmune diseases (Angell, 1996).

## Class-Action Lawsuits

A primary concern with these high-powered law firms and the considerable damage awards they procure is the fact that they create a powerful incentive, one in which the motivation to sue stems not from the grievous injustice perpetrated against a defenseless victim that cries out for restitution but instead from the self-interests of the law firms that bring the suits. By *The New York Times* estimates, approximately 10,000 class-action lawsuits are filed each year, with awards that measure in the billions of dollars, yet few substantial sums ever make it to victimized consumers (Browning, 2003). Indeed, this point is illustrated by the recent successful class-action lawsuit against the movie rental chain Blockbuster. Attorneys successfully sued Blockbuster for the high penalties that the company charged consumers who returned their rentals late. Under the terms of the settlement, those who had paid late fees were entitled to coupons of $12–$18. The share of the settlement for the attorneys who brought the lawsuit: $9.25 million (Fabrikant, 2001). With such an economic calculus, it is no wonder that law firms bring such suits against organizations and institutions with deep pockets.

Although an example such as the Blockbuster case appears to be one in which nobody got hurt, consider the case of the Firestone Wilderness tires (which will be addressed in more depth in chap. 6). When the story broke in Texas in early 2000, it was the first *public* sign that there was a problem with the safety of Firestone tires. However, according to Keith Bradsher (2001h) of *The New York Times,* one group of people already knew about the problem and indeed had established a national database to track it: trial lawyers. Their reason for not bringing their concerns to the National Highway Transportation Safety Board? There were not yet enough victims in the database to support a successful class-action lawsuit. The trial lawyers' plan was to wait until more injuries and deaths occurred before they came forward with the evidence.

The lure of a successful lawsuit has become nothing short of dramatic, and prone to abuses. Perhaps no other company in America faces as many lawsuits as Wal-Mart. The statistics are staggering. According to its own data, Wal-Mart was sued 4,851 times in the year 2000—or an average of 13 times a day—for every day of the year (Willing, 2001). Indeed, the huge target that Wal-Mart has become has given rise to the Wal-Mart Litigation Project, whose purpose is "an effort to gather, refine, and market information about lawsuits against Wal-Mart" (Wal-Mart Litigation Project, 2004, n.p.). Historically, the accepted wisdom has been to settle if the cost of litigation was thought to be higher than a proposed settlement amount. Given the staggering quantity of lawsuits, however, Wal-Mart instead has decided to fight rather than pay—even the small ones. The strategy, although risky in terms of public relations, does, according to the company, appear to be working.

One unique aspect of the scourge of class-action lawsuits is "venue shopping"—the practice of filing suit in a location that will most likely result in a favorable outcome for the plaintiff. According to a *Harvard Journal of Law and Public Policy* study, the most popular place to file class-action lawsuits is Madison County, Illinois (in which the largest town is that of Edwardsville; Liptak, 2002c)—an area of 30,000 people. Its reputation is such that people now drive to the community to see a pharmacist and ask for a prescription to be filled for only two pills, in hope of being included as part of a class-action lawsuit and thus be entitled to participate in any damage awards (Seglin, 2002). This also explains why lawyers suing three California-based companies (Intel, Gateway, and Hewlett-Packard) chose Madison County, Illinois, as the location. (Their claim was that the Intel Pentium 4 computer chip was not fast enough.) As one observer noted, "Why should a county judge in Illinois be interpreting California law with respect to whether the Pentium 4 processor is faster than the Pentium III processor"(Liptak, 2002c, pp. 3–11)?

Another aspect of venue shopping that leads plaintiff lawyers to seek places like Madison County is that federal courts have higher standards of "class certification" than do state courts (Liptak, 2002c). Professor Susan Kniak of Boston University observed that "Madison County judges are infamous for approving anything put before them, however unfair to the class or suggestive of collusion that is" (Liptak, 2002a, p. A14). Speaking to the issue of the abuse of class-action lawsuits, John Beisner, attorney and author of the Harvard study, summed up the problem at the root of much of the class-action lawsuit scourge: "There is mounting evidence that what happens in these cases is that the class does not get anything. It's a capital transfer from defendants to plaintiffs' lawyers" (Liptak, 2002a, p. A14). Time will tell if recent legislation that transfers class-action lawsuits from state to federal courts will limit such abuses (Morgenson & Justice, 2005).

## Punitive Damage Awards

To be sure, although trial lawyers are one piece of the puzzle, juries and their awards appear to be another part of the problem. Whereas few analysts have problems with compensatory damage awards (which attempt to pay compensation to victims for their injuries), punitive damage awards (whose purpose is to punish and act as a deterrent) are another matter (Davidson, Knowles, & Forsythe, 1998). In 1997, Chrysler was hit by a $262.5 million award in favor of a family whose 6-year-old died when thrown from a minivan, due to faulty rear-door latches. The problem with the award? The child, who had not been wearing a seat belt, was thrown out a side window and not the rear door (Ito, 1997). Other major awards include a $150 million judgment against General Motors for a failed door latch on a Chevrolet truck, and a $145 million award in punitive damages against State Farm Insurance Companies for not satisfactorily settling a claim from a policyholder who had a car accident (State Farm was also found liable for $2.6 million in compensatory damages; Liptak, 2002b). The granddaddy of all damage awards, however, came in 2002 against Philip Morris. An angry jury awarded a smoker damages of $28 billion—later settled at $28 million ("Smoker's Award Cut," 2002). Although companies rarely pay out the actual damages—indeed, most research suggests that the majority of judgments are ultimately settled for high five- or low six-figure amounts (Hughes, 1997)—it nevertheless follows that the landscape is dangerous for any organization or institution that miscalculates.

## Lawsuit as Corporate Strategy

It should be noted that the problem in the legal environment is not just (un)injured souls with "greedy lawyers" who sue companies in hopes of getting rich. Corporations are not poor, persecuted victims (itself a rhetorical strategy used far too often in news accounts). Undeniably, companies sue other companies, using litigation as a part of corporate strategy. Mutual funds regularly sue companies whose stock they own on grounds of securities fraud; such acts result in approximately one half of the awards paid in this area (Browning, 2003). Furthermore, companies are not above using the legal system against individuals, employing so-called SLAPPs (strategic lawsuits against public participation) that are designed to silence those who would challenge corporate power. The point of this brief review is that the legal landscape in which corporations must answer criticism for their actions is an unruly one, a context in which law and policy decisions are handed down by juries rather than by Congress or regulatory agencies. In a hyperlegal environment, is it reasonable to expect corporations to come clean and tell all? Such an environment is poisonous to the idea that individuals and organizations might be willing to "fess up" or take risks in their public statements, whereby they disclose the nature and the scope of their wrongdoing—even when there may be compelling reasons to do so. Nonetheless, there are organizations that appear to be willing to take the risk; this next section lays out the arguments in support of both a conciliatory approach and a less accommodative one.

## JUST HOW CANDID SHOULD ORGANIZATIONS BE? THE CASE FOR AND AGAINST FULL DISCLOSURE

### The Case for Full Disclosure

The research literature on crisis communication is replete with advice to practitioners that encourages them to be as candid as possible during an organizational crisis. Coombs (1999), for example, urged crisis managers to be proactive, to get all the bad news out as quickly as possible, to be sensitive to public concerns, and to offer sympathetic messages to those who may be affected by the crisis. Similarly, Pines (1985) endorsed a proactive communicative strategy; for example, he counseled would-be crisis managers to "retain control of the story" (p. 18)—something that can only be done by taking a public relations approach in which a company has a proactive message strategy that speaks directly to consumer and community concerns about the apologetic crisis.

There are a number of justifications for making the case that an organization should practice full disclosure during a crisis and ensure that information is issued as completely, accurately, and quickly as possible. Full disclosure does not mean telling every last detail; rather, it means that an organization's communication should be characterized as open, forthcoming, and constructively revealing information, which may include offering an apology.

Certainly, it goes without saying that if an organization is facing a crisis not of its own making and is instead the victim of an external agent, a policy of full disclosure is a wise course of action. As discussed in chapter 1, such was the situation the makers of Tylenol found themselves in after a consumer terrorist laced Tylenol capsules with cyanide in 1982, causing seven deaths in the greater Chicago area (Fearn-Banks, 1996). Johnson & Johnson, the parent company of McNeil Consumer Products Corporation (which was the maker of Tylenol), took a proactive stance to the crisis, and went out of its way to practice full disclosure, even to the point of providing reporters from *60 Minutes* and *Nightline* with broad access to company officials and facilities.

Another such rationale is that an organization must be careful to fully disclose information because, if it fails to, it risks alienating key stakeholder groups (Kauffman et al., 1994). Organizations have key constituents, such as employees and suppliers who support them throughout their existence. Yet, these groups pale when measured against the influence of consumers who are angry with an organization during a crisis. Indeed, the potential costs of liability may be small when measured against the costs that irate consumers can level against an organization. The annals of corporate history are replete with examples of organizations whose behavior was dramatically affected by the purchasing decisions or shunning of consumers. Exxon franchisees found themselves on the receiving end of such anger after the Exxon *Valdez* ran aground in Prince William Sound (Hearit, 1995a). Angry consumers cut up their Exxon gasoline charge cards and sent them back to the company en masse. Said another way, the marketplace is crowded and if customers are given reason to go elsewhere, they will; consequently, organizations caught in a crisis must demonstrate good faith with these groups by fully disclosing the details of their actions, even if less than flattering, and offer an apology. Such a stance, of course, privileges the long-term effects of corporate actions more than it does the more immediate legal concerns.

Another rationale for full disclosure is evidenced by the commonly accepted belief that once an organizational crisis occurs, due to investigative journalists as well as political and judicial pressure, all of "the facts" will be revealed anyway, so an organization should seek to build goodwill and maintain control of the crisis story (as much as is possible) by being the first to release the information. Again, history provides examples of personal and private details that come out after intense mediated, political, and/or legal scrutiny: Captain Joseph Hazelwood's arrest for drunken driving, President

Clinton's willingness to engage in immoral behavior while on the telephone with a fellow head of state, or the release of a private company memo demonstrating that Dow Corning had concerns about the safety of silicone breast implants (Hilts, 1992).

The research literature for full disclosure also asserts that by coming clean and apologizing, corporate officers risk less damage to their company's image. Bradford and Garrett (1995), in their discussion of message strategies employed by organizations during a crisis, found that the preferred message strategy desired by consumers is one of apology. In fact, they asserted that attempts to minimize, justify, or otherwise explain organizational actions without offering an accommodative apology tends to score worse in people's perceptions than does even a strategy of silence. In other words, consumers expect conciliatory statements after wrongdoing; anything less and they draw negative conclusions about an organization and its ethics. Hence, it is wise for an organization, in terms of its organizational image, to practice full disclosure coupled with an apology.

Concern for consumers is not the only justification for full disclosure. To fully disclose the facts and apologize is to preserve the relationship with the victims of the wrongdoing. To apologize is to remove the insult from the injury (Cohen, 1999). There are many examples of clients who win huge jury awards, and, on hearing the award, have remarked, "All I really wanted was an apology, and only when they would not apologize did I decide to sue." By apologizing, an individual or an organization is able to remove some of the hurt. Conversely, to not apologize is seen as a denial of respect to the victims; this adds more hurt to an already difficult situation. A subsequent virtue of full disclosure followed by an apology, then, is that it functions to prevent more litigation (Cohen, 1999). By apologizing, an individual or an organization is able to turn a foe into a friend, or, at a minimum, reduce the hostility that a legal antagonist might feel.

This conciliatory or apologetic response is likely to create the conditions by which it is possible to reach a settlement (Cohen, 1999). If a company with significant resources has indeed committed a grievous harm in which there are clearly identifiable victims, then it is a nonsequitur to assume that an organization is likely to escape such a situation without having to face any significant financial expenditures. Consequently, to apologize often succeeds in restoring the relationship such that negotiations can begin quickly in order to reach a private settlement and, thus, avoid costly litigation altogether. Goldberg, Green, and Sander (1987) described it this way: "[A]n apology alone is insufficient to resolve a dispute, but will so reduce tension and ease the relationship between the parties that the issues separating them are resolved with dispatch" (p. 221). An apology, then, functions to remove much of the poisonous tone and attitude that might otherwise surround such negotiations.

If an organization takes a conciliatory approach and fully discloses the facts, its victims may choose not to pursue legal remedies. Cohen (1999) asserts: "Taking the step to make a legal claim is often triggered by the injured party's anger. An early apology can help defuse that anger and thereby prevent a legal dispute" (p. 1022). Said another way, although apologizing may be an invitation on the part of some to bring a lawsuit, so too may not apologizing. Smart executives consider the calculus of the context of their wrongdoing, the needs and desires of the victims, the potential costs, and the degree to which an apology would potentially reduce the likelihood of legal action, and then make a calculated judgment that errs on the side of a conciliatory approach (Cohen, 1999).

There are other conditions that support full disclosure. Due to the presence of liability insurance, for instance, some organizations can afford to respond (Kauffman et al., 1994). After the Exxon *Valdez* oil spill, for instance, it eventually came out that Exxon had a $4 billion insurance policy—which roughly equaled the amount of claims and damages it faced. With such a fact in mind, the company should have done more to take a more conciliatory approach to managing its communication after the spill. The converse is true as well. Can an organization afford not to respond? That is, does it threaten the organization's very survival to not respond? The case of Arthur Andersen and its auditing work for Enron is instructive here, in that the company, out of liability concerns, chose to avoid a conciliatory response and negotiate a settlement with prosecutors; instead, the company ended up going to court and lost, and was eventually forced to forfeit its right to audit public companies after a guilty verdict.

Finally, as noted earlier, the costs of liability that organizations face are two types of judgments: compensatory and punitive (Davidson et al., 1998). The examples cited earlier of high jury awards were cases of high punitive damages in which juries sought to "teach a company a lesson" or wanted to "cause them pain just like they caused pain to the victims" due to a perceived lack of contrition and repentance. By issuing an apology, a company is seen as more conciliatory and less callous. Hence, even if a case does make it to trial, the apology, although it may not have brought about a settlement, is likely to perform in a positive way by reducing the likelihood of a high legal judgment against a company because it is seen to be apologetic (Cohen, 1999).

## The Case Against Full Disclosure/Apology

Although the arguments for full disclosure are compelling, the arguments against full disclosure are equally persuasive. Whereas there are many reasons not to disclose information during a crisis, there is one that really is primary and central to the position: Litigation brings with it huge costs to an organization, costs that are in addition to the potentially huge financial considerations (Kauffman et al., 1994).

Implicit to all of the concerns with full disclosure is the issue of liability. To apologize and admit guilt is to assume responsibility and culpability. To do so in a context in which the apology is spoken to the victim puts the apologist in a situation in which he or she has all but admitted responsibility and now faces legal liability. Legally speaking, an apology alone can be used as evidence of guilt. Cohen noted that the federal rules of evidence normally exclude "hearsay" as evidence of guilt; the one exception is in the case of apologies for which "an apology alone can be used as evidence against the defendant" (Cohen, 1999, p. 1029). A statement in which an individual or organization acknowledges guilt for an act and apologizes for it is indeed legally admissible.

There are other costs that come with litigation. One such cost is a chief executive's time. Time spent to prepare a response to a lawsuit is time that cannot be spent strategically responding to the varied needs of the marketplace. Second, the presence of lawsuits often is accompanied by another form of attention, that from state and federal authorities investigating the allegations of wrongdoing. A third cost of litigation is the actual cost of preparing and responding to allegations; attorneys' fees at firms with top reputations run to hundreds of dollars an hour. Such fees add up quickly when a company hires entire teams of lawyers. A fourth reason for not fully disclosing all the facts of a case is that the more information that is disclosed, the more likely an organization is to be questioned about it during "discovery." In other words, disclosure of information about organizational wrongdoing is a direct invitation for further plaintiff inquiries on a particular or related problem.

The question of liability is undergirded by a compelling justification for not fully disclosing all that is known about a crisis: The fact of the matter is that before the law, a company's legal responsibility is to its shareholders and not to the general public. Disclosing information that is damaging to shareholder interests is, in a sense, a violation of that legal responsibility (Epstein, 1972). Currently, there is no law or regulation that requires organizations to take into account the needs of other constituent groups. The law protects the rights of capital, not communities in which capital operates.

There are other persuasive reasons not to practice full disclosure. One such point is that there is no way to know when corporations have been successful by withholding information (Kauffman et al., 1994). Unquestionably, given the large number of corporations and the multiplicity of acts they are capable of, it is not inconceivable that there are organizations who did not practice full disclosure and "got away with it." Like a good conspiracy theory, the lack of evidence is, in effect, support for the position (Hofstader, 1964).

Although such may be the case, there are other rationalizations for the position. One is that what a company discloses may end up shocking, appalling, or angering key constituents (Kauffman et al., 1994). As noted in chapter 2, Ford Motor Company performed a cost/benefit analysis in which management compared the costs of providing a technological fix to the problem of the propensity of the Ford Pinto to explode in rear impact collisions to the costs of payments to victims and their families in the event of harm or death, and that Ford chose to offer payouts over a fix. The revelations of such a calculus caused considerable damage to Ford's image for years (Kauffman et al., 1994). This choice brought about outrage among Ford owners and the general public. Similarly, in the 1930s through the 1960s the federal government conducted a series of experiments designed to test the long-term effects of syphilis on victims. The revelation that the government participated in a study that chose *not* to treat African-American men caused outrage among the African-American community, and in future years, created the basis for the belief among some African-Americans that the government created crack cocaine in order to imprison or kill large numbers of African-American men (Harter, Stephens, & Japp, 2000).

An additional and correlated reason for not fully disclosing information is that of context. In an antitrust case, for example, a low-level staffer's memo that speaks in hyperbole about dominating and controlling the market might be taken as representative of a company's position as a whole. Or a minority, although eventually correct position about a problem with a certain product can become "proof" that a company knew about the problem years before it was willing to deal with it.

Moreover, to come clean and apologize might be considered weakness on the part of some, and provide strategic opportunity for one's opponents. Such was the case with Senator Trent Lott. His serial apology for his remarks at Strom Thurmond's 100th birthday party (that the country would have been better off if Thurmond had been elected), coupled with his poor record on civil rights issues, created a context in which he was weakened politically to the point where he eventually ended up losing his position as Senate Majority Leader (Applebome, 2002). As well, Cohen (1999) referenced the case of the Liggett Tobacco Company, which revealed its past wrongdoings; the result was that it laid itself open to the fury of rival tobacco companies. The firm, which has a considerably smaller market share than its competitors, broke ranks in 1997 and admitted that smoking causes cancer. Because of this admission, other tobacco firms have attempted to isolate the company both legally and economically.

Finally, to open up and apologize may put an individual or organization in a position whereby it voids its insurance coverage. Most insurance company policies are written in such a way that the apologist is faced with a "general duty of cooperation with the insurance company in the defense of a claim" (Cohen, 1999, p. 1025). Some even go so far as to prevent the apologist from taking on liability without the consent of the insurance company. Although the cases in which an insurance company is likely to void a policy are limited, this is nonetheless a legal concern for individuals and organizations to consider.

## CRISIS COMMUNICATION CHOICES

Organizations face a variety of competing concerns in a crisis situation: the needs of competing constituencies, the organization's legal obligations to shareholders, liability, and the desire to not offend media and key constituent groups. What, then, should organizations and institutions that are caught in a crisis say?

## When to Apologize

There are a number of contexts in which liability concerns do not prohibit organizations from taking full and public responsibility for their actions; that is, there are situations in which individuals, organizations, and institutions can "safely" apologize and assume full responsibility. One such context is those crises that observers view largely as "media flaps"—those instances in which an organization has done wrong but faces no victim that has received significant (and especially bodily) harm. One such example is the case of Chrysler, when it was disclosed in 1987 that the company had systematically unhooked odometers and executives had driven the cars—in some cases up to 400 miles—and then reconnected the odometers and sold the automobiles as new (Hearit, 1994). Although the company eventually was charged and pleaded guilty to mail fraud, the liability concerns were minimal. The company replaced cars in the most egregious examples, but for most consumers Chrysler simply offered free checkups and extended their warranties, as well as paid $16.4 million in fines to settle the issue. Similarly, AT&T, after its customers experienced a service interruption, found it necessary to apologize and assume responsibility (Benoit & Brinson, 1994). The company simply reimbursed its clients for the time in which service was interrupted and faced no long-term liability issues for the service disruption. Such stories garner a great deal of media attention, but in and of themselves generate no real victims and, hence, find their liability concerns to be minor or nonexistent.

Similarly, a second context in which an organization might find it in its best interest to deliver an apology is when the determination of compensation is relatively straightforward or when the actual damages can be determined and calculated in a relatively uncomplicated manner (Wagatsuma & Rosett, 1986). Such a case might involve an injury that is caused by an organization but results in very little suffering. Compensation may be required to pay for missed work, but beyond that little additional reparation is required, particularly any kind of punitive damage award.

One context in which apologies tend to solve rather than create liability concerns are in defamation lawsuits. Given that the "crime" is, in effect, one of speech, it is not a stretch that another form of speech, an apology, can be used to mitigate damages in a defamation suit (Wagatsuma & Rosett, 1986). The case of *Dateline NBC*'s apology to General Motors after rigging tests to make sure that GM's C/K trucks exploded in an exposé segment is an example of this; the apology made by Stone Phillips and Jane Pauley functioned to mitigate the need for damages to be paid by the errant broadcaster (Hearit, 1996).

Another context in which it is safe to issue an apology is as part of a larger legal settlement (Cohen, 1999). Although it tends to negate the effect of being a "voluntary" apology, time has shown that apologies are important enough to be included as part of negotiated agreements. Settlements vary as to whether said apologies are to be private or public.

A final context in which it is useful to offer an apology can be found in those situations in which guilt can be proved regardless of an apology (Cohen, 1999). Such was the case in 1992 of the Sears Repair Centers that were accused by the Attorney General of California with systematically defrauding customers by charging them for repairs that they did not really need. Sears initially attempted to argue that it had simply engaged in "preventative maintenance"; it quickly became evident that a strategy in which it acknowledged that some "mistakes were made" would aid a quicker resolution of the crisis (Hearit & Courtright, 2003b). In instances such as this—in which guilt is relatively straightforwardly determined—it is in the best interests of an individual or an organization to "come clean" and issue an apology. Such an organization will be sued successfully with an apology or without one; and, as noted earlier, to offer an apology is likely to help limit punitive damages.

## When Not to Apologize

Although there are situations in which it is recommended that an organization can "safely" apologize, it also follows on a purely strategic level that there are instances in which an individual or organization is probably wise to accept legal advice not to apologize. (chap. 4 addresses the ethical side of this equation.)

One such example occurs in those situations in which it is difficult to determine the level of compensation that would be required to rectify the situation. Most efforts to determine reasonable compensation for injury or death do so through a calculus of age, income, and time lost (indeed, the whole field of forensic accounting has emerged in recent years); in other instances it is a profoundly difficult equation. Although it may be reasonably uncomplicated to determine the earnings potential of a successful business executive in his or her 50s, it is comparatively more difficult and problematic to determine the value of a child (economically), or a child's lifetime earning potential, when no career had been chosen. Similarly, when damage is not to people but the environment, the difficulty of determining damages becomes profoundly more knotty and difficult.

Similarly, a second situation in which it is strategically undesirable to apologize occurs in those instances in which a large class of people qualify for victim status: An apology would be used as proof as culpability. Such a decision to apologize would be likely to set in motion a chain of events that would result in a substantial negative judgment that would, in effect, bankrupt the organization or institution.

## Contexts With No Easy Answer

Yet, what about those situations in which the question as to whether to fully disclose and issue an apology is not clear-cut? How, then, should an organization respond? In an examination of what companies say in such a context, Tyler (1997) observed that because there is a dilemma between two equally unattractive alternatives—that of incurring liability versus that of incurring public anger and distrust—the preferred communicative response by corporate officials tends to be an equivocal one. Such a response is characterized by organizational officials who express sorrow for what has happened without saying clearly whether the company was responsible for the act. Such was the case of earlier-mentioned Toshiba, which extended its "regrets" for what had happened and promised that the company was actively engaged in efforts to make sure the illegal sale of sensitive material never happened again—yet, it did so with a carefully worded statement to make sure that the company assumed no liability from the statement by acknowledging fault for the wrongdoing (Hearit, 1994). Unfortunately, to engage in too much equivocation results in the message being rejected as insincere (Tyler, 1997).

However, there are credible efforts that seek to linguistically separate the sorrow for an offense from a statement that accepts responsibility (Englehardt et al., 2004). This tack is rooted in the idea that an apology tends to function to bring parties together and reduce some of the anger that comes from a wrong. Such a response was shown by Fitzpatrick (1995), who maintained that crisis managers can be apologetic for an incident without taking the blame for it. Similarly, Cohen (1999) argued for the presence of a "safe apology." Specifically, he asserted that the idea of benevolence can be separated from the idea of responsibility; that is, an individual or an institution can apologize ("I'm sorry") without assuming guilt ("I did it; I'm responsible"). Recent efforts by the states of Massachusetts, Texas, and Hawaii to legally ensconce apology into their respective state laws seek to codify into law this distinction between an apology as a statement of concern or regret and a formal acknowledgment of culpability. In other words, these states have attempted to differentiate between benevolent expressions of kindness and "embedded admissions of fault" (J. R. Cohen, 2002, p. 829). Currently, the laws are in flux and represent a patchwork of different ideas. Incongruently, for example, a physician's offer to pay medical bills is not viewed as an admission of fault, but sending flowers to someone can be construed as an admission of responsibility.

Even if a company offers a "statement of regret"—which Hearit (1994) described as a carefully crafted statement whereby organizations voice and articulate concern for the victims while avoiding direct statements of responsibility—such an accommodation falls short. It must be accompanied by a corrective-action strategy whereby an organization articulates the efforts taken to ensure that the problem will not recur and that the problem's underlying causes have been addressed.

## CONCLUSION

This chapter has discussed how organizations are to address the competing interests of their stakeholders (customers, clients, communities)—toward whom they have a moral responsibility—with those of the shareholders—toward whom they have legal and fiduciary responsibilities (Epstein, 1972). In so doing, it has shown that there are a number of situations and contexts in which, from a legal perspective, an organization can and should come clean and fully apologize. These are situations in which the wrong is such that to not fully apologize will risk alienating customers permanently; when damage to a company's image is as financially devastating to a company's bottom line as is a legal judgment; when apologizing is likely to dissipate anger, so that people do not end up suing to bring about a settlement; to lessen the likelihood of punitive damages; when the damages are easily calculated; when an organization can be sued successfully without making an apology; and in defamation lawsuits as well as media flaps in which there is no real legal liability. Conversely, when damages are difficult to calculate it is probably in a company's best interest to avoid an apology. For those cases that are in between, research has shown that companies tend to take a more equivocal approach whereby they do not deny guilt but neither do they accept it. The next chapter goes beyond the legal issues of each individual case and asks the ethical question as to whether an individual or organization *should* apologize.

Perhaps the most creative example of an organization negotiating this difficult terrain of whether to admit guilt or not can be found in the case of British Petroleum after an oil spill off the coast of San Diego, California, not long after the Exxon spill in Prince William Sound. Company officials went public with a statement that said, "Our lawyers tell us it's not our fault, but it sure feels like our fault and we'll do everything we can to fix it" (Sandman, 1993, p. 64).

# 4

# Apologetic Ethics[1]

Therefore, if you are offering your gift at the altar and there remember that your brother has something against you, leave your gift in front of the altar.

First go and be reconciled to your brother; then come and offer your gift.

Matthew 5:23–24 (*The Holy Bible*, 1973/1984)

Unlike individuals, when organizations and institutions are caught in a crisis they face a difficult legal dilemma. As noted earlier, the legal terrain that organizational officers must negotiate is difficult and complex, and one misstep is likely to result in considerable liability costs. Yet, although legal judgments are indeed costly, the damage an organization may face to its carefully constructed image is no less expensive should the organization choose not to "do the right thing" in the eyes of media and consumers. Indeed, it appears as if companies that engage in wrongdoing and do not "come clean" often face a decade's worth of anger from key publics, anger that is likely to be abated only when another organization commits a more egregious error that supplants the previous transgression in the public's consciousness. Whereas chapter 3 attempted to address what an organization caught in a crisis legally *might* say while navigating the problem of liability, attention here is now turned to what an organization *should* say, taking into account the ethical responsibility of individual and corporate apologists. At root, this chapter suggests that when speaking ethically, as in the chapter-opening example, the emphasis should be on reconciliation.

The question of ethics concerning apologetic communication is complicated. This chapter reviews some of the competing approaches to public relations ethics, with an eye toward the context of crisis management, and then proposes casuistry as a method by which to develop an ethical standard for apologetic communication. A casuistical approach is one that grounds such exemplars in relevant moral considerations. Casuistry is valuable in this context because it can be used to develop a normative standard, or para-

---

[1]This chapter was written with Sandra L. Borden.

digm, by which to judge apologetic communication. Subsequently, this chapter reviews recent developments in public relations ethics, and then follows with the proposal of casuistry as a vehicle by which to evaluate the ethics of apologetic discourse. This is accomplished by the specification of an ideal ethical standard regarding both the manner and content of the communication as well as an attempt to explain some complicating circumstances that may warrant a deviation from the ideal.

## PUBLIC RELATIONS ETHICS

The topic of ethics in public relations has undergone substantial development in recent years. Although this review is not meant to be exhaustive, it does attempt to explicate major developments in the field (for recent detailed reviews, see Curtin & Boynton, 2001; Day, Dong, & Robins, 2001; Seeger et al., 2003; Seib & Fitzpatrick, 1995). Specifically, there are a number of major schools of thought regarding how ethics intersects with public relations (Curtin & Boynton, 2001).

One approach to public relations ethics is the advocacy model. This approach argues that organizations are free to have their own distinct points of view and, as a result, are entitled to representation and counsel (Barney & Black, 1994; Edgett, 2002). It is the ethical duty of public relations counsel to energetically defend a client's point of view to the public. Lying or the use of deception would, of course, be considered an unethical form of persuasion in this model.

More socially responsive ethics have been proposed as well (Daugherty, 2001). Grunig's excellence theory (1992a; Bowen, 2004) argues that organizations should act only in a way that gives equal consideration to both a company's interests as well as the public interest. Similarly, K. A. Leeper (1996) applied concepts of communitarianism to public relations exchanges, maintaining that organizations have an obligation to mitigate the effects of corporate actions on the communities that they affect. More recently, Fitzpatrick and Gauthier (2001), for instance, developed an approach for public relations counselors rooted in three tenets: avoid or at least minimize harms while promoting benefits, show respect for persons (i.e., treat people with respect and dignity), and practice distributive justice (i.e., distribute the benefits and burdens of an action as fairly as possible).

Others relate general ethical theory to public relations crises, applying both teleological and deontological approaches to provide crisis managers with meaningful guidance. Pratt (1994), for instance, used a situational analysis method to assess the ethics of Perrier in 1990 when the company disclosed that it had discovered the presence of benzene in its water source. Similarly, Williams (1997) used both teleological and deontological standards to offer an ethical analysis of the discourse surrounding the Intel

Pentium chip controversy of 1994. In so doing, both Pratt and Williams argued that, when constituting their response to a crisis, organizations and their managers must consider both the motives for their decisions as well as the outcomes that their decisions have on stakeholders.[2]

More specifically related to the study of ethics as a distinctively communicative phenomenon, there are those who take a discursive approach to ethics. One example of this kind of approach seeks to apply the work of Habermas (1979) or other critical theorists to a public relations context (R. V. Leeper, 1996). In the same way, Botan (1997), van Es and Meijlink (2000), and Kent and Taylor (2002) attempted to utilize a communication approach to develop a public relations ethic; they proposed the use of dialogic ethics, first articulated in a communication context by Johannesen (2001). The dialogic approach asserts that people are not to be exploited by corporations and given limited communication choices but instead should be nurtured and actualized. In addition, individuals should not be treated as a means to an end, but instead should be given the freedom to question the assumptions behind the communication. Finally, the emphasis during a communication exchange should be on mutually creating meanings rather than using communication as merely information transfer. To date, this approach has not been applied to the crisis context, although one suspects that when an organization's very survival is at stake, the response is unlikely to be consistent with a dialogic approach to ethics. This, of course, begs the question of whether a dialogic approach is to be recommended.

Although these and other ethical analyses are useful to demonstrate the ethical considerations relevant to individuals and organizations that communicate regularly with core stakeholders, they are less helpful when applied to a crisis situation. These models are primarily designed to address the ethics of typical, everyday kinds of communication, rather than those crisis situations in which an individual's or an organization's high-priority values (i.e., health, survival) are threatened (Weick, 1988). Such a threat means that an organization in a crisis situation faces a direct communication conflict between the ethical and the economic (although such conflicts make up the day-to-day business of a company, they are more immediate and intense during a crisis). Hence, for an ethical analysis, such as Kernisky's (1997), to be useful, it must speak directly to the context in which an organization's very survival is at stake, and the organization's standard ways of communicating are dramatically changed (i.e., are reduced and more centralized; Billings, Milburn, & Schaalman, 1980).

---

[2]When we refer to "stakeholders," we mean it in the sense of parties who have a moral claim on the apologist by virtue of having a stake in the apologist's actions. Perhaps they are affected directly by the apologist's actions, or maybe they are in a relationship with the apologist, or perhaps they have certain rights in play. In any case, our conception of stakeholders is not limited to those one might pay attention to strictly from a self-interested point of view.

Moreover, it is important to realize that an important distinction needs to be made between the ethics of the act triggering the apologia versus the ethics of the communication after the act. This book attempts to cover the broad range of apologetic communication, including individuals, corporations, and institutions that face severe ethical criticism. By and large, it deals with the guilty (although, as demonstrated in chaps. 5, 6, and 7, it is fair to question whether said individuals and institutions are indeed guilty of the criticism in some cases). As a result, any ethic developed here should be recognized to be a *communication* ethic that deals with the communication after the (alleged) wrongdoing, rather than the ethics of the alleged wrongdoing itself. Said another way, this chapter seeks to sketch out an approach that provides a standard by which to judge the communication that occurs after an ethically questionable act. Individuals and organizations, then, may follow up their ethically questionable act with unethical or ethical communication.

## CASUISTRY

The case-based approach of this book is highly compatible with an ethical decision-making procedure known as *casuistry*. Casuistry has become increasingly popular since 1988, with the publication of the influential *The Abuse of Casuistry* by Jonsen and Toulmin. It has been applied to journalism, public policy, medicine, research ethics, and other fields. (For more on casuistry, see Arras, 1993; Boeyink, 1992; Borden, 1999, 2002; Keenan & Shannon, 1995; Kirk, 1936; Leites, 1988; Miller, 1996.) The study of casuistry represents a rich and historical ethical tradition that dates from the Middle Ages and the Renaissance, with roots in classical rhetoric (Jonsen & Toulmin, 1988).

The idea of casuistry is that it is possible to develop ethical cases that serve as paradigms, or exemplars, of demonstrably moral or clearly immoral acts. Jonsen and Toulmin (1988) argued that "these type cases are the markers or boundary stones that delimit the territory of 'moral' considerations in practice" (p. 307). Hence, to take what we know about individual and corporate communication resulting from an ethical challenge, it is possible to develop a paradigm, or standard, by which to judge crisis communication. We intend to articulate what is ethically ideal (Borden, 2002). However, by comparing ethically ambiguous cases to this ideal, future analyses will be able to specify *degrees* of ethical communication: what is more ethical and what is less ethical, how far one can depart from the ideal and still remain in the realm of what is ethically acceptable, and, finally, what measure of difference from the ideal results in a paradigm shift from ethically acceptable to ethically prohibited. This permits a more nuanced perspective on the moral choices of individuals and institutions caught in a wrong than do analyses that oversimplify the process of ethical evaluation as consisting only of black-and-white decisions.

Casuistry is an inductive method similar to the analogical reasoning used in case law. The method starts with a situation in which the ethical considerations are so clear-cut that different people can readily agree on whether it is ethically acceptable. This so-called "paradigm case" then functions as a standard against which to measure more complex, ethically perplexing situations. To the degree that a more difficult case resembles the paradigm in terms of its ethically relevant features, the second case will receive the same assessment as the paradigm—much as a precedent functions in legal reasoning. In other words, if the paradigm case is found to be ethically sound, an essentially similar case also will be judged ethically sound (Jonsen & Toulmin, 1988).

To the degree that a more difficult case differs from the paradigm in terms of its ethically relevant features, the second case will receive a different assessment. Said another way, if the paradigm case is found to be ethically sound, an essentially different case will be deemed ethically deficient. It is crucial to specify which aspects of the paradigm case matter to its ethical assessment. Otherwise, it is easy to get distracted by merely superficial differences (e.g., whether an instance of plagiarism involved an article about fish rather than an article about cars). Once these relevant characteristics have been adequately articulated, one has a somewhat more general basis to compare cases while at the same time retaining a direct link to the specifics that give ethical principles concrete, practical meaning (Boeyink, 1992).

A key insight of the method is that general principles are not always the most helpful starting point for ethical decision making. This is especially true in situations in which it is difficult to agree at the outset on a priori assumptions (Jonsen & Toulmin, 1988). That being said, we believe that the judgments one reaches with casuistry ultimately rely on the larger world of ideas provided by ethical theory, but only opaquely unless the casuist makes an effort to make these other ethical ideas transparent (Borden, 1995). Casuistry fell into disuse after its high point in the Middle Ages precisely because it failed to consider the broader perspective provided by ethical ideas embodied in theories such as consequentialism and deontology (Jonsen & Toulmin, 1988). Therefore, we inform our application of casuistry with ethical standards reflecting relevant considerations from deontology, consequentialism, and care ethics. These standards, explained later in this chapter, include respect for autonomy, minimizing harm, and nurturing relationships.

Bound up with rights to reparation are the right to know and the right to be protected from unnecessary or undue harm flowing from the duties of fidelity and nonmalfeasance (Ross, 1930). Both of these are inevitably involved in any apologetic episode, because harm has occurred and may be prevented in the future depending on the ethical nature of the apologia. Also, the apologist has information that the injured party is entitled to know in order to understand what has happened and to make a reasonable assessment of the damage that has been wrought and what might be done to repair it. In short, the victim needs the information to exercise his or her autonomy. Duties of justice also are relevant in a variety of ways, because the apologists often are in a position to take unfair advantage of the victims as the vulnerable parties in a crisis communication context. The victims, therefore, are entitled to protection from abuse of power. Also, the offenses that are the subject of apologia often involve the fair distribution of goods, such as the monetary worth of products or stock. Finally, there is the issue of everyone getting their due—the victims receiving their compensation, and the apologist receiving his or her punishment.

Feminist ethics also calls our attention to the importance of relationships and the experience of caring and being cared for within those relationships (Noddings, 1984). The strength of the relationship between each injured party and the apologist varies, but in each case there is a preexisting relationship that has somehow been disturbed by the apologist's offense and that probably would continue to be mutually beneficial and satisfying if it could somehow be restored or, at minimum, placed on the public record. Therefore, some of the characteristics of the ideal paradigm speak directly to the dynamics of the relationship between apologist and injured parties, including the inevitable loss of trust that accompanies betrayal. The offense, in other words, is not just against the people and groups involved, but, in a sense, against the very relationship itself.

The paradigm locates the ethical analysis in the primacy of the victims; that is, in those who have been most wronged and who least willingly consented to the risk of injury (see chap. 2). Although the paradigm case thus gives primacy to the victims—and the need for reconciliation between the apologist and the victims—it should not be taken to mean that the victims are the only parties of interest. All stakeholders—be they stockholders, communities, suppliers, watchdog groups, governmental agencies, or even the media functioning as accusers in an apologetic crisis—have an interest in a restorative outcome to the crisis. Thus, even though attention tends to focus most heavily on the victims during an apologetic crisis, we presume that all stakeholders deserve moral consideration.

Audience interest in a positive conclusion to a crisis is supported by recent research. Bradford and Garrett (1995), for instance, dealt with the important question of audience expectations during allegations of ethical misbehavior on the part of organizations. They found that not just victims but consumers in general regularly look for organizations caught in a wrong to be direct and to take a conciliatory approach to their wrongdoing in an apology. Any attempt by an organization to explain or justify its misdeeds is rated by stakeholders as negatively as is choosing a strategy of silence.

One example supports this point. During the Intel Pentium chip controversy, the constant barrage of criticism by consumers drove the price of

Intel's stock into a downward spiral. Only after Intel apologized, the case was settled, and irate consumers could return their computers for a replacement chip did the value of Intel's stock return to its precrisis level (Hearit, 1999). Hence, by ethically responding to the victims in the case, even stockholders were able to achieve a positive outcome to the apologetic crisis.

Now that we have articulated some of the relevant ethical considerations, we can begin describing an exemplary, or paradigmatic, apologia when the individual or institution is guilty of the perceived offense. We begin with a discussion of the morally relevant characteristics that have to do with the manner, or form, of the communication.

## MANNER OF THE COMMUNICATION

Several characteristics of the paradigm case have to do with the *manner* of an apologia itself. Ideally, an ethical apologia is:

- Truthful.
- Sincere.
- Timely.
- Voluntary.
- Addresses all stakeholders.
- Is performed in an appropriate context.

### Truthful

Truthfulness suggests that an apologia should be characterized by a disclosure of useful information and not omit key facts that, when revealed, would fundamentally change how others view the apologist's actions. (Note: The topic of disclosure is addressed more fully later in this chapter.) A major component of truthfulness is that an individual or an organization caught in a crisis should not engage in deception. If an apologist chooses to lie, such a choice should only be made as a last resort and then only for reasons that would survive public scrutiny—of which there are very few. It should be noted here that the criterion is truthfulness, rather than Truth, which avoids a whole host of philosophical problems (Bok, 1989).

The criterion of truthfulness does acknowledge the propensity of individuals and organizations to "strategically name" their wrongdoing (Hearit, 1994). Yet, truthfulness requires that the names submitted by apologists must bear some resemblance to the reality of the "facts of the case," while acknowledging that "Even if a given terminology is a reflection of reality, by its very nature as a terminology it must be a selection of reality, and to this extent it must function also as a deflection of reality" (Burke, 1966, p. 45). The definitions proffered by apologists are anything but neutral—they are strategic (Cox, 1981; Schiappa, 2003) and contain an argument inherent in them (Crable & Vibbert, 1985). To affix a name to something is to engage in a largely persuasive act that contains an attitude toward the object—and gets at the difficulty in coming up with a neutral determination of what an act means.

The case of the Audi 5000 in the late 1980s is instructive. Critics charged that the automobile was prone to "sudden acceleration"; that is, it would accelerate when the car was idling, with a driver's foot on the brake. This technological problem, it was alleged, resulted in injuries and deaths across North America. Audi countered this definition with the claim that, according to their independent testing, the incidents under question were the result of "pedal error," in which drivers put their foot on the accelerator instead of the brake—a contention that was later supported by the federal government (Hearit & Courtright, 2003a). In this case, Audi's communication met the criterion of truthfulness.

A negative example of truthfulness was the 1992 case in which Sears Auto Repair Centers were alleged by the California Attorney General's office to have defrauded customers by charging them for repairs that they did not need. Sears responded to the allegations that it was engaging in "preventative maintenance" (Hearit & Courtright, 2003b). It was a clear case of a company trying to put a positive spin on a situation with a language choice that bore no representation to the actual facts of the case. Hence, this criterion acknowledges the reality-creating nature of definitions while requiring that organizations and individuals choose a definition with which informed auditors are likely to agree, rather than claim that an apologist has overreached.

## Sincere

A second characteristic of the ideal apologia is that it be performed with sincerity. An apologia typically is understood as an attempt to express regret for wrongdoing, to communicate an understanding of the offense's impact and antecedents, and to generally make things right (Hearit, 1994). Whenever an apologist lacks any real regret, understanding, or a true intention of making things right, the recipients of the communication are misled and deprived of their due. Their right to autonomy—to make informed, free choices about their own lives, including any action they might want to take against the apologist or to restore the relationship—is compromised. Furthermore, such deficient motivation potentially causes harm by leading the recipients to make future decisions based on false premises such as deception. Perhaps the recipients, trusting erroneously in the apologist's sincerity, postpone or cancel actions that would guard them against a financial loss or provide them with legal relief. There also is a sense in which victims are entitled to an offender's regret for wronging them.

Three components are involved in the performance of a sincere apologia. First, an individual or an organization must demonstrate a good-faith effort to achieve reconciliation. The point is that there must be an actual motive (as opposed to unknowable motivations), knowable through the apologist's discourse and actions (Burke, 1969), to express genuine regret and achieve a reconciliation. This often is demonstrated in the corrective action that an organization has taken to resolve a problem, as well as the availability for third-party verification. A second component of this idea is the recognition that the demonstration of sincerity is indeed rooted not just in operational performance but also in communicative performance. A good example of this is the case of American Airlines in 2003, which, shortly after requesting and receiving wage concessions from its mechanics' and flight attendants' unions, turned around and gave bonuses to key executives to induce them to stay with the company during a difficult time. When the incongruence of these actions came to the fore, instead of simply issuing a news release or placing an advertisement in media outlets, CEO Donald Carty immediately went before microphones and cameras and apologized with demonstrable remorse for the insensitivity and wrong-headedness of the company's actions (Reed, 2003).

A final component of performing sincerity is that the apologist shows evidence of a true desire to reconcile with offended stakeholders, rather than acting in such a way that it is evident that the apologist's only desire is to escape from the media glare. Again, the case of Intel, with its flawed Pentium II chip, is a useful example. When the company finally relented to demands from disgruntled consumers that the company replace the chip that caused inaccurate calculations, the company stated that it still thought that the problem was overblown but would nevertheless replace the chips. In effect, Intel missed an opportunity to restore positive relations with reconciliation and instead followed a path that would simply put the issue to rest and get the company off the front page of the newspaper's business section (Hearit, 1999).

## Timely

A third characteristic of the paradigm case is that the apologetic response be timely—that is, it is performed as soon as the offender recognizes the offense. On first glance, this would appear to be a relatively straightforward condition—as soon as an offense is made known to or recognized by the offender, then a response should follow. If an apology comes too late, after key stakeholders have had to continually call for it, such an individual or an organization would be (rightly) perceived to not want or to resist reconciliation, and thus to have a tin ear. This, if true, would violate the victims' right to have their offense acknowledged, and it communicates implicitly a lack of concern about the victims' injury. It also devalues the relationship between the apologist and the victims by implying that reconciliation is not worthwhile and by corrupting the experience of "knowing each other" that exists to varying degrees in any relationship.

Finally, there is a consequential aspect to this paradigm characteristic. If the apologist fails to deliver a response in a timely manner, the victims are deprived of certain options to deal with any damage caused by the offense, potentially at the cost of significant financial, emotional, and other types of harm. The efforts by President Clinton to apologize for the Tuskegee experiments came quite late and, as a result, most of the victims had already passed away (Harter et al., 2000).

Although slowness of response is a key problem, the converse can present its own set of issues. An individual or an organization that responds too quickly can be perceived as trying to "put out a fire" or "get it over with quickly," rather than as seeking to achieve reconciliation in an offended relationship. It also may be imprudent to respond if vital information is unavailable. In this way, in apologetic crises time is structural rather than linear; that is, it is less about the clock and more about when moral guilt is able to coalesce in the minds of stakeholders and when the information is needed. Thus, what is required is a communicated response in an appropriate point in time.

## Voluntary

A fourth criterion for an ethically ideal apologetic response is that the communication proffered by the apologist be voluntary; that is, it must be performed without actual or anticipated coercion. By this, the idea is that the apologist has decided to offer an apology on the basis of moral reflection.

A voluntary apologia communicates a sincere desire to reconcile, rather than an opportunistic attempt at damage control. Without this criterion, the victims have little reason to trust the apologist's words or actions, whether they constitute the expressed desire to reconcile or actual promises of compensation. And, if the response is involuntary, the victims have reason to feel insulted as parties to a relationship in which their needs are not valued and the mutual commitment that is supposed to characterize relationships is, and maybe never was, present.

A final aspect by which to assess the voluntary nature of the apologetic discourse is that of tone. Part of the process of remorse is a certain degree of humility—as opposed to anger. In President Clinton's first apologia for the Monica Lewinsky scandal, on August 17, 1998, the presence of anger directed at Independent Counsel Kenneth Starr was reflective of an involuntarily delivered apologia—one proffered for political, not moral, reasons.

## Addresses All Stakeholders

A truly ethical apologetic response must speak to the concerns and interests of all parties who have been offended. This is simply a matter of being morally accountable to those who have a legitimate moral claim. Yet, when speaking of contexts of wrongdoing, the problem typically is rooted in the fact that individuals and corporations have natural constituencies. It is the propensity of apologists, when caught in a crisis, to speak only or at least primarily to their natural or most immediate constituencies, rather than to all those stakeholders whom the apologist has wronged—those who have a moral problem with the apologist's acts.

Such was the case with the settlement by Merrill Lynch in May 2002. The company engaged in negotiations with New York Attorney General Elliot Spitzer for the practice of falsely talking up the value of telecommunications stocks to individual investors—and thus ultimately defrauding them when the boom went bust—in order to gain lucrative investment banking fees from those same companies. Merrill Lynch agreed to pay a $100 million fine without acknowledging that it had done anything wrong. The beneficiaries of the $100 million, however, were not the retirees who lost significant portions of their life savings; instead, the monies went into the treasury of the State of New York (Hearit & Brown, 2004). An ideal apologia would have found a way to address issues of compensation to those who were actually wronged by the company's actions. In this particular case, individual investors have had to turn to the courts to sue Merrill Lynch for fraud.

## Appropriate Context

A final paradigm characteristic that addresses the manner of apologetic speech concerns the site, location, or medium chosen. There are a couple of factors that are worth noting. First, the forum as such must be accessible to all stakeholders. That is, it must be conducted in such a way that all who were wronged have genuine entrée to the apology. With major offenses, such as President Clinton's admission of an inappropriate relationship with Monica Lewinsky, a televised apologia is necessary. In many instances, an advertisement in regional or national newspapers is appropriate. Second, when the victims are smaller in number and can be constituted as a group, a more private occasion may be desirable. Such was the case with the Christian & Missionary Alliance, which apologized in the late 1990s for abuses that occurred in the schools in which children of missionaries in Africa were educated. In addition to a public apology in denominational publications, the church invited the victims to a conference center in suburban Atlanta and provided a personal, private apology in the context of a religious service (Courtright & Hearit, 2002).

In sum, for apologetic discourse to be considered ethically ideal, it must be truthful, and sincerely and voluntarily delivered in an appropriate time. It must also address all stakeholders and be performed in an appropriate context. Although these characteristics are critical, on their own they are incomplete. Just as important is the content of what is said in an apologetic statement.

## CONTENT OF THE COMMUNICATION

Several characteristics of the paradigm case have to do with the *content* of the apologia itself. Ideally, an ethical apologia:

- Explicitly acknowledges wrongdoing.
- Fully accepts responsibility.
- Expresses regret.
- Identifies with injured stakeholders.
- Asks for forgiveness.
- Seeks reconciliation with injured stakeholders.
- Fully discloses information related to the offense.
- Provides an explanation that addresses legitimate expectations of the stakeholders.
- Offers to perform an appropriate corrective action.
- Offers appropriate compensation.

### Explicitly Acknowledges Wrongdoing

The best apologia, ethically speaking, makes no bones about the fact that an offense has been committed—wrongdoing is not merely implied in the wording so that the recipients have to "fill in the blanks." Ethically, such clarity prevents possibly misleading the recipients of the apologia. But, more important, it respects the right of those who have been wronged to have their injury acknowledged and "owned" by the offender. In short, this characteristic validates the moral claims of the injured parties. Such was the approach taken by the Chrysler Corporation in 1987 to revelations that it had disconnected odometers on cars, driven them for an average of 40 miles (although in some cases the mileage was as much as 400 miles), and then rehooked the odometers and sold the cars as new. CEO Lee Iacocca directly admitted to the wrongdoing; he remarked, "Disconnecting odometers is a lousy idea. That's a mistake we won't make again at Chrysler. Period" (Hearit, 1994, p. 114).

### Fully Accepts Responsibility

Ideally, the apologia not only makes clear that an offense has been committed but also that the apologist is guilty of committing it. This requirement discourages the common practice of scapegoating, in which the apologist tries to rhetorically displace the blame onto a single individual or unit in a large organization. It also discourages disassociation, in which the apologist uses strategic ambiguity to distance himself or herself from the offense and thus avoid, or mitigate, blame (Hearit, 1995a). This requirement acknowledges the need for honesty, opens up opportunities for self-improvement, and, again, respects the right of injured parties to validate their moral claim. With revelations that the Toshiba Machine Company had sold top-secret milling equipment to the then-Soviet Union in 1987, the Toshiba Corporation went out of its way to announce that its top two executives would resign. The company noted that in the Japanese business world there was no higher form of apology (Hearit, 1994). Such a strategy demonstrated that the company and its leadership fully assumed responsibility for the misdeeds.

## Expresses Regret

Having admitted the offense and then responsibility for it, the apologist now is encouraged to convey dismay at causing harm and failing in his or her responsibilities. This restores trust with the injured parties by acknowledging the injury as a moral offense. It also implicitly reinforces the relationship by suggesting that the offense is an anomaly, and not "the way things are going to be from now on." In other words, once everyone gets past this rough patch, the injured parties can go back to depending on the apologist with an increased amount of confidence. Such was the tack taken by executives at Texaco after allegations in 1996 of racism on the part of key executives, who called African-American employees "black jellybeans" that were "glued to the bottom of the jar" (Brinson & Benoit, 1999, p. 484). The company relied heavily on strategies of mortification, and the company chair, Peter Bijur, went out of his way to demonstrate his regret for what had occurred, admitting that he was "ashamed" (Brinson & Benoit, 1999, p. 493).

## Identifies With Injured Stakeholders

In order to show that the individual or organization truly "gets it," the apologist ideally should express empathy with the injured parties. This means that the apologist should frame the offense from the point of view of the injured parties. This is a necessary step in order to comprehend the depth and effect of the offense in a way that honors the experience of those who have been wronged. Without such an appreciation, appropriate (felt) regret may not even be possible. Such an appreciation also will help the apologist choose the appropriate words, context, and tone to convey regret in a way that feels legitimate and proportionate to the offense. Identification also suggests acknowledging that the relationship will never be exactly the same again because of the loss of trust associated with the injury. Perhaps it was his assuming such a stance that made the aforementioned case of Don Carty's apology at American Airlines so remarkable. Carty went out of his way to acknowledge that it was wrong to give out retention bonuses to senior executives when other employees were being asked to accept cutbacks (Reed, 2003).

## Asks for Forgiveness

The ultimate goal of an apologia is to "make things right again." If the apologist is guilty of breaking faith with stakeholders, an actual apology will be necessary for reconciliation to take place. This works in tandem with the other characteristics to encourage a restoration of the damaged relationship. It says to the injured party, "I want to start over. I want to know I have your trust again." Asking for forgiveness is important even when the prospects for forgiveness are slim (maybe justifiably so). In other words, the relationship may realistically have no future, yet it is ethically desirable to express to the injured parties that they are, in fact, valued and that their opinion of the apologist matters. This honors the history between the apologist and the injured parties, including the trust that has been violated with the accompanying harms and feelings of violation. One of the factors that makes the 2001 apology by the Roman Catholic Church so memorable (as fully explicated in chap. 7), is the fact that the Church so directly asked for forgiveness from God and from those it harmed for multiple sins and offenses (Stanley, 2000b).

## Seeks Reconciliation

An ethical apology will help to effect the repair of the injured relationship. Assuming that this relationship was mutually beneficial to begin with, it is in the best interest of all involved to get back to where the relationship was before the wrongdoing—or to make it better, by starting over with the insights that come from having weathered a storm in the relationship. As with other characteristics, this is an important step even when reconciliation is unlikely because it validates the worth of the injured parties. The aforementioned Christian & Missionary Alliance (C&MA) case is admirable in the fact that the institution did not simply apologize but went out of its way to restore those who had been harmed into full fellowship with the church (Courtright & Hearit, 2002). The C&MA invited victims to a retreat, and apologized both privately and publicly, in an effort to promote reconciliation on the part of the denomination for its role in the misdeeds.

## Fully Discloses Information Related to the Offense

Full disclosure of information as a characteristic presumes a degree of discretion as far as what kind of information should be shared, how soon, and in what form. In other words, the apologist is not expected to be rash in releasing sensitive information, for example. Some information should be evaluated carefully to determine whether it is accurate, whether its release would violate someone's confidentiality or unduly harm someone, and if the injured parties are even entitled to it. That being said, this characteristic discourages the apologist from releasing pertinent information in a piece-meal fashion just to avoid conflict or embarrassment or to deny other parties' rights. Full disclosure respects the injured parties' right to an account of the offense. This step also may help to prevent further harm by giving those injured an opportunity to stem or reverse their losses, for example. It does, however, also provide those injured with resources to punish the apologist by seeking legal and financial penalties. In other words, such information may be used as legal evidence. Kauffman et al. (1994) rightfully pointed out that assessment of this criteria is difficult, given the fact that it is impossible to know when corporations have hidden information from those whom they have harmed. Nonetheless, organizations can meet this criteria by revealing all details that are relevant to victims.

## Provides an Explanation That Addresses Legitimate Expectations of the Stakeholders

An apologist must meet the legitimate expectations of all stakeholders. This characteristic simply encourages the apologist to organize the apology within a framework that is meaningful to the injured parties. Closely linked with identification, this characteristic encourages discussion of the offense, its causes, and its effects in terms of the responsibilities the apologist has violated. An injured party should not have to wonder, "What does this have to do with *me?*" Whether it be a failure to maintain confidentiality, to give truthful recommendations, or to correct mistakes as soon as possible, the explanation should make clear what exactly the apologist has done wrong regarding the injured parties. Such was the weakness of the apology of the Exxon Corporation after the oil spill in 1989. The company took out a response in *Time* magazine whereby it apologized to "the people of Alaska" but left those who were most directly harmed—the fishermen who made their livelihood from Prince William Sound—unaddressed in the advertisement and subsequent communications (Hearit, 1995a).

## Offers to Perform an Appropriate Corrective Action

Performance of corrective action consists of expressing that one has learned one's lesson, is committed to not repeat the offense, and wants to avoid the circumstances that contributed to the offense. This gives the injured parties reason to have confidence in the apologist again, to be open to rebuilding the damaged relationship, and it also reassures them that "at least some good came out of this." It additionally affirms to them that the apologist has good intentions, that is, the apologist will meet his or her responsibilities well and will try to constantly improve. This also is practically beneficial to the apologist, who has a stake in the maintenance of the relationship and who wants to perform his or her duties optimally in the future. Such was the strategy taken by Jack in the Box after a tragic *E. coli* crisis killed three children in the Pacific Northwest in 1993. The company, along with its parent corporation, Foodmaker, became a leader in developing innovative technology to ensure that the problem would not recur (Ulmer & Sellnow, 2000).

## Offers Appropriate Compensation

*Compensation* refers to the repayment of an actual debt now owed to the injured parties (e.g., giving a credit for an unfair charge) and/or self-imposed suffering that is roughly proportional to that of the injured parties. This may take the form of financial liability, but it also may be primarily ritualistic, such as an advertising campaign that exposes the apologist to shame. In this way, an apologist may offer compensation in the form of proportional humiliation (Courtright & Hearit, 2002). Few examples of compensation are made public due to the fact that such an outcome is usually the result of private negotiations between a company and its victims. It is important to note that such compensation does not have to take the form of a financial settlement. The earlier-mentioned Chrysler odometer example is a case in which a company found nonfinancial ways to offer compensation—Chrysler offered a free checkup and extended warranties for those whose cars had been "tested" (Hearit, 1994).

The idea of casuistry is that it presents a standard by which to adjudicate ethical questions. This chapter has applied casuistry to the problem of apologetic discourse in situations in which the individuals or organizations are guilty of the allegations leveled against them. However, one of the advantages of casuistry is that it gives real weight to real-world circumstances. The next section attempts to address those complicating circumstances that might legitimately warrant departures from the ideal we have described.

### COMPLICATING CIRCUMSTANCES

In a casuistical analysis, it is the particular constellation of characteristics possessed by the paradigm case that makes its moral clarity so compelling. In other words, it is the whole package, rather than any one item, that settles an ethical judgment about the paradigm case. Therefore, failing to meet one or several of the ideal paradigm's characteristics is not necessarily ethically fatal. Rather, such departures may characterize a rhetorical choice as being less ethical than the paradigm case, but still ethically acceptable. Of course, enough departures from the ideal may warrant pronouncing a given rhetorical choice as downright unethical. Some apologia may only meet about half the ideal criteria. In such cases, an apologist may have to reflect on the relative centrality of the paradigm's characteristics in order to decide whether a rhetorical choice is still acceptable. At this stage of development, we propose that there are at least five complicating circumstances, which concern corporate discourse more than individuals, that could justify departures from the paradigm case while still retaining the essential ethical character of an apologia. (We recognize the possibility that there are other factors that may emerge.) They are the following:

- Catastrophic financial losses.
- Grave liability concerns.
- A moral learning curve.
- The problem of full disclosure.
- Discretion.

## Catastrophic Financial Losses

First is the recognition that organizations may be in financial trouble. Such organizations, although able to provide a heartfelt and penitent apology, may nevertheless be in no position to offer financial compensation to the victims of its wrongdoing. One such example could be a not-for-profit organization such as a church or a social service agency that depends on its donors for survival; in such a case, compensation would divert funds from the performance of social good. In this sort of situation, an organization may look for nonfinancial ways by which to compensate for its wrongdoing, such as offering to create a memorial to the victims. It is a well-accepted ethical standard that one may not be required to perform an action of which one is incapable.

## Grave Liability Concerns

Second, and related to the first, is the problem of liability and its impact on the apologetic exchange. Individuals and organizations are legally responsible for their actions. The presence of liability law is such that when said apologists commit a wrong, there often is a financial cost to their wrongdoing, in terms of incurring legal liability for their actions. It is our position that such individuals should be held responsible and be expected to own up to liability. However, we do recognize the fact that there are certain instances of wrongdoing in which the liability is so great that the consequences to an organization's very survival would be grave. Such was the case with the aforementioned case of Merrill Lynch. Attorney General Elliot Spitzer acknowledged that the guilt of Merrill Lynch, as well as that of brokerage firms, was so great that entire companies could have been closed, or he could have legally indicted the firms for fraud, which would have, in itself, been a form of a corporate death penalty (Hearit & Brown, 2004). As a result, the problem of liability does present a complicating and hence mitigating circumstance by which to judge the ethical choices of the apologists.

Although not ethically ideal, catastrophic liability may move an apologist to offer a statement of regret for its actions while being careful not to assume full (legal) responsibility (Hearit, 1994). It would then be left up to the courts to adjudicate the question of civil liability. One variation on this idea might be for an apologist to engage in a legal settlement with authorities that provides some financial penalty or compensation while not opening the organization up to full legal liability, because doing so would bankrupt the organization. However, if an organization is in a situation in which nondisclosure could be fatal or lead to further substantial injury, an organization is in a situation in which it must tell all—there is no room for ethical exceptions (Kauffman et al., 1994).

## Moral Learning Curve

A third complicating factor has to do with the nature of the relationship with the injured parties. In some cases, time may have passed, and the injured parties have long since passed away. Although the ethical ideal is to address an apologia to the victims or the surviving members of a victim's family, it is recognizable that individuals or institutions may not be fully aware of their guilt, or they may develop a response to their actions that changes over time as they come to recognize their guilt and hence decide to proffer an apology. In such a case, a late apology is better than no apology at all. This is because individuals and organizations often go through a "moral learning curve" in which they initially do not recognize the harm that their actions have caused. Only after time and reflection does the need for an apology become apparent. This factor attempts to account for such a situation.

Such was the case of the Catholic Church in its decision to offer an apology as it prepared for the new millennium (this case is covered in more detail in chap. 7). It recognized that many acts committed in the defense and propagation of the Gospel may have, over time, hurt the very people that the Catholic Church was trying to convert ("Excerpts From the Apology," 2000). Hence, despite the fact that the victims of the Catholic Church's acts were harmed generations before, it was nonetheless appropriate for the Church to offer an apology in order to "make right" what it had done in the past.

Another example of a moral learning curve was demonstrated by the Denny's restaurant chain. The company, as a result of a number of lawsuits and significant social sanction, was shown to have regularly practiced discrimination toward its African-American customers throughout the 1990s. Recognizing the gravity of its problem and the fact that the company was indeed guilty of discrimination, Denny's communicated its corrective action by instituting a wholesale cultural change in the way that it treated all of its customers, hired a minority advertising agency, and significantly increased the number of minorities in managerial and board positions. By doing so, Denny's was able to articulate how it was able to leave behind its legacy of discrimination and is now considered one of the top companies in America for employees of color to work at (Adamson, 2000; Chin et al., 1998). Such an example recognizes that managers of organizations are, on reflection, able to account for and respond to the wrongs that have been committed previously.

## The Problem of Full Disclosure

To what degree does an organization qua organization fully know the extent of its wrongdoing? Simply put, although discrete individuals might know the extent of an organization's wrongdoing, damaging or incriminating information may not be available to the dominant coalition within a company or organization at the time of critical decision. In some cases the knowledge may be present albeit buried in volumes of paperwork, or in other instances the cause might be more insidious. Individuals within an organization have their own agendas and often work to hide or cover up information that could be damaging to themselves or the organization.

Furthermore, to what degree do materials that come to light constitute "proof" of organizational knowledge of wrongdoing? For instance, in a product safety incident, suppose a memo surfaces in which an individual raises questions as to the safety of a product. Critics may immediately hail the memo as proof that a company knew of its wrongdoing, although at the time it was written such a memo may have represented one individual's opinion, which was seriously taken into account and then dismissed.

Additionally, as pointed out in chapter 2, task differentiation has an impact on the identification of organizational responsibility and guilt in that it functions to diffuse responsibility. Few individuals in an organization have the whole picture of how all aspects of a product might go together. As a result, a defective product might add up to a harm, although the designers and engineers who made the product were careful in all of their individual decisions.

## Discretion

Finally, we do acknowledge that the confidentiality of the victims is such that it may warrant that an organization not go public with a full disclosure or apology. In such instances, we recognized the need to respect the confidentiality of the victims or be indiscreet. Such was the case with the previously mentioned Christian & Missionary alliance. In coming to terms with the abuse suffered by missionary children at the Mamou Alliance Academy in Mamou, Guinea, from 1950 until 1971, the C&MA chose to apologize privately to the victims at a conference center in Atlanta (as well as to offer counseling and other remedies) for the wrongdoing that occurred. Yet, the denomination did publicly acknowledge and detail the wrongdoing, all the while being careful not to reveal the identities of any of the victims due to the stigma that they would face (Courtright & Hearit, 2002).

## CONCLUSION

This chapter has addressed how individual and organizational apologists should respond to allegations of wrongdoing by featuring ethics in their responses. In so doing, it has laid out a method by which to ethically judge the apologetic decision making offered by individuals and organizations, and at the same time has acknowledged the fact that there are complicating factors that affect such decision making.

All things being equal, victims should be the first priority for an organization caught in a crisis. The paradigm relies on this assumption. However, the paradigm acknowledges the validity of other stakeholders. What do we propose when the interests of the various stakeholders are fundamentally different, and perhaps incompatible? This becomes an issue particularly in the area of financial compensation, where there is only so much money to go around, regardless of the legitimate claims of various stakeholders. How should we prioritize after privileging the victims? A feminist ethics approach gives more consideration to those stakeholders with the closest relationships to the apologist and/or the relationships with the best prospects of being mutually satisfying in the long term. A utilitarian calculus is one in which an apologist strives to achieve the most net benefit overall. In this solution, as in the first, some stakeholders will come out better than others, but the apologist's resources will be distributed in such a way as to maximize the benefit for the greatest number of stakeholders, while minimizing overall harm. Stakeholders are prioritized according to the consequences they will experience from the apology, rather than on the basis of prior factors such as consent or extent of injury. This could conceivably mean that some stakeholders benefit more from the apology than do the actual victims; however, this result may be too counterintuitive in view of all the ethical factors we have considered so far.

Optimally, we may be able to achieve some kind of balance wherein the interests of the various stakeholders are resolved in a manner approaching equilibrium. Nothing is "taken away" from some stakeholders in order to give more to others in this scenario. Rather, all stakeholders get some consideration, although probably not everything they desire or deserve. However, this sort of solution probably is not possible in crisis situations involving high costs and scarcity conditions. In such situations, some way of prioritizing among the competing interests at stake will be necessary. In the spirit of the paradigm case, we suggest using the same criteria as before: who has been most wronged and who has least willingly consented to the risk of injury. We could thus come up with a list of stakeholders in descending order of importance. Those at the top of the list would receive the most consideration, rhetorically and financially.

This chapter concludes the theoretical portion of this book. The next chapter begins a three-chapter section that analyzes apologetic communication in an attempt to assess the ethical quality of public statements in instances of allegations of individual, corporate, and institutional wrongdoing.

# 5

# Apologia and Individuals

## Politicians, Sports Figures, and Media Celebrities

There was a man who had two sons. The younger one said to his father, "Father, give me my share of the estate." So he divided his property between them.

Not long after that, the younger son got together all he had, set off for a distant country and there squandered his wealth in wild living. After he had spent everything, there was a severe famine in the whole country, and he began to be in need. So he went and hired himself out to a citizen of that country, who sent him to his fields to feed pigs. He longed to fill his stomach with the pods that the pigs were eating, but no one gave him anything.

When he came to his senses, he said, "How many of my father's hired men have food to spare, and here I am starving to death! I will set out and go back to my father and say to him: Father, I have sinned against heaven and against you. I am no longer worthy to be called your son; make me like one of your hired men." So he got up and went to his father.

But while he was still a long way off, his father saw him and was filled with compassion for him; he ran to his son, threw his arms around him and kissed him.

The son said to him, "Father, I have sinned against heaven and against you. I am no longer worthy to be called your son."

But the father said to his servants, "Quick! Bring the best robe and put it on him. Put a ring on his finger and sandals on his feet. Bring the fattened calf and kill it. Let's have a feast and celebrate. For this son of mine was dead and is alive again; he was lost and is found." So they began to celebrate.

Luke 15:11–24 (*The Holy Bible*, 1973/1984)

The story of the prodigal son is ultimately one of reconciliation, a reconciliation that only comes after the realization that the son's acts have dishonored the father and made the son unworthy of his inheritance. In a generous act of grace, the father chooses not to take into account the wrong he has suffered but instead accepts the apology and offers forgiveness. Indeed, this parable illustrates the transforming power of an apology, how it can repair a damaged relationship and restore fellowship between the offender and the offended. (For the psychological research on the transformative effects of apology, see Bennett & Dewberry, 1994; Bennett & Earwaker, 1994; Enright & Fitzgibbons, 2000; Enright & North, 1998; Lazare, 1995; Petrucci, 2002; Takaku, 2001; Weiner, Graham, Peter, & Zmuidnas, 1991; and Worthington, 1998.)

Apologies are not just used in private exchanges but also have been shown to repair relationships between public officials and their constituencies. Probably the most (in)famous apologia is Richard Nixon's well-known "Checkers" speech, in which the then-vice president defended himself from Democratic-party charges that he misused a special campaign fund. After he denied the charge and detailed his financial status, Nixon declared that he had indeed accepted one gift from a Republican contributor—a cocker spaniel named Checkers—and that because his kids liked the dog so much, he refused to return the gift. The effort by Nixon was successful enough to save his place as the vice presidential nominee on the 1952 Republican ticket (Rosenfield, 1968).

Similarly, Senator Edward Kennedy delivered an oft-referenced apologia on July 25, 1969, after campaign worker Mary Jo Kopechne died in a car accident that occurred while the two drove home after a late-night party. In this address viewed by 35 million people, Kennedy presented himself as a tragic victim of events that were beyond his control, and alluded to the possibility of a mysterious curse that hung over his family (Butler, 1971; Ling, 1972). He concluded the speech with an appeal for the support of the people of Massachusetts and asked that they help him to decide whether he should retain his Senate seat. Public response to his speech was overwhelmingly positive; consequently, Kennedy was able to stay in the Senate.

Historically, politicians who sought to justify their (mis)behaviors, such as Nixon and Kennedy, constituted the bulk of mass-mediated apologiae up through the 1980s. Although no longer the only form of justificatory communication, apologiae and apologies that emanate from individuals still constitute a significant portion of all apologetic address. The research on apologetic discourse also mirrors this fact; all scholarly articles published in communication journals between 1950 and 1990 reviewed the efforts of individuals (Hearit, 1992). Only after events such as the Tylenol tampering episodes or the Exxon oil spill in Prince William Sound did researchers begin to turn their attention to other forms of apologetic address.

By convention, an apology is principally an interpersonal exchange between two individuals, one who has been wronged and another who is in
need of absolution. However, events like those faced by Nixon and Kennedy
have functioned to turn a context that previously was a private exchange
into a public one. Subsequently, it is one that pursues not the repair of relationship but that of an image—not with a friend or partner but with a constituent group. And, rather than being a tête-à-tête that is kept private,
contemporary apologiae are adjudicated in such a way so that all can see.
Accordingly, this chapter first surveys the academic research on the topic of
individual apologia and then applies it to three types of actors for whom
apologiae and apologies have shown themselves to be increasingly relevant:
political, sports, and media personalities.

## INDIVIDUAL APOLOGIA THEORY

### Dyadic Exchanges

The definitive characteristic of an apologia is that it is a response to a
"kategoria"—an accusation that constitutes an ethical attack on someone's
character (Ryan, 1982). In the seminal monograph on the topic, Ware and
Linkugel (1973) wrote: "In life, an attack upon a person's character, upon
his worth as a human being, does seem to demand a direct response" (p.
274). The use of a direct response—an apologia—seeks to help individuals
clear their names. Undeniably, the motive behind an apologia is the purification of a damaged image (Fisher, 1970).

Expanding on Ware and Linkugel's original conception, Kruse (1981a)
argued that apologetic exchanges are characterized by three requirements.
First, they require the presence of an ethical charge of wrongdoing. Second,
they necessitate a context in which an audience expects a message to be
apologetic; the purification of a persona is the principal justification for this
sort of reply. Third, they cannot be delivered by another but must be made
by the self in defense of the self. Given the interplay between the accuser and
the accused, in many ways apologetic discourse is fundamentally dyadic—it
seeks the repair of the relationship between the offender and the offended.
The deliverance of an apology cannot be delegated or passed off to another,
nor can the acceptance of an apology and the concomitant offering of
forgiveness be made by someone other than the offended (Tavuchis, 1991).

The nature of an ethical allegation is not limited to criticisms against a
person's character but may also be taken to include policies held by an individual. In a further development of the situation of apologetic response,
Ryan (1982), for instance, maintained that a perspective that views apologia
only as a response to a charge against an individual's character is unneces-
sarily limiting. Consequently, he offered a broader definition, one that in-

cludes an attack on a person's policies (as well as character). From Ryan's frame of reference, what constitutes an apologia is the presence of an attack that cannot go unanswered. Perhaps Kruse (1981a) was the most definitive on the subject; she asserted that, from a critical standpoint, the key point is that public criticisms have been leveled against individuals that cause observers to believe them to be unethical—and hence warrant a response.

## The Language of Apologetic Speech

It is in the realm of the substance of apologetic speech that most scholarly development has occurred. Here, scholars have attempted to articulate the many strategies that apologists have to draw from in formulating their responses. Ware and Linkugel (1973) articulated the most prolific model that details the "factors" used by apologists caught in a wrong. In particular, they concluded that apologists feature one or a combination of four factors when responding to allegations of wrongdoing: denial, bolstering, differentiation, and transcendence. The first, denial, occurs when an accused rejects or repudiates the charges leveled against him- or herself. Ware and Linkugel (1973) noted that many individuals, if unable to deny an act, use denial of intent as a strategy to diffuse hostility. A second factor, bolstering, is an identification strategy that seeks to reinforce past relationships. A third factor, differentiation, is a redefinition strategy that attempts to change the context in which an idea is understood, whereas the final factor, transcendence, also seeks to change the context but in this case to a much larger or conceptual one. These four factors, then, are used in combination to determine the posture that an apologist takes toward his or her wrongdoing.

Although Ware and Linkugel's (1973) factors have been most influential—indeed, most studies published until the 1990s tended to utilize this approach—the schema is not without difficulties. First, given its simplicity, it is often applied as a template, resulting in unimaginative analysis. Second, and more important, there are a number of strategies that researchers have since catalogued that show the presence of many more strategies of apologetic address. Others have noted the presence of a wide variety of other strategies, among them justification, mortification, scapegoating, and even silence (Brummett, 1980; Coombs, 1995; Hearit, 1994, 1996; Notz, 1997).

The fullest form of the strategies used by apologists in responding to allegations of wrongdoing comes from Benoit's oeuvre (1995; Benoit & Brinson, 1994; Benoit, Gullifor, & Panici, 1991; Brinson & Benoit, 1996, 1999), articulated under the rubric of image repair theory (2000). He argued that when allegations have been leveled against an individual, he or she seeks to save face by responding with one or a combination of the following five strategies: denial, evasion of responsibility, reduction of offensiveness, corrective action, and mortification. The first, denial, has two forms. Simple denial occurs when individuals deny having perpetrated the alleged act of wrongdoing (Brinson & Benoit, 1996) or at least dispute that they were responsible for it (Benoit, 1995). When unable to deny, individuals often shift the blame, a strategy by which they attempt to scapegoat another party.

To evade responsibility for their actions, apologists often use one of four strategies (Benoit, 1995). First, they may claim that they were provoked—and simply, although regrettably—they responded. A second strategy is one of defeasibility; here, individuals seek to evade responsibility with the claim that events were really beyond their control. Relatedly, apologists often define their behaviors as an accident for which they should not be blamed. Finally, Benoit argued that, in defense of their reputations, individuals sometimes claim that their intentions were good but the act was misunderstood or had unforeseen consequences.

When individuals are unable to escape responsibility for their actions, Benoit (1995) posited that they often seek an alternative strategy by which they try to reduce the offensiveness of their actions in order to make their transgressions appear less problematic. The first way individuals do this is to bolster—an identification strategy that reminds the offended of a previously positive attitude toward the alleged wrongdoer. Minimization is another strategy whereby individuals seek to argue that the consequences of an act are not as serious as originally believed. A third approach, differentiation, seeks to distinguish one act from similar acts, whereas transcendence attempts to differentiate by changing the moral context of the act. Fifth, Benoit argues that when all else fails, some individuals resort to attacking their accusers whereas others rely on a subsequent strategy in which they offer compensation in order to repay the damages caused by the negative actions.

A fourth vehicle that those caught in a wrong use to repair their ruined reputations is a strategy of corrective action (Benoit, 1995). Here, they promise to fix the problems that led to the wrongdoing in order to make those problems unlikely to recur.

A final strategy, mortification, occurs when individuals apologize and ask for forgiveness (Benoit, 1995). Such a strategy takes responsibility for the negative acts and seeks a pardon from another. This practice is frequently linked with a strategy of corrective action (Benoit, 1995).

Benoit's (1995) project has been of tremendous use to scholars in apologetic communication; it is no understatement to say that it has become the definitive work on the strategies used by apologists. Although a number of criticisms have been leveled against Benoit's image repair theory (i.e., he rediscovered Aristotle's *topoi*, or stock lines of argument), the bulk of studies published in crisis management, apologia, and defensive communication all owe a significant debt to the thoroughness of his project (see Benoit, 2000; Burns & Bruner, 2000; Simons, 2000).

## Third Parties

As a starting place, apologiae deal with the relationship between the offender and the offended. To be sure, in her articulation of the generic parameters of apologetic discourse, Kruse (1981a) was adamant that an apologia can only be delivered by the accused; no third party can deliver an apologia on behalf of another. Yet, the late 20th century undeniably witnessed the introduction of third parties into apologetic exchanges. Perhaps owing to the fact that we live in a "corporate" society, when an individual wrongs another there seems to be no shortage of people who then step forward and say they were wronged as well. That is, due to individuals' membership in groups and constituencies, they now place themselves in the midst of apologetic exchanges that historically have been between two parties.

Third-party identification and participation is particularly true in at least three ways. First, third parties often insert themselves in the role of "victims." In other words, third parties, usually in the form of a group or coalition (social movement), claim that the actions of another wronged them. Hence, although they were not addressed as individuals in the wrongdoing, their membership in an offended group gives them opportunity to claim offense. John Rocker's interview with *Sports Illustrated*—discussed at length later in this chapter—is one such example of a context in which a whole host of individuals and groups were able to claim offense by Mr. Rocker's ill-conceived statements.

"Professional critics" are a second form of third parties who inject themselves in apologetic exchanges. These pundits are third-party observers who write or produce commentary about the actions of wrongdoing on the part of guilty parties and then propose public social sanction against them. Professional critics seek to function as moral lecturers. In so doing, they perform a vital role of "certifying" that an offense requires an apology; once an apology is given, they serve as judge and jury as they label the apology as either acceptable or unacceptable.

Finally, a third feature of current apologiae that involves third parties is the introduction of third parties in the role of defense. No longer is it enough for apologists to defend themselves; now third parties regularly run to the defense of the accused and offer an explanation that accounts for the wrongdoing. In so doing, they attempt to offer a form of third-party credibility to buttress the position of the apologist, be it in the form of a news conference or writing an op-ed piece in the wrongdoer's defense.

Although their reflection of the social mores of the day is positive, overall the introduction of third parties has a desultory effect. It is important to note that, by and large, third-party apologists are not interested in the positive resolution of the moral conflict; rather, in their injection into the apologetic exchange, they have their *own* interests to serve, and do so. Tavuchis (1991) argued, "But what is of crucial structural import here is the conversion of what was a relatively private, dyadic conflict between two parties, sequestered from outsiders, into a public dispute involving specific others with interests and commitments of their own" (p. 51). Such an addition into the exchange fundamentally changes its dynamic nature; the addition transforms the exchange from focusing on social reconciliation to the point whereby it slows down or permanently hampers any form of reconciliation and, more likely, seeks to increase the anger and self-righteousness of both the accused's and the victim's respective social constituencies. When made into a public spectacle, an apology is no longer a vehicle by which to bring reconciliation but rather an "angry demand for a symbolic surcharge in the form of a humbling confession" (Tavuchis, 1991, p. 58). As shown to be the case later in this chapter, especially with the example of President Clinton, calls by third parties for apologies are not attempts to bring social reconciliation but instead are "sanctimonious demands for further punishment and public humiliation" (Tavuchis, p. 56)—in a phrase, a rhetorical trap.

In so doing, third-party participation places an emphasis on punishment of the wrongdoer rather than on the reconciliation and repair of the relationship, which goes against the spirit of an apology. Such a move transforms the apologist from one of two participants in a social drama to a condensation symbol for a whole host of social wrongs and definitions. Sadly, then, the apologist loses any sense of control as an agent and is less likely to stop the exchange with an apology.

Furthermore, too much beating up on an apologist can have a refractory effect by creating sympathy for the apologist: If a wrongdoer is seen to be beaten on, issues of public honor and public shame then become more paramount, turning the villain into a victim. Defiant apologiae become sources of pride to rally around, such as was the case with basketball star Latrell Sprewell, who in 1997 became a symbol of an African-American male standing up and striking back against the White establishment when he responded to the incessant taunts of Golden State Warriors' head coach P. J. Carlesimo by physically attacking the coach.

The heavy participation of third parties in the apologetic exchange follows a predictable script and, in all three cases that this chapter examines, it did indeed function to turn the villain into a victim. This probably was one of the unintended consequences that the Republican majority faced when it voted to impeach President Clinton after the Lewinsky scandal, a case this chapter now explicates.

## CASE STUDIES OF INDIVIDUAL
## APOLOGETIC ADDRESS

### President Clinton

In many ways, 1998 was a Dickensian year. The economy was chugging along at a sustained and growing pace and the stock market was reaching record highs. Yet, events in January transpired that plunged the nation into a year-long odyssey though the trials and travails of a weakened president whose actions left a permanent stain on his office. In the course of events, President Clinton made six major statements that counted the sum and substance of both his apologiae. This analysis seeks to give historical context and explicate all six statements as well as focus analysis on the three major apologetic statements he made. (For more on Clinton's apologiae, see Blaney & Benoit, 2001; Kramer & Olson, 2002.)

*Initial Allegations and Apologetic Responses.*   On January 21, President Clinton was accused of having an affair with a 21-year-old intern, Monica Lewinsky (Clines & Gerth, 1998). In addition to allegations of an affair, serious political charges arose suggesting that the president may have obstructed justice in an effort to conceal the affair from the public and from lawyers for Paula Jones, who was pursuing a sexual harassment lawsuit against him for an alleged incident that took place while he was governor of Arkansas. As a result, Independent Counsel Kenneth Starr—already investigating the president for the failed Whitewater deal—was authorized to investigate whether or not the president had suborned perjury by encouraging Lewinsky to lie under oath to protect him.

In an interview with PBS's Jim Lehrer, the president seemed to respond to the story as if he was measuring and formulating his story as he went along. To allegations of an extramarital affair with a 21-year-old and that he had suborned perjury in an effort to cover up the affair—allegations universally believed to be wrong—President Clinton utilized a strategy of denial. He replied, "That is not true. That is not true. I did not ask anyone to tell anything other than the truth. There is no improper relationship, and I intend to cooperate with this inquiry. But that is not true" ("The President Under Fire," 1998c, p. A24). When pressed by Lehrer to explain what he meant by "no improper relationship," President Clinton utilized a strategy of differentiation. He replied, "Well, I think you know what it means. It means that there is not a sexual relationship, an improper sexual relationship, or any other kind of improper relationship" ("The President Under Fire," 1998c, p. A24). In other words, he was careful not to deny any relationship, only one that was an "improper" sexual one.

In an interview later that day with National Public Radio's Robert Siegel and Mara Liasson, the president reaffirmed this strategy of denial to a question as to whether he had had an affair with Monica Lewinsky:

> No. That's not true either. And I have told people that I would cooperate in the investigation, and I expect to cooperate with it. I don't know any more about it than I've told you, and any more about it, really, than you do. But I will cooperate. The charges are not true. And I haven't asked anybody to lie. ("The President Under Fire," 1998c, p. A24)

Less than a week later, President Clinton seemed more sure of himself and issued his more forceful and perhaps his most memorable statement on the allegations surrounding the Lewinsky affair. Again, using a strategy of denial, he responded with a wag of the finger:

> But I want to say one thing to the American people. I want you to listen to me. I'm going to say this again: I did not have sexual relations with that woman, Miss Lewinsky. I never told anybody to lie, not a single time. Never. These allegations are false. And I need to go back to work for the American people. ("The President Under Fire," 1998a, p. A14)

Buoyed by the strong denial, using all the ceremonial power of the presidency, Clinton lieutenants were able to go on the offensive and offer strong third-party support of the president. First Lady Hillary Rodham Clinton appeared on the *Today* show to discuss the charges. Responding to a question from Matt Lauer, Mrs. Clinton reiterated the president's denial: "… I think the important thing now is to stand as firmly as I can and say that, you know, the President has denied these allegations on all counts, unequivocally" ("The President Under Fire," 1998b, p. A22). Additionally, she pointed out that Clinton friend Vernon Jordan "has helped literally hundreds of people" ("The President Under Fire," 1998b, p. A22), and thus his helping Miss Lewinsky would not have been unusual. She then proceeded to issue a scathing use of a counterattack strategy on Independent Counsel Kenneth Starr for his $30 million investigation of the Clintons, and claimed that he was "politically motivated" and "allied with the right-wing opponents of my husband," concluding that, all told, the actions of Kenneth Starr and others adds up to a "vast right-wing conspiracy that has been conspiring against my husband" ("The President Under Fire," 1998b, p. A22).

Clinton's first opportunity to address his wrongdoing in January 1998 must be considered a complete moral failure, because he denied any wrongdoing (wrongdoing to which he eventually admitted). As it relates to the manner in which his apologia was delivered, it fails: The apologia was not truthful; it was not sincere, but instead was manipulative in his attempt to define the relationship as "not improper"; nor did it address all moral claimants.

In terms of the content of the apologia, it did not explicitly acknowledge any wrongdoing whatsoever, nor did it fully accept responsibility, nor issue any regret, nor ask for forgiveness. Evidently, this was a case in which the president was of the mindset that the complicating factor of discretion and his subsequent right to privacy (and that of Ms. Lewinsky) gave him permission to be less than forthcoming as to the nature of the wrongdoing. However, it does appear that, in a case involving the president of the United States, discretion as a complicating factor is likely to be defined very narrowly.

### *Apologetic Response to Allegations of Witness Tampering.*
President Clinton's next major statement on the Lewinsky scandal occurred on February 7, and was prompted by allegations that he was guilty of witness tampering. Specifically, the allegations stipulated that he had attempted to influence the testimony of his personal secretary, Betty Currie. After his 6-hour deposition in the Paula Jones sexual harassment case, he called Mrs. Currie into work the next day—Sunday, January, 18, 1998—to go over the testimony that he had presented, which raised questions as to whether he was attempting to influence her recollection of events. It was reported that the president walked his secretary through the answers he had given in his deposition, and that there was at least one critical incident in which his interpretation differed from hers. Acting as a third-party apologist, White House press secretary Michael McCurry suggested a more innocuous interpretation of events: the president was attempting to influence his own memory of the circumstances of the case.

In his own defense, President Clinton denied any wrongdoing; he insisted, "I never asked anybody to do anything but tell the truth" (Broder, 1998a, p. A1). He further ruled out any chance that he might resign:

> To give in to that would be to give in to everything that I fought against and that got me into this race in 1991 to try to run for President in the first place. I have tried to bring an end to this sort of thing in our public life. I've tried to bring the American people together. I've tried to depersonalize politics and take the venom out of it. And the harder I've tried to do it, the harder others have pulled in the opposite direction. (Broder, 1998a, p. A8)

He then added some bolstering, focusing on his relationship with the American people: "And I would never walk away from the people of this country and the trust they placed in me" (Broder, 1998a, p. A8).

Not only did he rule out resignation, but Clinton's lawyers went on the offensive, using a third-party defense. Again relying heavily on a strategy of counterattack, Clinton's personal lawyer, David Kendall, decried the tactics used by Independent Counsel Kenneth Starr. Specifically, he argued that the independent counsel had illegally leaked grand jury testimony to media sources and, consequently, Kendall was pursuing a contempt citation against Starr (Broder, 1998a).

*August 17 Televised Apologetic Address.*    Although the story did not go away, it certainly died down a bit until August 1998, when it became evident that President Clinton would testify before a grand jury in response to the emergence of DNA evidence on a blue dress owned by Ms. Lewinsky. Given that the president had agreed the previous week that he would testify, and amid growing speculation that his testimony would likely admit that he lied to the American people about his relationship with Monica Lewinsky, there was a mounting expectation that he would make a public address to account for the inconsistency.

In an interview on *Meet the Press,* Senator Orrin Hatch, chairman of the Senate Judiciary Committee, laid a rhetorical trap for the president, and Clinton surprisingly took the bait. Specifically, Hatch suggested that if the president would make a full mea culpa, in the process he would likely diffuse the desire to impeach him (Seelye, 1998). He asserted, "If he comes forth and tells it and does it in the right way and there aren't a lot of other factors to cause the Congress to say, 'This man is unfit for the Presidency and should be impeached,' then I think the President would have a reasonable chance of getting through this" (Seelye, 1998, p. A1).

In the event the President was forced to admit he had lied, according to Hatch, "just a mere apology is not enough here; he'd have to really pour his heart out to the American people," suggesting that Clinton admit he lied to protect his wife and daughter (Seelye, 1998, p. A12).

The initial response to Hatch's offer was to reject it, continuing with the strategy of denial. Spokesperson Barry Toiv replied, "The President has told the truth about this and he will continue to do so. I have no reason to think that he has changed in any way" (Bennet & Van Natta, 1998, p. A1).

Events begin to change on August 7, when Monica Lewinsky testified in federal court that she had indeed had an affair with the president (Van Natta & Bennet, 1998). By August 14, stories were leaked that the president was considering acknowledging that he had had an affair with Ms. Lewinsky (Berke, 1998).

Finally, on August 17, the president testified for 4½ hours before a grand jury and acknowledged that he had had an intimate relationship with Monica Lewinsky. Concomitant with the testimony, he entered the public crucible in a nationally televised speech, partially written by Mrs. Clinton, to recount his testimony and acknowledge the affair to the American people (Abramson, 1998). In a defiant apologia, the president first began with a strategy of confession regarding the relationship with Ms. Lewinsky: "Indeed I did have a relationship with Miss Lewinsky that was not appropriate. In fact it was wrong. It constituted a critical lapse in judgment and a personal failure on my part for which I am solely and completely responsible" ("Testing of a President," 1998a, p. A12).

In effect, he admitted the relationship and fully acknowledged the wrongdoing. Regarding the allegations that he encouraged others to lie, he continued with a strategy of denial; he stated, "But I told the grand jury today, and I say to you now, that at no time did I ask anyone to lie, to hide or destroy evidence, or to take any other unlawful action" ("Testing of a President," 1998a, p. A12). Not to be too humble and conciliatory, Clinton then turned his attention to the familiar strategy of counterattack toward Independent Counsel Kenneth Starr. He charged:

> I had real and serious concerns about an independent counsel investigation that began with private business dealings 20 years ago—dealings, I might add, about which an independent Federal agency found no evidence of any wrongdoing by me or by wife over two years ago. The independent counsel investigation moved on to my staff and friends. Then into my private life. And now the investigation itself is under investigation. This has gone on too long, cost too much, and hurt too many innocent people. ("Testing of a President," 1998a, p. A12)

President Clinton then utilized a strategy of differentiation whereby he distinguished between his public and private life by pleading for the return of his personal privacy: "Now this matter is between me, the two people I love most—my wife and our daughter—and our God. It's nobody's business but ours. Even Presidents have private lives" ("Testing of a President," 1998a, p. A12). Coupled with the public apology, news reports revealed that the president spent much of the weekend preceding his testimony acknowledging the relationship and apologizing to friends and close advisors (Berke & Van Natta, 1998).

Reaction to the speech was predictable. Professional critics lined up on each side. Republican Orrin Hatch of Utah, who had said the president should come clean and "pour his heart out," was reported to have commented, "Wasn't that pathetic? I tell you, what a jerk. That's the biggest mistake he's ever made" (Sack, 1998, p. A16). The speech did not even address Democratic expectations. Rep. Charles Rangel of New York said, "I thought there would be more humility. But he was forceful enough. I don't know really whether that works or not. I think it works for the people who wanted to get it behind us" (Sack, 1998, p. A16).

Judging by the reactions of others, this second major apologetic statement offered by President Clinton, after he testified before a grand jury, would still have to be considered morally unacceptable, although it was a considerable improvement over his initial denial. In this case, he began to come to grips with his wrongdoing, but did not do so fully. As is commonly known, this is when he first began to acknowledge his wrongdoing, but clearly had not come to the place of full repentance.

As to the manner of his apology, for the first time he was truthful, in that he acknowledged what most Americans suspected all along—that he had indeed had a sexual relationship with Ms. Lewinsky. As to sincerity, it is here where the apology began to break down; when people judged his performance, they did not see humility and repentance performed but instead saw defiance, due to his heavy use of counterattack against Kenneth Starr. Of course, given that almost 8 months had transpired, the apologia was very late. He apologized to the Lewinsky family, his own family, and the American people, and in so doing began to address all moral claimants. Finally, his decision to deliver the apology from the White House was an acceptable context.

Regarding the content of the apologia, again, the apologia presented a major improvement, although it left much to be desired. First, President Clinton did explicitly acknowledge his wrongdoing, discuss his regret, and accept responsibility; but he did so in such a way that he continued to utilize strategies of shifting of the blame and launching a counterattack against Independent Counsel Kenneth Starr. In this way, Clinton's apology was not as successful at meeting expectations as it might have been (Gronback, 1999). The purpose of his apology was to repair his relationship with the American people. In so doing, be began to bring about reconciliation. However, he offered no corrective action. All in all, the apology would have to be viewed as morally unacceptable due to the fact that it lacked contrition.

*Apology at King Celebration.* Either recognizing from public outcry that the previous admission was not enough or realizing that multiple apologies would be necessary, President Clinton revisited the topic of apology in remarks he made at the Union Chapel in Oak Bluff, Massachusetts, on the 35th anniversary of Dr. Martin Luther King, Jr.'s, "I Have a Dream" speech. In a speech that focused on the mutual interdependence of all Americans, he turned the topic to that of forgiving enemies. He ritualistically revisited and reaffirmed his need for mortification when he intoned:

> All of you know I'm having to become quite an expert in this business of asking for forgiveness. And I—it gets a little easier the more you do it. And if you have a family, an Administration, a Congress and a whole country to ask, you're going to get a lot of practice.

> But I have to tell that in these last days it has come home to me again, something I first learned as President, but it wasn't burned into my bones—and that is that in order to get it, you have to be willing to give it.

And all of us—the anger, the resentment, the bitterness, the desire for re-
crimination against people you believe have wronged you—they harden the
heart and deaden the spirit and lead to self-inflicted wounds.

And so it is important that we are able to forgive those we believe have
wronged us, even as we ask for forgiveness from people we have wronged.
("In Clinton's Remarks," 1998, pp. A1, A10)

In this way, Clinton used a strategy whereby he encouraged people not to
judge him, but instead to forgive him, as he was learning to forgive those
who he felt had harmed him.

*Moscow Press Conference Apology.*    The president's next remarks on the
topic occurred when he gave his first public press conference since acknowledging the affair, albeit in Moscow. When questioned about whether his admission of a relationship with Monica Lewinsky had expressed enough
contrition, he replied, "I have acknowledged that I made a mistake, said that
I regretted it, asked to be forgiven, spent a lot of very valuable time with my
family in the last couple of weeks and said I was going back to work" (Broder,
1998b, p. A1). At this stage, Clinton was in danger of delivering a serial
apology in that his major apology before the nation clearly had not put the issue to rest.

*Prayer Breakfast Apology.*    Frustrated at the unwillingness of President
Clinton to offer contrition, Senator Joseph Lieberman, a Democrat from
Connecticut, took to the Senate floor to denounce the behavior of the president. Lieberman challenged him on the point that Clinton had long known
the boundaries of a private life of a president and acknowledging that he had
failed profoundly as a role model for the American children and as a representative of the American people; he concluded his remarks arguing that
Clinton's "behavior is not just inappropriate, it is immoral" ("Excerpts From
Senator Lieberman's Talk," 1998, p. A18). Lieberman charged:

Just as the American people are demanding of their leaders, though, they are
also fundamentally fair and forgiving, which is why I was so hopeful the President could begin to repair the damage done with his address to the nation on
the 17th. But like so many others, I came away feeling that for reasons that are
thoroughly human, he missed a great opportunity that night. He failed to
clearly articulate to the American people that he recognized how significant
and consequential his wrongdoing was and how badly he felt about it.

He failed to show, I think, that he understood his behavior had diminished
the office he holds and the country he serves and that it is inconsistent with

the mainstream American values that he advanced as President. And I regret that he failed to acknowledge that while Mr. Starr and Ms. Lewinsky, Mrs. Tripp and the news media have each in their own way contributed to the crisis we now face, his Presidency would not be imperiled if it had not been for the behavior he himself described as wrong and inappropriate. Because the conduct the President admitted to that night was serious, and his assumption of responsibility inadequate. ("Excerpts From Senator Lieberman's Talk," 1998, p. A18)

Whether it was a political calculation for fear that he was losing his liberal base (similar to what ultimately forced Richard Nixon's resignation), or a real acknowledgment on the part of the president of profound regret, Senator Lieberman's speech compelled Clinton to shift his tone and publicly apologize for the first time. When asked at a picture-taking session with the Prime Minister of Ireland, Bertie Ahern, if he had heard the senator's pointed criticisms, Clinton responded, "I've been briefed on them and basically I agree with what he said" (Broder, 1998c, p. A1). He continued by saying he was "sorry" for the first time; he declared: "I've already said that I made a bad mistake, it was indefensible and I'm sorry about it .... I'm very sorry about it. There's nothing else I could say" (Broder, 1998c, p. A1).

Apparently finally slouching toward fully acknowledging his wrongdoing, President Clinton was reported to have apologized to House Democrats at a private White House meeting later that week, and then to donors in Orlando later that afternoon, admitting, "But I let you down. And I let my family down and I let this country down. But I'm trying to make it right. And I'm determined never to let anything like that happen again" (Bennet, 1998, p. A1).

Finally, on September 11, the president gave the performance that he should have given all along. Speaking to a group of religious leaders at the National Prayer Breakfast at the White House, he fully utilized a strategy of mortification, took responsibility for his wrongdoing, and showed a spirit of humility whereby he demonstrated that he really was sorry:

> I have been on quite a journey these last few weeks to get to the end of this, to the rock-bottom truth of where I am and where we all are. I agree with those who have said that in my first statement after I testified, I was not contrite enough. I don't think there is a fancy way to say that I have sinned.
>
> It is important to me that everybody who has been hurt know that the sorrow I feel is genuine: first, and most important, my family; also my friends; my staff; my Cabinet; Monica Lewinsky and her family; and the American people. I have asked all for their forgiveness. But I believe that to be forgiven, more than sorrow is required, at least two more things.

First, genuine repentance: a determination to change and to repair breaches of my own making. I have repented.

Second, what my Bible calls a broken spirit: an understanding that I must have God's help to be the person that I want to be, a willingness to give the very forgiveness I seek, a renunciation of the pride and the anger which cloud judgment, lead people to excuse and compare and to blame and complain. ("Testing of a President," 1998b, p. A12)

Press accounts also revealed that Clinton had selected two religious leaders to keep him accountable (Goodstein, 1998).

In assessing this final apology, Clinton's confession finally reached the standard of the ethically ideal. He took responsibility for his wrongdoing, sought full forgiveness from those he had wronged, and again demonstrated that if he was to be forgiven he must also forgive. As to the manner of the apology, first, it was truthful. Although it was late, he came clean on his need for repentance and consequently offered a sincere apology that all those present saw as heartfelt and honest. Although it might have been a response to Senator Lieberman's call for a full apology, this apology does have the marks of being a voluntary apology in a way that the one after his August grand jury testimony did not (rather, the August apology appeared to be strategic). This apology fit the context and the ritualistic nature of the form; he was in a room filled with ministers who were in a position to judge his repentance.

Concerning the content of his apology, it is here where President Clinton's apology clearly does reach the standards of the ethically ideal. First, he explicitly acknowledged his wrongdoing, fully accepted responsibility and expressed regret for what he had done, and asked for forgiveness. For the first time, he provided an explanation and apology that addressed the expectations of the American people as to what he needed to say. Finally, it was revealed shortly thereafter that he had developed accountability partners, which represented a form of a corrective action strategy by which he was able to put in place measures to ensure that the wrongdoing did not happen again.

It is important to note that the apology did go a long way to healing the "breach"; however, an apology is a social exchange, and although it may have been effective, this apology did not heal the political and legal consequences of his act. On September 11th, Kenneth Starr released his 445-page report that made an argument for impeachment, describing in intimate detail 10 sexual encounters between President Clinton and Monica Lewinsky (Broder & Van Natta, 1998). This led to the decision of the House of Representatives to impeach Clinton, in a December 19 partisan vote, for perjury and obstruction of justice (Mitchell, 1998). The impeachment issue went to the Senate, where former Arkansas Senator Dale Bumpers, a third-party advocate, gave an impressive and forceful speech of defense that made a com-pelling case for acquittal (Apple, 1999). Finally, the whole ordeal ended on February 12, when the Senate voted for acquittal on the two articles of im-peachment (Mitchell, 1999). President Clinton, after the vote, went to the Rose Garden, where he made the following remarks: "I want to say again to the American people how profoundly sorry I am for what I said and did to trigger these events and the great burden they have imposed on the Con-gress and on the American people. This can be and this must be a time of reconciliation and renewal for America" (Bennet & Broder, 1999, p. A1).

The apologies delivered by President Clinton show an individual who vi-olated most of the characteristics of an ethical apology at first, but eventu-ally worked to get it correct. With humility and conciliation he was able to eventually meet the generic expectations of the American people.

Some situations that require apologiae, like President Clinton's, are in-deed serious, dealing with issues of legality or moral imprudence. Other is-sues that may necessitate a discourse of defense are best characterized as media-flaps—times when impudent individuals open their mouths and, through ill-chosen language, immediately create for themselves a mael-strom of criticism. Such was the situation faced by relief pitcher John Rocker in late 1999.

## John Rocker

In the December 22, 1999, edition of *Sports Illustrated,* John Rocker, a relief pitcher for the Atlanta Braves, gave an interview with writer Jeff Pearlman that touched off a firestorm. In the wide-ranging interview, Rocker spoke about his opinions of women drivers as well as anyone who speaks Spanish. However, he saved his toughest remarks for a question as to whether he would ever want to play in New York City:

> I would retire first. It's the most hectic, nerve-racking city. Imagine having to take the [Number] 7 train to the ballpark, looking like you're [riding through] Beirut next to some kid with purple hair next to some queer with AIDS right next to some dude who just got out of jail for the fourth time right next to some 20-year-old mom with four kids. It's depressing. (Pearlman, 1999, p. 62)

In addition, he added:

> The biggest thing I don't like about New York are the foreigners. I'm not a very big fan of foreigners. You can walk an entire block in Times Square and not hear anybody speaking English. Asians and Koreans and Vietnamese and

Indians and Russians and Spanish people and everything up there. How the hell did they get in this country? (Pearlman, 1999, p. 62)

Besides offending the aforementioned groups, in a single interview Rocker also insulted Asian-American women, the Japanese, and African-Americans, when he called his teammate Randall Simon "a fat monkey" (Pearlman, 1999, p. 64). He also offended others by spitting into a toll booth while driving his car and making an obscene gesture at a driver who had honked at his car.

Given that Rocker's remarks were widely reported and seemed intended to be rude to as many people as possible, reaction to the article was predictable and swift. Those close to baseball and Rocker commented, as did those who had little connection to the events. Baseball commissioner Bud Selig called Rocker's remarks "inappropriate and offensive" ("Rocker Blasts New York," 1999, p. D2). Atlanta Braves teammates also distanced themselves from Rocker's remarks. Brian Jordan told a local radio station that "You can't respect a guy that makes comments like that publicly" ("Rocker Blasts New York," 1999, p. D2), while the Braves organization, in the person of General Manager John Schulerholz, was quick to point out that Rocker's comments "in no way represent those of the Atlanta Braves organization" ("Rocker Blasts New York," 1999, p. D2). Even then, Senate candidates Rudolph Giuliani and Hillary Rodham Clinton got into the act. Mrs. Clinton stated, "These bigoted remarks were outrageous and unacceptable and send a terrible message to kids. New Yorkers are proud of the city's diversity" ("Rocker Blasts New York," 1999, p. D2). Mr. Giuliani remarked, "The Braves have some great players who are immigrants and foreigners, so maybe that kind of tension created on a team is the reason why the team underperformed in the World Series throughout the decade" ("Rocker Blasts New York," 1999, p. D2).

*Initial Apologia.*    Clearly chastised, Rocker released a statement that acknowledged his remarks had gone too far:

> While I have evidenced strong competitive feelings about New York fans in the past, and take responsibility for things I have said publicly, including the *Sports Illustrated* article, I recognize that I have gone way too far in my competitive zeal. Even though it might appear otherwise from what I've said, I am not a racist. ("Rocker Blasts New York," 1999, p. D2)

In the statement, he offered a strategy of mortification for going too far in his remarks, but also utilized a strategy of denial whereby he rejected that his remarks were racist in their intent.

As far as this analysis is concerned, when the ethical approach developed in chapter 4 is applied to this first apology by Rocker, it fails on both the manner as well as the content—the apology is ethically unacceptable. As to the manner of the apology, it does appear to be truthful on the surface as well as timely, although clearly it was not a voluntary apology; Rocker did not come off as someone who realized he was wrong and his conscience was pricked, but rather as someone who faced the harsh glare of an unwanted media spot-light. Furthermore, Rocker did not apologize directly to those he offended, but rather offered only a generalized apology. As far as context, the apology came through a released statement rather than directly from Rocker speak-ing before cameras, so it fails in terms of being not the best environment for him to make the address, nor did it come close to fitting the criteria of being well performed.

As to the content of Rocker's statement, the apologia is best described as incomplete. Although he accepted responsibility for what he said, he did not specifically apologize for his hurtful words, nor did he explicitly acknowl-edge that he had done wrong (beyond his admission that he had gone too far). Furthermore, he did not ask for forgiveness, nor pursue a relationship with the injured parties. Finally, his apology did not meet the expectations for such an offense, nor did he seek to provide any corrective action.

*Mediated Firestorm.*   Rather than quelling the controversy, Rocker's ini-tial apologetic performance did little more than fuel the fire that had ignited around him. Personal and professional critics joined in the chorus of criti-cism against Rocker, claiming to be wronged or offended, or offered to parse Rocker's comments to reveal what Rocker had really meant. Jim Schultz, the public relations director of the Braves, noted that the organization's of-fices were flooded with calls from people who identified themselves as mem-bers of one of the groups Rocker criticized and who promised never to watch a Braves game on television again. Hank Aaron, a senior vice president with the Braves, communicated that he was "sickened" by Rocker's commentary and openly wondered if Rocker would be allowed to stay in baseball (Chass, 1999, p. D1). Bill Campbell, the Atlanta mayor, added to the criticism: "We regard ourselves as a city of great tolerance. This is the birthplace of Dr. King; the civil rights movement sprang from the loins of Atlanta." Campbell called Rocker's remarks a "personal tragedy" that was "largely the product of ignorance" (Chass, 1999, p. D1). *The New York Times* writer George Vecsey opined that the use of the word *Beirut* was a "white code word for a neighbor-hood of color" (Vecsey, 1999, p. D1).

In one of the stranger turn of events, sensing the public outcry, Commis-sioner Bud Selig called Rocker's remarks "reprehensible" and "completely inexcusable" and ordered Rocker to undergo psychological testing before the league made a decision on how Rocker would be disciplined (Curry, 2000a, p. D1), apparently mistaking a sociological problem for a personal pathology (Poussaint, 2000). Selig commented:

I am profoundly concerned about the nature of those comments, as well as by certain other aspects of his behavior. As a result, following consultation with the Major League Baseball Players Association, I have determined that Mr. Rocker will undergo a psychological evaluation, which I expect to be concluded expeditiously. At that time, I will take what ever action that I consider to be necessary. (Curry, 2000a, p. D4)

The punishment, according to Sam Kasten, Braves president, would now be meted out by Major League Baseball and not the Braves, because Rocker's comments had tarnished the entire league (Curry, 2000a). Rocker could be banned from baseball, which would be justified by Paragraph 3(a) of the Basic Agreement:

> The player agrees to perform his services hereunder diligently and faithfully, to keep himself in first-class condition and to obey the club's training rules, and pledges himself to the American Public and to the club to conform to high standards of personal conduct, fair play and good sportsmanship. (Curry, 2000b, p. D1)

The decision to require psychological testing for prejudiced comments set off a firestorm of controversy, in a small way turning the victimizer into the victim. The consensus was that racism and xenophobic views, although troublesome, do not constitute mental illness (McKinley, 2000; Poussaint, 2000). Dr. Daniel Borenstein, then president-elect of the American Psychiatric Association, opined, "A tendency toward bias is a normal human characteristic. An extreme form of bias is racism, but none of that is a mental disorder in itself" (McKinley, 2000, pp. 4–5). *The New York Times* columnist Robert Lipsyte described the decision to pursue psychological testing to be "almost Soviet"(Lipsyte, 2000, pp. 8–13).

*Apologetic Interview With Peter Gammons.*     Apparently fearing that a severe penalty would be forthcoming, and that eating some humble pie was in order, Rocker agreed to be interviewed on ESPN by Peter Gammons on January 12th, his first interview since the crisis had erupted the previous month. In this interview, he gave more attention to the symbolic aspects of his performance. He first used a strategy of denial when he claimed his remarks had been "grossly misrepresented" (Olney, 2000, p. D2). He then quickly turned to a fuller strategy of mortification: "All I can do is apologize and offer my deepest regrets" (Curry, 2000c, p. D3). Rocker then attempted to differentiate how his remarks should be understood. Rather than being seen as a general outburst against ethnic minorities and other groups, he insisted that his remarks really needed to be understood in the context of how he had been treated by New York baseball fans during the previous season—being spit on, having beer dumped on him and batteries thrown at him—and that his remarks should really be seen as a "forum to try to retaliate at all the wrongs and injustices that had been done towards me and towards my teammates and it went a little too far" (Curry, 2000c, p. D3). In effect, he used a strategy of good intentions whereby he claimed that he had really just been trying to defend his teammates and had been misunderstood, in terms of how people interpreted his remarks. He explained his comments by denying any intention of wrongdoing:

> The last thing I want to do is offend people and ostracize myself. I like being around people and like being accepted by people, and if I had ever felt any of these comments would ostracize myself and take me back and put me on a pedestal segregated, I certainly never would've said it because that wasn't my intent. (Curry, 2000c, p. D3)

He completed the mortification by adding that if he heard someone make comments made about him of the sort that he made, he would think such a person was a "complete jerk" (Olney, 2000, p. D2).

As to his comments about calling teammate Randall Simon a "fat monkey," he again used differentiation when he replied that it was "clubhouse humor" and the reporter "took it literally" (Curry, 2000c, p. D3; "Teammate of Rocker," 2000, pp. 8–11). Finally, when asked by Gammons if he was a racist, Rocker again turned to denial when he replied, "I think I made myself pretty clear. Absolutely not" (Curry, 2000c, p. D3). In response, *Sports Illustrated* writer Jeff Pearlman noted, "I can say, without a doubt, that I did not goad him into saying anything" (Olney, 2000, p. D2).

One measure of the quality of the apology was the reaction of those closest to him. In this case, the truthfulness of Rocker's remarks have to be called into question. Rocker's Atlanta Braves teammate, Randall Simon, for instance, rejected Rocker's characterization, thus keeping the story alive. Simon claimed that Rocker never had much of a relationship with people of color on the team: "He knows we've never had a relationship like that. He has no relationships with the black guys or the Latin guys on the team. He's lying to try and cover himself. He has a lot of guts to say that" ("Teammate of Rocker," 2000, pp. 8–11). Furthermore, Simon threatened, "I swear to you if he said that to my face I'd tear him up, and one of us would be suspended right now" ("Teammate of Rocker," 2000, pp. 8–11).

The assessment of Rocker's first apology showed that it was a failure and did not meet the criteria for an ethical apology. This second apology, although not ethically ideal, did reach standards of moral acceptability. As to the manner of the apology, he chose a much more appropriate context, submitting to an interview with a respected sports journalist, who acted in a priestly role (Lessl, 1989). This enabled Rocker to speak in such a way that he was able to be judged as to the quality of his performance. In this fashion, he demonstrated contrition and remorse. In so doing, he was capable of more directly addressing all moral claimants and offering an apology to them.

The content of this interview also represented a significant improvement. First, he directly apologized, explicitly acknowledged his wrongdoing, and offered regret. Furthermore, he identified with the injured parties, acknowledging that he would see himself as a "complete jerk" if he were on the other side. However, Rocker's heavy use of differentiation was such that it called into question the degree to which he fully accepted responsibility, in that he continued to claim that he had been misunderstood.

*Public Chastisement.*    Professional third-party victims continued to get involved. The controversy continued on January 18th when approximately 75 people, carrying signs such as "Fire John Rocker" or "M.L.B.—Major League Bigot," protested outside of CNN's headquarters in Atlanta ("Turner Supports Rocker," 2000, p. D4). They protested the fact that Time Warner, which owns both *Sports Illustrated* and the Atlanta Braves (Chass, 1999a) had done nothing to discipline the troubled reliever (perhaps the controversy was a new form of integrative product and marketing …; Araton, 1999).

Media mogul Ted Turner kept the controversy alive when he appeared on CNN's *Moneyline*. "I think he was off his rocker when he said those things," said Turner ("Turner Supports Rocker," 2000, p. D4). He added that the reliever had since apologized for his offensive remarks and deserved another chance.

On February 1, 2000, Commissioner Bud Selig finally handed down his penalty: He suspended Rocker for 73 days (45 days of spring training and 28 days of the regular season), fined him $20,000, and required him to undergo "sensitivity training" (Chass, 2000a, p. A1). This marked the first time a player had ever been disciplined for the use of offensive speech. In handing down his punishment, Selig announced:

> Major League Baseball takes seriously its role as an American institution and the important social responsibility that goes with it. We will not dodge our responsibility. Mr. Rocker should understand that his remarks offended practically every element of society and brought dishonor to himself, the Atlanta Braves and Major League Baseball. (Chass, 2000a, p. A1)

In his response, Rocker objected to the harsh penalty, and asserted that he had addressed the problem:

> I do not believe it is appropriate that I should be harshly disciplined for my misguided speech unaccompanied by any conduct on my part. I have previously apologized for my unfortunate remarks and stand by my apology. (Chass, 2000a, p. D6)

Concurrently, the players' union announced that it would challenge the suspension by filing a grievance, due to the severity of the punishment and given the fact that it involved speech and not behavior. It is interesting to note that other players had been suspended for shorter periods of time for drug use.

The fact that Rocker was suspended, and harshly, for his speech, brought a predictable outcry—and functioned, in many ways, to invert the story and make him a media poster boy for the First Amendment, once again turning the victimizer into the victim. Ever-present Alan Dershowitz, a Harvard Law School professor, published an editorial in which he argued that although Rocker works for a private organization, and hence, First Amendment protections do not apply, "to conclude that baseball has the right to suspend Rocker does not mean that it was right to do so" (Dershowitz, 2000, p. A21). Dershowitz said that instead Major League Baseball should have announced that it was "committed to freedom of speech and that comments of individual players should not be misunderstood as reflecting the opinions of Major League Baseball" (Dershowitz, 2000, p. A21).

*The New York Times* editorialized that although Selig was right to "condemn" Rocker for his remarks and to "order counseling and therapy for a troubled young man," the editors were "troubled by its [Major League Baseball] decision to go the additional step of fining Rocker for a mistake that involved offensive speech rather than physical misconduct or violations of the law" ("The Difficult Case," 2000, p. A14). Such a move "diminishes the principle that the best response to hateful speech is constructive speech and public condemnation" ("The Difficult Case," 2000, p. A14).

On March 1, arbitrator Shyam Das announced his decision to lessen John Rocker's suspension by two thirds. In his action, Das reduced Rocker's suspension to the first 2 weeks of the regular season, and allowed him to join his team at spring training almost immediately—thus reducing a 73-day suspension to a total of 27 days. Furthermore, he reduced the fine leveled by Selig from $20,000 to $500, yet upheld baseball's authority to require Rocker to attend a diversity training program—a form of corrective action externally imposed (Chass, 2000b). In allowing an almost 2-week spring training suspension to stand, Das did uphold the right of the commissioner to punish a player for his speech, although Selig's original suspension was considered too severe (Chass, 2000b). Fan reaction to the reduction was divided: Some thought that Rocker should have been suspended for a year and permanently labeled as a "racist," whereas others argued that he should be free to say what he wanted. One New York Mets fan, Mike Sullivan, remarked, "What he said was really stupid, but there's no law against being stupid"(Koeppel, 2000, p. D3).

*Spring Training Apology.*    When Rocker was allowed to rejoin his team at spring training, the atmosphere was a bit of a carnival, with more than the usual number of reporters following the team (Curry, 2000d). In keeping the story alive, Rocker published a 300-word column in the *Atlanta Journal-Constitution* on March 2 that functioned to turn his earlier efforts into a serial apology. He continued on with his strategy of mortification. He wrote:

> In a December issue of *Sports Illustrated,* I made several comments of which I am ashamed …. My comments concerning my team were totally unprofessional and out of line. To the Braves management, to Bobby Cox and to the entire team, I am extremely sorry for the stress and confusion I have brought on the entire Braves organization. (Curry, 2000d, p. D3)

At spring training, on his first day, Rocker faced his teammates and felt the need to deliver another apology in a team meeting. Apparently close to shedding tears, he reportedly said, "Please, guys, let me play" (Araton, 2000, p. D1). At the meeting, called by Manager Bobby Cox, he spoke to his teammates for 10 minutes, telling them he was sorry and that his remarks were not intended to be malicious. After he talked, six players spoke, alternating between lecturing Rocker and acknowledging the need to forgive and move on (Curry, 2000e). Rocker also approached Randall Simon, whom he had called a "fat monkey," and said, "I want to apologize to you"; Simon saw remorse and pain (Araton, 2000, p. D1). After the clubhouse session, Rocker addressed reporters and read a two-page statement that was similar to the article he had published in the *Atlanta Journal-Constitution.* In it, he apologized again, this time to the Braves and their manager, to AIDS patients, and for not being a role model (Curry, 2000e).

This third and final apology was probably the best one he delivered. It also met standards for being ethically ideal, because rather than having it be a mediated apology, Rocker instead spoke directly to his teammates, a group of claimants to whom Rocker had caused considerable grief, and straightforwardly apologized to them—although the content of the apology was reported to media. In this apology, Rocker met the manner criterion by directly apologizing in an appropriate context, and did so with a sincere performance; by most accounts he was close to tears.

As to the content, this apology also was much better. He explicitly acknowledged that what he had said was wrong, that the remarks were his, and that he was truly sorry. In particular, he directly addressed those whom he had specifically hurt, including teammate Randall Simon, his manager, and the entire organization. Perhaps the factor that demonstrated Rocker's repentance best was his stance: He listened and stood "in the dock" while he was reprimanded by some of his teammates. He did not offer any corrective action, however, although some might consider his sensitivity training to be a form of corrective action.

On March 14, Rocker pitched in his first spring training game against the Detroit Tigers. As he entered the game, he received a standing ovation from the 10,078 fans in Disney Stadium. He retired the three batters he faced. On the insistence of Bobby Cox, he addressed the reporters after the game. He said, "The best thing I got out of [this situation is] that it showed you people in the media that not everybody's against me. I've been running into nothing but positives ever since all this happened" (Chass, 2000c, p. D4).

*Developments and Distractions.* Perhaps due to feeling pressure from the controversy, Rocker faced a tough start to the season in which, unlike the previous year in which he had 38 saves, he gave up 25 walks and 18 hits in 18 innings (Chass, 2000d; Vecsey, 2000). The story reignited on June 4 when Rocker discovered that Jeff Pearlman, the reporter from *Sports Illustrated* who had interviewed him, was in the Braves clubhouse. Rocker challenged, "This isn't over between us. Do you know what I could do to you?" (Vecsey, 2000, p. D1). He then demanded that Pearlman not be allowed into the clubhouse. GM John Schuerholz announced, "We immediately began to address the matter internally and are continuing to do so. We will do everything in our power to insure that similar incidents do not occur in the future" (Vecsey, 2000, p. D2). Commissioner Bud Selig released a statement that said he was "saddened by the regrettable incident" (Chass, 2000d, p. D1).

The Braves reacted to the outburst quickly; management fined Rocker $5,000. The team also demoted him to Richmond in the International League, using his erratic pitching as a cover for the move. In announcing the decision, Schuerholz said:

> The environment to do that [avoid controversy and focus on baseball] doesn't exist here. We don't have the luxury for guys to work their ways through tough times. We decided he needs to pitch consistently to do that. We think he will do that and be as good as he was last year. (Chass, 2000d, p. D1)

Although many thought that Rocker would stay in the minors for 4 weeks until the Braves completed a series with the New York Mets, Rocker's stay at Richmond was brief; it lasted only 6 days, and he received the call on June 13 to return to the Braves after successfully completing a save ("Braves Recall Rocker," 2000, p. D7).

*Final Denouement.* Perhaps in an attempt to prove that he was not prejudiced and had no problem associating with the minority groups of which he criticized—and to directly identify with the injured parties (but in a move that again functioned to keep the story current)—Rocker announced when the Braves arrived in New York that he would ride the No. 7 train to the team's game in Shea Stadium (Chass, 2000e). Rocker reportedly told *USA Today's Baseball Weekly,* "The first day I get to New York, I'm getting on the 7 train. I'm taking it to Shea Stadium. I won't be in a cab. I won't be on the bus. I'll be on that train. And I'm looking forward to it" (Chass, 2000e, p. D2). Mayor Rudolph Giuliani said that the city would try to persuade him and the Braves not to go that route. Later, Giuliani announced that the typical security detail of 45 would be increased to 400 to 500 officers—including some in plainclothes (Chass, 2000e, p. D2). Mets' center fielder Darryl Hamilton remarked that Rocker seemed to be going out of his way to create attention and even putting himself at risk:

> There are too many security risks involved. On the baseball field, you've got some type of protection. If you're talking about riding the subway, you are on someone else's turf. I still can't understand why the guy is bringing more attention to himself than is needed. Get four games over with, and get out of here. (Chass, 2000e, p. D2)

To prepare for the visit, the Mets undertook some serious security measures, most near the dugout in the Braves bullpen. The organization added fences and a roof over the mound as well as stationed a significant police presence there (Kepner, 2000). Additionally, better judgment did prevail and Rocker decided not to take the No. 7 train, although the city did increase dramatically the number of police officers at the games (Flynn, 2000).

Before the first game, Rocker read a statement to the press, which was later shown to the stadium amid a chorus of boos. In the statement, Rocker offered a strategy of mortification: "My comments weren't made with intentions of malice. However, many people perceived these comments to be malicious and for this, again I apologize" ("The Apology," 2000, p. 1D). He continued with a strategy of bolstering in which he noted that "the overwhelming majority of the people in this city are extremely charismatic and full of personality, although a bit spirited at times, but that doesn't make them bad people" ("The Apology," 2000, p. 1D). He proceeded to play in the eighth inning, during which he was able to retire the side without giving up any hits—his only appearance in the series due to an open callus on his left thumb (Chass, 2000f). All in all, what was viewed to be a showdown between New Yorkers and Rocker had all finished quietly.

The final apologia under analysis was not a case of breaking the law nor merely a media flap, but instead was a situation in which a national historian with an impeccable reputation was accused to have engaged in a very fresh-man-level form of error, that of plagiarizing the work of others. This situa-tion, like Rocker's, drew a great deal of media attention.

## Doris Kearns Goodwin

The most unlikely apologiae of 2002 came from allegations of plagiarism by two nationally recognized authors of history. In January 2002, Fred Barnes noted in the newsmagazine the *Weekly Standard* (Crader, 2002) that noted World War II chronicler Steven Ambrose, in his book *The Wild Blue* (2001), had plagiarized sections of Thomas Childer's (1996) *Wings of Morning*. Ambrose largely shrugged off the allegations; he claimed that the similarities in the passages were not a big deal, and that he had referenced Childer's work (Crader, 2002). With the exception of a few critical news stories—in which Ambrose admitted that he had quit writing "serious" history a long time ago—and perhaps aided by the fact that he was dying of lung cancer, the apologia appeared to perform suc-cessfully. But on the heels of allegations of Ambrose's plagiarism came additional charges in the *Weekly Standard* that another historian, the critically acclaimed Pulitzer Prize-winning author Doris Kearns Goodwin, had plagiarized passages in her 1987 book *The Fitzgeralds and the Kennedys* (Crader, 2002). Given the repeated nature of the offense, and that plagiarism appears to be about the only transgression that all university faculty generally agree is unethical, coupled with the rarity of catching a professor in a wrong, the allegations were tailor made to cre-ate a mediated crisis for Goodwin.

*A Small Magazine and a Big Target.* In an article in the *Weekly Standard* entitled "A Historian and Her Sources," Crader (2002) detailed passages in *The Fitzgeralds and the Kennedys* (1987) that were conspicuously similar to some in Hank Searls' *The Lost Prince: Young Joe, the Forgotten Kennedy* (1969) and some from *Times to Remember* (1974), the autobiography of Rose Ken-nedy. Although those passages demonstrated conspicuous similarities, it was the allegations of plagiarism from Lynne McTaggart's book *Kathleen Kennedy: Her Life and Times* (1983) that proved to be the most damaging. The *Weekly Standard* detailed the charges:

> McTaggart, for example, writes that
>
> > her [Kathleen's] closest friends assumed that she and Billy were "semiengaged." On the day of the party reports of a secret engagement were published in the Boston papers …. The truth was that the young couple had reached no such agreement. (p. 65)

The corresponding passage in Goodwin's (1987) book differs by just a few words:

> her [Kathleen's] closest friends assumed that she and Billy were semi-engaged. On the day of the party, reports of a secret engagement were published in the Boston papers …. The truth was that the young couple had reached no such agreement. (p. 586)

McTaggart:

> Hardly a day passed without a photograph in the papers of little Teddy, taking a snapshot with his Brownie held upside down, or the five Kennedy children lined up on a train or bus. (p. 25)

Goodwin:

> hardly a day passed without a newspaper photograph of little Teddy taking a snapshot with his camera held upside down, or the five Kennedy children lined up on a train or bus. (p. 523)

McTaggart:

> Mrs. Gibson gave a tea in her honor to introduce her to some of the other girls—hardly a routine practice for new recruits. (p. 130)

Goodwin:

> Mrs. Harvey Gibson gave a tea in her honor to introduce her to some of the other girls—hardly a routine practice for new recruits. (p. 666)

(Crader, 2002, pp. 12–13)

Furthermore, Crader (2002) argued that there were "dozens more such parallels" in the book (p. 13), and that there were 40 notes in the 2001 edition of *The Fitzgeralds and the Kennedys* that were not in the 1987 edition. He also pointed out that the preface to the 2001 edition also contained a curious statement not present in the earlier edition: "In the preparation of this work, I was grateful for Lynne McTaggart's biography, "Kathleen Kennedy: Her Life and Times," which is the definitive biography of Kathleen Kennedy and which I used as a primary source for information on Kathleen Kennedy, both in my research and in my writing" (Crader, 2002, p. 13). Yet the date of the preface was given as "November 1986," not 2001.

The allegations were particularly embarrassing due to the fact that in 1993 Goodwin had taken Joe McGinniss to task for plagiarizing one of her books in his book *The Last Brother*, a profile of Sen. Edward Kennedy. In an interview with the *Boston Globe* in 1993, she intoned, "He just uses it flat out, without saying that it came from my work. I just don't understand why that wasn't done" (Kirkpatrick, 2002a, p. A10).

Crader (2002) then contacted the parties involved. McTaggart would not offer comment; Simon & Schuster spokesperson David Rosenthal admitted to the errors and began to offer a third-party defense of Goodwin. Rosenthal said, "In the original book there were some mistakes made. Those mistakes were corrected" (Crader, 2002, p. 13). He then used a strategy of differentiation that accounted for how the "mistakes" were made while he preserved Dr. Goodwin's scholarly credibility: "Doris acknowledged the mistake to McTaggart, and they reached an understanding on how those mistakes should be corrected. The error was inadvertent. Back then, Doris kept notes on long legal pads and some papers got shuffled. It was corrected as soon as she became aware of the error" (Crader, 2002, p. 13). The two parties, according to Rosenthal, were able to resolve the issues between them.

When contacted, Doris Kearns Goodwin offered a similar defense to that of Rosenthal as to how the plagiarized material found its way into the book. Her response was short on mortification but long on differentiation: "I wrote everything in longhand in those days, including the notes I took on secondary sources. When I wrote the passages in question, I did not have the McTaggart book in front of me. Drawing on my notes, I did not realize that in some cases they constituted a close paraphrase of the original work" (Crader, 2002, p. 13).

Following up on this assertion that the plagiarism was inadvertent, Goodwin claimed to fix it as soon as it was brought to her attention: "I acknowledged immediately that she was right, that she should have been footnoted more fully. She asked that more footnotes be added and a paragraph crediting her book. This was done in the paperback edition" (Crader, 2002, p. 13).

Finally, Goodwin concluded with a strategy of corrective action, claiming that she had "learned" from her mistakes and, consequently, they were unlikely to recur. She responded, "This was brought to a satisfactory conclusion 15 years ago. And learning from this, I have made it a constant practice to use quotations in the text itself and to have the original source directly in front of me when I am writing" (Crader, 2002, p. 13). When asked by Crader why the passages in question were referenced but not quoted, Goodwin answered, "Had she asked for more quotations in the text, I would have done it" (Crader, 2002, p. 13).

From an ethical context, this first apologia is difficult to assess, especially if one takes Goodwin's point that this was an already settled matter that was satisfactorily resolved. This, of course, gets at the difficult nexus when private matters become public ones. However, given that Goodwin is the closest scholar America has to a national historian, and given that her books often are viewed as authoritative statements on the subjects she writes about, it is not stretch to conclude that this private matter between two historians is indeed worthy of public consideration and adjudication. When considered in this way, her first apologia must be assessed to be ethically unacceptable.

As it concerns the manner of Goodwin's apologia, it appears to have met the criterion of truthfulness (although questions would be raised later as more facts came out), sincerity, timeliness, being voluntary, and being offered in an appropriate context, in that she did acknowledge that issues had been raised by McTaggart regarding similarities in their respective books, and, working with her publisher, quickly acted to give credit to McTaggart in subsequent editions of the book. It is important to note, however, that Goodwin failed on the criterion of addressing all stakeholders, in that consumers of her work were not informed of the plagiarism.

Similarly, Goodwin met some of the criteria of the content of an ethical apologia, but failed on critical ones. She did accept that she was responsible for the almost identical quotations in her book, and explained that this was caused by the fact she used to take notes in longhand. Furthermore, she demonstrated that corrective action was taken in fixing the shortcomings as soon as they were disclosed, and that she now uses a computer scanner to ensure that the problem is unlikely to happen again. What is troublesome, however, is that Goodwin never fully acknowledged wrongdoing by admitting that she had plagiarized, clinging precariously to the term "close paraphrase," which does not do justice to the similarities. Nor did Goodwin express regret and ask for forgiveness in such a way as to meet consumers' expectations that she might take responsibility with an acknowledgment that her standards had fallen short.

*Apologetic Campaign Part I: Time Magazine.*    Sensing a potential media firestorm and the delicious schadenfreude of a teacher caught by the trap of plagiarism, Goodwin immediately went on the offensive, and began an orchestrated public relations campaign to restore her damaged reputation. To this end, she made a start by publishing an article in *Time* (Goodwin, 2002). What is notably absent in the article is any statement of mortification or even regret. Indeed, in the article she described what had happened to her as "caught up in the swirl," as if she were not a central character in the drama, and she issued a counterattack against the *Weekly Standard* for publishing "an article reviving the issue" long after "the matter was completely laid to rest" (Goodwin, 2002, p. 69).

Her apologia began by briefly acknowledging that an offense had been committed. She wrote:

> Fourteen years ago, not long after the publication of my book *The Fitzgeralds and the Kennedys*, I received a communication from author Lynne McTaggart

pointing out that material from her book on Kathleen Kennedy had not
been properly attributed. I realized she was right. Though my footnotes re-
peatedly cited Ms. McTaggart's work, I failed to provide quotation marks for
phrases that I had taken verbatim, having assumed that these phrases,
drawn from my notes, were my words, not hers. I made the corrections she
requested .... (Goodwin, 2002, p. 69)

In this response, she minimized the problem by simply describing it as a case
of failing to use quotation marks in a few places and for a few phrases. She
then immediately turned to a strategy of transcendence, whereby she noted,
"The larger question for those of us who write history is to understand how
citation mistakes can happen" (Goodwin, 2002, p. 69). In other words, she
argued that the issue should not be about any guilt that Doris Kearns
Goodwin might hold but instead be about how all historians have to be careful about this problem. In so doing, she redefined plagiarism as nothing more
than "citation mistakes" (Goodwin, 2002, p. 69).

Goodwin then proceeded to launch into an extended explanation in
which she took the ironic stance that the explanation for her mistakes was
the thoroughness of her work. For instance, she wrote that "the research and
writing for this 900-page book, with its 3,500 footnotes took place over 10
years" and that "After three years of research, I discovered more than 150
cartons of materials that had been previously stored in the attic of Joe Kennedy's Hyannis Port house .... It took me two additional years to read, cate-
gorize and take notes on these documents" (Goodwin, 2002, p. 69).

She continued, "During this same period, I took handwritten notes on perhaps 300 books .... Notes on all these sources were then arranged chronologi-
cally and kept in dozens of folders in 25 banker's boxes" (Goodwin, 2002, p. 69).

But it is here where her explanation faltered. She revealed:

> As a final protection, I revisited the 300 books themselves. Somehow in this pro-
> cess, a few of the books were not fully rechecked. I relied instead on my notes,
> which combined direct quotes and paraphrased sentences. If I had the books in
> front of me, rather than my notes, I would have caught mistakes in the first place
> and placed any borrowed phrases in direct quotes. (Goodwin, 2002, p. 69)

Goodwin then finished her apologia with an extended conclusion in
which she utilized a strategy of corrective action designed to reassure that
the problem would no longer recur, and claimed that "The only protection
as a historian is to institute a process of research and writing that minimizes
the possibility of error" (Goodwin, 2002, p. 69). In this section, she talked
about how the mistakes were ones of using hand written notes, how she had
since shifted to the use of a "computer for both organizing and taking notes"
(Goodwin, 2002, p. 69), and that her research practice was to "now rely on a

scanner, which reproduces the passages I want to cite, and then I keep my own comments on those books in a separate file so that I will never confuse the two again" (Goodwin, 2002, p. 69).

She then finished with the statement that "In the end, I am still the same fallible person I was before I made the transition to the computer, and the process of building a lengthy work of history remains a complicated but honorable task" (Goodwin, 2002, p. 69).

Instead of putting the issue to rest, Goodwin's second and what must be considered her major apologetic statement actually functioned to give the story legs, for it took an issue in a small-circulation public affairs magazine and published a response to it in a large, general-circulation magazine. Furthermore, the explanations offered there raised more questions than they answered. For this reason, her second apologia, like her first, fell short and must be considered ethically unacceptable.

As to the manner of her defense, credit must be given to Goodwin for voluntarily publishing the article and attempting to clear her reputation in a timely way. She did appear to be truthful and account for what had happened, and, in this case, she switched from the term "close paraphrase" to "citation mistakes," an improvement in the language she chose to address her mistakes. In so doing, she was able to better address all stakeholders and defend the "brand" that her name had become. The location of the defense in *Time* also was appropriate, in that it is a magazine whose readership would likely read her books.

However, when the content of Goodwin's apologia is considered, it tends to fall short, in that she did not seem to meet the ritualistic requirement that she view the problem as serious if not sacred and "stand in the dock"; instead, she appeared to treat the process lightly. She did express regret for what had happened and that she had "become the story." In addition, the evolution of her language from "close paraphrase" to "citation mistakes" was a considerable step toward accepting responsibility, although it still was some distance away from admitting that she had committed plagiarism and needed to ask for forgiveness. Yet, even though she appeared to accept responsibility for the errors, she failed to do so. Note, for instance, the reliance on the passive voice in her explanation that "a few of the books were not fully rechecked." There is no actor in the sentence. It could be read that she had a research assistant who failed to check the books—an admission that would counteract her claim of *personal* thoroughness, or it could be read that she failed to check the books. Either way, she assumed no personal guilt or responsibility for the mistakes. Neither did Goodwin seek to restore her relationship with injured stakeholders; instead, she described the lesson to be learned as one related to how historians can write better history. Additionally, as is shown shortly, she did not fully disclose all of the facts that surrounded the case, in that she employed a staff of researchers. Finally, Goodwin continued to not meet the public expectation for even some degree of contrition.

*Major Admissions: The New York Times Interview.* To many, Goodwin's explanations and lack of contrition continued to ring hollow. And in an attempt to beat Philip Nobile—an Internet "reporter" who seemed to make it his personal crusade to make Goodwin accountable (or just embarrass her)—to the punch (Kirkpatrick, 2002d), she offered a third apologetic statement to put the issue to rest. In it, she disclosed in an interview to *The New York Times* that the plagiarism of McTaggart's work and others was more widespread than initially thought (Kirkpatrick, 2002b). Indeed, she admitted that she and her researchers had discovered approximately 50 borrowed passages, as well as some in other books, although she refused to say which ones because she and her staff were still examining them (Kirkpatrick, 2002b). She also disclosed that her changes in her research methods, specifically computerization, did not occur until after she published *No Ordinary Time,* which won her a Pulitzer Prize in 1994—not in 1987, as she had said earlier.

In admitting that the problem was not due to longhand note taking, she was forced to admit that her research standards were not up to par: "The mechanical process of checking things was not as sophisticated as it should have been" (Kirkpatrick, 2002b, p. A10). She also revealed that she employed a team of four research assistants—three full time and one part time—and that one had been her lead assistant on the publication of *The Fitzgeralds and the Kennedys.*

Yet, it was in her discussion of the research assistants that Goodwin utilized a strategy of scapegoating to preserve her reputation; she claimed that the problems of the plagiarism of McTaggart's book resulted when one of her research assistants lost McTaggart's book and, as a result, it could not be checked for accuracy (Kirkpatrick, 2002b). The answer to why either of them did not simply locate a new copy of the book was not revealed in the interview.

*Moral Outrage.* Rather than solving the problem, Goodwin's explanations seemed to simply fan the flames and prolong the reporting on the story. Such an explanation on the part of Goodwin—that she did not commit plagiarism (a word noticeably absent from her apologia)—sparked cries of incredulity and brought with it a bad review of her attempted repair of her public persona. In an editorial in *USA Today* (a paper with its own history of plagiarism) that examined Goodwin's case as well as that of Steven Ambrose, the paper remarked, "They're wrong. Just as they misled readers in passing off dozens of sentences, paragraphs and phrases as their own best-selling work, now they're trying to mislead the public by redefining plagiarism" ("Purloined Letters," 2002, p. A12).

Then, the editorial referenced the undergraduate handbook for students in writing classes at Harvard. It continued:

"May be they [Ambrose and Goodwin] need to return to the basics. If you 'don't use quotation marks you are plagiarizing, even if you do cite' the source, according to the handbook for Harvard's required composition course. Students who flout the rule are booted from school ...." ("Purloined Letters," p. A12).

The paper then reminded, "Goodwin should be aware of that. She taught at Harvard. And, in fact, she probably is. She and her publisher paid a 'substantial' sum to one writer from who she cribbed, and they now are preparing to destroy old copies of a Goodwin book that doesn't include the right quote marks" ("Purloined Letters," 2002, p. A12).

The editorial concluded, "All of the blame shifting, excuse making and half-apologizing disserve readers in the same way the initial offense does. They're denied the truth. That means returning the author's credibility to its original state will be difficult" ("Purloined Letters," 2002, p. A12).

The consequences of the wrongdoing began to have an effect on Goodwin's reputation almost immediately: Within that week she was removed from her role as a commentator on *The NewsHour with Jim Lehrer,* and an invitation to deliver a commencement speech at the University of Delaware was rescinded (Kirkpatrick, 2002c; Mehegan, 2002a).

Another commentator, Jonathan Yardley of the *Washington Post,* in a column entitled, "In Search of the Appropriate Euphemism," also took Goodwin to task for her admittance that she had "borrowed" material but refused to acknowledge that she had indeed plagiarized. In referencing this decision, Yardley wrote:

> Whether this [*The Fitzgeralds and the Kennedys*] is in truth "her own book" would seem to be a dubious proposition in light of the admission that Goodwin and her assembly line—three full-time researchers, according to the *New York Times,* and one part-timer—had "borrowed" the words and ideas of others, but one is forced to acknowledge that "borrowed" is about as ingenious a euphemism as one can imagine, right up there with "friendly fire" and "courtesy call" and "collateral damage." It simultaneously admits the offense and denies: Yes, something was taken, but since it was merely "borrowed," it can be given back with no harm done. Why, it really didn't happen at all. (Yardley, 2002, p. C2)

He concluded with the assertion that, at root, the problem was that Dr. Goodwin was a celebrity researcher who had achieved a certain amount of brand identity; her name was, in effect, "a product called Doris Kearns Goodwin" (Yardley, p. C2).

The allegations continued to take their toll. On March 5, the Pulitzer board, headquartered at the School of Journalism at Columbia University, forced Goodwin out of participation in the 2002 awards, although the board allowed her the face-saving stance of writing a letter stating her intentions to withdraw (Mehegan, 2002b). In its announcement of the move, the board revealed, "Ms. Goodwin will not attend the annual meetings on April 4 and 5 when the 18-member Board makes its decisions" (Mehegan, 2002b, p. E4). The board also made public the letter from Dr. Goodwin, which offered her detailed explanation: "Because I am so distracted by the media focus on my work, I do not feel capable of giving the considerable time needed to make the proper judgments on the many books and newspaper entries that deserve our full and complete understanding" (Mehegan, 2002b, p. E4). John Carroll, the board chairman and *Los Angeles Times* editor, acknowledged that the board would take "time to weigh the issues and determine what action, if any, should be taken" (Mehegan, 2002b, p. E4).

*Damage Control in Minnesota.* With the move by the Pulitzer board, the allegations reached a crescendo—Goodwin was confronted once again with the need to revisit the issue in a public forum. The context was a speech: Originally, she had planned to deliver a lecture entitled "Democracy in Times of Crisis"; instead, she changed her topic to address the controversy in a speech entitled "The Writing of History: Problems and Pleasures," her fourth apologetic statement, which was delivered to a supportive audience at the College of St. Catherine in Minneapolis/St. Paul.

Although this was her fourth apologetic statement, she offered no new comments, instead ritualistically reassembling earlier stated arguments. In her address, Goodwin talked a great deal about her love for history and how her background as a girl growing up on Long Island led her to study and to communicate history. After sharing a number of anecdotes, she addressed the recent controversy that surrounded her work. She stated, "If I stumbled, the reputation for integrity I have worked for all my life will sustain me" (Grossman, 2002, n.p.). She used a strategy of differentiation by which she said that her primary material for her book *The Fitzgeralds and the Kennedys* was the "dozens of cartons stored at Hyannis Port for 50 years" (Grossman, 2002, n.p.). She repeated earlier explanations for her wrongdoing that it was rooted in the fact that she took notes in longhand (before the advent of computers), and that in the writing of the history she had inadvertently failed to distinguish between some of her own personal notes and observations with the writing of others (Mehegan, 2002c). In addition, she offered a corrective action strategy by which she reiterated that she was now using a scanner to take notes: "I now use scanners to make copies" of pages she is taking notes on, "and keep my notes in an entirely separate place" (Mehegan, 2002c, p. A3).

Finally, in examining the "maelstrom" that she was facing, Goodwin responded as if it were all done and that she was now at the point of having learned from it, noting "when you are confronted with a mistake of the past, admit it, talk about it. You cannot change the past. You can rectify the present and make it better for the future" (Grossman, 2002, n.p.). However, there were times, she admitted, "when I wondered if it would have been better to have said nothing, because otherwise it seems to get worse" (Mehegan, 2002c, p. A3).

*Critics Close to Home.*    Yet again, the speech failed to satisfy her critics, resulting in a second negative review. This time, it came from the student newspaper at Harvard University, *The Harvard Crimson.* The editorial staff of the *Crimson* urged her to step down from the Board of Overseers, a 29-member body that governs the university (Mehegan, 2002d). The editorial began by reviewing the material on plagiarism found in the Faculty of Arts and Sciences Handbook for Students, and concluded that "Students who, for whatever reason, submit work either not their own or without clear attribution to its sources will be subject to disciplinary action, and ordinarily required to withdraw from the College" (The Crimson Staff, 2002, n.p.).

The problem the paper had with Goodwin is that:

> Goodwin's plagiarism of sentences, nearly verbatim, from source materials is inexcusable. As an overseer, Goodwin is a leader an academic community, the foundation of which is integrity in independent scholarship. As a leader, she should recognize that her action is unbecoming an Overseer and resign her post immediately, sending the clear message to the campus that she understands the gravity of the offense she has committed. (The Crimson Staff, 2002, n.p.)

After noting that even Goodwin had acknowledged that the problem was deeper than a few cites in one book, the *Crimson* continued: "Even though the plagiarism was apparently unintentional, Goodwin's gross negligence—losing primary works, not checking citations before publication"constitutes the lack of respect and appreciation of others' work that cannot be condoned by anyone who purports to be a model for the Harvard community" (The Crimson Staff, 2002, n.p.).

Finally, the editorial ended by noting that, according to another Harvard publication, *Writing With Sources,* any student who plagiarizes will have a report attached to his or her records that he or she was "required to withdraw for academic dishonesty." The editorial then concluded: "With this policy, it is clear that the College does not think that students who have committed plagiarism should be able to proceed, unaffected, with their career goals. Why then, should an adult who is more experienced, much less a professional historian, continue in her position in the University without consequence?" (The Crimson Staff, 2002, n.p.).

The controversy continued when the University of Kansas rescinded an offer to Goodwin to speak as part of the Presidential Lecture Series at its Dole Institute of Politics, as a result of her admissions ("KU Revokes Invitation to Author," 2002). Even the high-powered lobbying of Senator Edward Kennedy with that of former Senator Bob Dole was not successful at getting the rescission overturned (Kirkpatrick, 2002d).

Even McTaggart got back in the act; she published an editorial in *The New York Times* in which she reviewed her experiences in her case against Goodwin. First, in addressing Goodwin's claim that she was fixing the problem by adding footnotes, McTaggart wrote, "Plagiarism is the dishonorable act of passing someone else's words off as your own, whether or not the material is published. Merely footnoting the copied words does not cure the wrong. In cases where the words are protected by copyright, copying in more than minimal amounts is illegal, regardless of whether the copying was unintentional" (McTaggart, 2002, p. A15).

At root, McTaggart argued that it is ultimately the words that authors own:

> Writers don't own facts. Writers don't own ideas. All that we own is the way we express our thoughts. Plagiarism pillages unique expressions, specific turns of phrase, the unusual colors a writer chooses to use from a personal literary palette. Of course, in popular histories familiar facts and scenes are often retold, but this is not plagiarism if the telling is done in a writer's own words. (McTaggart, 2002, p. A15)

And, in a parting shot, McTaggart asserted:

> But it is important not to excuse the larger sins of appropriation. In this age of clever electronic tools, writing can easily turn into a process of pressing the cut-and-paste buttons, or gluing together the work of a team of researchers, rather than the long and lonely slog of placing one word after another in a new and arresting way. (McTaggart, 2002, p. A15)

In a telephone interview with the Boston Globe, McTaggart reported that there were 173 occasions in which Goodwin "lifted" (Mehegan, 2002e, p. E1) material from McTaggart. It was only when McTaggart threatened to sue for copyright infringement did Goodwin agree to fix passages in her book and acknowledge in a revised forward that McTaggart was "a primary source for information on Kathleen Kennedy, both in my research and my writing" (Mehegan, 2002e, p. E1). McTaggart continued, "I am not interested in her being demonized or crushed by this .... I was not interested in being vindictive, but because there was so much, I wanted justice, the recognition that this was wrong" (Mehegan, p. E1).

*Apologetic Campaign Part II: David Letterman.*     Yet, Goodwin would not go quietly into the night. She continued her campaign to restore her damaged image by appearing on the *Late Show With David Letterman*. When asked about the plagiarism, she responded, "I will confess that it was sloppiness …. There was no intent to do this" (Globe Staff, 2002, p. C18). She continued on with the fact that she believed the high-quality work that she had done in the past would sustain her reputation. In addition to an appearance on the *Late Show With David Letterman*, word leaked that Goodwin had hired a public relations consultant, Robert Shrum, and made use of her relationships with high-powered people (Kirkpatrick, 2002d)—an e-mail campaign was said to be in the works to have her reinstated on *The NewsHour with Jim Leher*. These moves did not sit well with her historian colleagues. A past president of the American Historical Association, Robert Darnton, commented, "If she is organizing a P.R. campaign to exculpate herself, that strikes me as unprofessional conduct" (Kirkpatrick, 2002d, p. 18).

In perhaps the closest thing to an end to the story, the *Boston Globe* reported that Goodwin sent a letter to the Pulitzer board on May 29 in which she resigned from her service to the awards, 3 years into a 9-year commitment. In her resignation letter she wrote, "After the controversy earlier this year surrounding my book 'The Fitzgeralds and the Kennedys,' and the need to concentrate now on my Lincoln manuscript, I will not be able to give the board the kind of attention it deserves" (Kahn, 2002, p. F1). As to the question of whether she was forced out, board administrator Seymour Topping said that no board actions preceded Goodwin's decision, but that there was consensus, nonetheless, to accept her resignation.

*Final Charges and Apologetic Defenses.*     Still the story did not die, for later that summer the *Los Angeles Times* published an article alleging that Goodwin's book on Franklin and Eleanor Roosevelt, *No Ordinary Time,* which had won Goodwin her Pulitzer, contained "nearly three dozen instances where phrases and sentences in Goodwin's book resembled the words of other authors" (Beam, 2002, p. C13; King, 2002). In this case, the biggest issue was a paragraph that was "almost verbatim" from *Eleanor and Franklin,* by Joseph Lash (1971), that was not placed in quotation marks. There were other instances in which, similar to earlier allegations, Goodwin (or her researchers) used similar sentences but changed words here or there.

Judging by the response, it appears that this allegation was what Goodwin had feared all along, because it applied to the book that had earned her the Pulitzer. The denial this time came not from Goodwin but instead from another third-party source—her attorney, Michael Nussbaum, who told *The New York Times* that the *Los Angeles Times* piece was "junk journalism …. Any time you put passages together side by side, yes, the inference will come forward that because the passages resemble one another there must be something wrong with the scholarship" (Beam, 2002, p. C13). Nussbaum's law firm, Ropes & Gray, was hired to go through the book and check it. He said that the firm "looked at every single footnote without exception and then went to every source to see if the footnote was correct, proper, and met the highest standards of scholarship. We gave "No Ordinary Time" a clean bill of health, and we stand by that" (Beam, 2002, p. C13).

Yet, the story continued to have legs. In October, *The New York Times* published an article on moral decline and cheating in America, and placed alongside the article pictures of Goodwin, Kobe Bryant (basketball star and accused rapist), Dennis Kozlowski (the former head of Tyco, who stole millions from the company), and comparable others (Lee, 2003).

This brought about a third-party defense on Goodwin's behalf by some of the most noted historians in the nation, who took issue with Goodwin's inclusion among "some of the most notorious scoundrels in America" (Schlesinger, Brinkley, Dallek, & Halberstam, 2003, p. A18). They wrote:

> We write as historians to attest to our high regard for the scholarship and integrity of Doris Kearns Goodwin and to protest vigorously your article "Are More People Cheating?" (Arts & Ideas, Oct. 4), with the photograph of Ms. Goodwin displayed in the company of some of the most notorious scoundrels in America.
>
> Cheating is a deliberate intent to deceive or defraud. Plagiarism is a deliberate intent to purloin the words of another and to represent them as one's own.
>
> Ms. Goodwin did not intentionally pass off someone else's words as her own. Her sources in her 1987 book, "The Fitzgeralds and the Kennedys," were elaborately credited and footnoted. Her errors resulted from inadvertence, not intent.
>
> She did not, she does not, cheat or plagiarize. In fact, her character and work symbolize the highest standards of moral integrity.
>
> Arthur Schlesinger, Jr.
> Douglas Brinkley
> Robert Dallek
> David Halberstam
> New York, Oct. 9, 2003. (Schlesinger et al., 2003, p. A18)

The letter was also signed by 10 other historians and authors. In effect, they argued that although Dr. Goodwin had made some errors, she should not be punished severely because her offense lacked intentionality.

Goodwin continued her efforts to rehabilitate her image. In February 2003, she published an editorial about Abraham Lincoln in *The New York Times*. In it she extolled the virtues of Abraham Lincoln and his view of America, and noted that he had once thought that America's brightest days and biggest opportunities were behind him. In applying this epideictic address to contemporary Americans, she wrote:

> Before Sept. 11, many of us might have felt, as young Lincoln did when he was young, that the "field of glory" had been harvested by previous generations—that the times seemed somehow trivial. But then the wheel of history turned again. With the war against terror, and the anxieties provoked by warnings of future attacks on American soil, our generation has been provided with its own historic challenge. While our worries are great, even greater opportunities exist for leaders and citizens alike to win the lasting glory. Let us hope that we, and those who lead us, will, like Lincoln, be inspired by the noble ambition to accomplish reputable deeds worthy of remembrance. (Goodwin, 2003, p. A21)

Goodwin's final attempts to put the issue to rest—her interview with *The New York Times*, the speech in Minnesota, and her appearance on the *Late Show With David Letterman*, as well as her editorial published by *The Times*—are assessed here as a group. Together, unlike the cases of President Clinton and John Rocker that tended to evolve and become more conciliatory, Goodwin's final apologiae most resemble that of a campaign in that they seem to follow one script, with minimal deviation—from her first apologia in *Time* to her editorial in *The New York Times*. In this way, this analysis concludes that her subsequent efforts after her primary public apologia in *Time* continued to fail to meet the standards of ethical acceptability.

As it relates to the manner of her apology, for instance, the criterion of truthful appears to be fine on the surface, in that she admitted the presence of mistakes on her part and references that it was a historical matter that was (thought to be) settled. However, there was some evolution as evidenced in her making appearances such as her speech in Minnesota as well as her appearance on the *Late Show With David Letterman*, in which she did acknowledge she was embarrassed by what had gone wrong and did strike a posture that demonstrated some contrition, although there was no clear evidence of mortification. As to the timeliness of her response, she appeared to respond very quickly, taking an attack on her reputation as a charge that required a response—maybe too quickly, in that it caused her to hire public relations counsel to "manage" her wrongdoing rather than coming clean about it. This is seen in her attempts to be preemptive, in which, anticipating a negative story that was about to come out against her, she contacted *The New York Times* and broke the story herself. Her historian peers' defense of her plagiarism in their letter to the editor of *The New York Times* also employed a well-known technique by which to add third-party credibility to one's claims.

As to the content of her apology, it was here where she failed and did so in substantive ways. First, she never explicitly acknowledged her wrongdoing. At best, she claimed it was a case of not footnoting as fully as she should have, as she employed the term "citation mistakes" and always tried to avoid using any noun to describe what sin she committed—for which she was taken to task in the previously mentioned editorial in the *Washington Post*.

Furthermore, she did have the problem of coming to grips with accepting full responsibility. Her explanations for her wrongdoing appeared to change as the story unfolded. Initially, it was only on one book. Then, it was the fact that it occurred before the use of computers and scanners was widespread. Next, it became a situation in which there was more than one book involved, although Goodwin was always careful to draw a line around her 1994 Pulitzer prize-winning book, *No Ordinary Time*, claiming that it was vetted by attorneys. Then, it was a case in which she disclosed that the wrongdoing was much larger than it first appeared—although that admission was only to preempt a news article alleging so. Even when she acknowledged the problem was widespread, she was careful not to accept full responsibility. In *The New York Times* interview, she blamed the errors on a lost book and scapegoated one of her research assistants (who presumably still worked for her). Never once did she give a full admission of responsibility in which she admitted to "plagiarism," which is what her constituents were expecting. She did claim that she had utilized corrective action; she was now more rigorous in her methods and utilized computer technology and a scanner to ensure accuracy.

To her credit, Goodwin did not dismiss the allegations as did Steven Ambrose. She did acknowledge that some mistakes were made, but probably felt to fully admit to the wrongdoing would destroy her scholarly reputation and career. Furthermore, she made herself available for public questioning; she did not run nor hide, and she maintained a schedule of public appearances (although some say too many, because she was not taking a posture of humility). Furthermore, she did have the books in question pulled by Simon & Schuster and began the process of offering a corrected edition. She also suffered the public humiliation of resigning from boards as well as having a number of speaking invitations rescinded.

As to the presence of complicating issues, expense does not appear to be one; Simon Schuster announced that it would cost only $10,000 to destroy unsold copies of the offending work. The issue of a moral learning curve here is most troubling in the sense that, as a professor—as pointed out by *The Harvard Crimson*—she should have known better than to commit an offense tolerated not even in a first-semester freshman at Harvard.

## CONCLUSION

All in all, these three apologiae demonstrate a number of interesting features. First, apologists seem to slouch toward a fuller acknowledgment of their wrongdoing. In most cases, individuals start with a strategy of denial, or—in the case of Goodwin—a denial of intention, and only when that strategy of denial does not work do they seem to be willing to come to grips with the nature of their wrongdoing. There truly does seem to be the presence of an evolution in their responses. This may be due to the fact that an initial strategy of denial seems like a helpful first attempt; and if it works, the problem goes away quietly. But if it does not work, the initial plan to deny may be quickly discarded even as a more conciliatory stance is tried. On the other hand, critics should recognize and acknowledge the presence of a moral learning curve (as articulated in chap. 4): As events unfold and people are placed in the crucible, they confront the possibility that they are indeed responsible for the wrongdoing. Also, it should be noted that only as the apologiae reach the standards of ethically ideal do media and public critics tend to be fully satisfied.

Second, third-party apologists regularly are present in all three cases, be they in the form of spokespersons, attorneys, friends and colleagues, or those who claim offense. In this way, the research literature should go beyond Kruse and her claim that apologiae only come from apologists; although they are not self-defenses per se, they are nevertheless a critical part of the apologetic exchange, and scholars are wise to take them fully into account when analyzing apologetic interactions.

Finally, what is evident in individual apologia is the presence of a public relations campaign in which all three apologists discussed in this chapter demonstrated that they have advisors, handlers, attorneys, and counselors who, in effect, write scripts for them to follow. In most cases, the script changes based on events, and rare is the apologetic performer who can stay "on message" even as new revelations come forward. In this sense, individual apologiae continue to be illustrative of the ongoing corporatization of discourse, and the emergence of a managerial rhetoric—even in the case of individuals.

# 6

# Apologia and Organizations

## Retail, Manufacturing, and Not-for-Profits

When Aaron has finished making atonement for the Most Holy Place, the Tent of Meeting and the altar, he shall bring forward the live goat.

He is to lay both hands on the head of the live goat and confess over it all the wickedness and rebellion of the Israelites—all their sins—and put them on the goat's head.

He shall send the goat away into the desert in the care of a man appointed for the task.

The goat will carry on itself all their sins to a solitary place; and the man shall release it in the desert.

Leviticus 16: 20–22 (*The Holy Bible*, 1973/1984)

The act whereby the guilt of the people of Israel was transferred to a goat was a purification ritual that is the antecedent of the modern idea of a scapegoat. The purpose of such cleansing was not to reconcile the community to God and achieve forgiveness of sins, as does an atonement ritual, but rather it was a ritual that purified the congregation because it removed the sin from the camp.

Concomitantly, the notion of a scapegoat has significant application to contemporary society, because modernity is characterized by its hypercorporate character. And, of course, when wrongdoing occurs, organizations are in need of symbolic cleansing, in that the only way to remove guilt from the organization is to get rid of the offending actors through a process remarkably similar to the ancient idea of a scapegoat.

In fact, as Western society has undergone a transition from an individual- to an organizational-based society, so too has discourse evolved from

121

an individual-driven rhetoric to a corporate form of discourse—with its heavy emphasis on the purification of the congregation. Although corporations created and disseminated this form of discourse for the better part of the 20th century, only recently have students of communication begun to focus on rhetoric that emanates from a corporate source.

A number of scholars argue that corporate discourse is a completely different phenomenon than the rhetoric that emanates from an individual source (Cheney, 1992; Crable, 1986; Sproule, 1988). Indeed, Sproule maintained that the field of modern communication has witnessed a paradigmatic shift from an individual to a managerial form of discourse. Specifically, he asserted that modern communication is an image-based rhetoric, rooted in entertainment. It is an ideological form, one that supplies prepackaged conclusions and emphasizes identification and likeability rather than ethos. Rather than appealing to a generalized audience, it instead seeks to narrowly segment audiences in order to pull the levers of persuasion. This managerial style of persuasion has affected individual, corporate, as well as institutional discourse. This chapter reviews the academic research on organizational apologia, which concerns for-profit companies as well as so-called third-sector organizations—not-for-profit organizations that play an integral role in contemporary society and commerce. It then draws application to three contexts: a media-flap in a retail environment, a manufacturing crisis that cost lives and millions of dollars, and a not-for-profit case that got caught up with many of the emotions that surrounded the terrorist attacks of September 11, 2001.

## CORPORATE APOLOGIA THEORY

### Contexts

By its very nature, criticism leveled against an organization is valuative; it argues that a company has violated a social convention by its actions. Such charges assert that organizational acts lack a basic level of competence or represent a disregard for stakeholders (Hearit, 1995a). Generally speaking, these accusations fall into four categories: accidents, product safety incidents, scandals and illegalities, and social irresponsibility (a model that accounts for the bulk of the different "forms" of response; for more on the ways scholars have organized the problem of contexts in order to account for every different type of context an organization might face, see Coombs, 1995, 1998; Hearit, 1999; Marcus & Goodman, 1991; Seeger et al., 2003). In accidents—due to an act of God or a failure of human interaction with technology—a misfortune has occurred that has caused harm to innocents or the environment. Although they are unexpected and typically one-time events, their causes tend to be systemic and the fault of the system (Perrow, 1984). This largely is related to the problem of complexity, because as complexity increases so too do opportunities for accidents. Accident victims quickly secure legal counsel to pursue compensation for harms they have suffered (Lieberman, 1981). They leave available to apologists a wide range of rhetorical latitude in which to locate responsibility; such "causes" range from blaming "disgruntled employees" to labeling an accident "an act of God," although American organizations are much more likely to locate blame in individuals at the switch rather than the Japanese tendency to locate responsibility in those at top (Sugimoto, 1999).

Product safety incidents, on the other hand, appear to take just the opposite tact. Rather than being the result of a dramatic, one-time event, product safety incidents tend to coalesce slowly as similar revelations from disparate sources begin to surface, as was the situation with the Dow Corning breast implant case (Brinson & Benoit, 1996). Like those injured by accidents, victims of faulty products are likely to be represented by legal counsel. However, the causes of product safety incidents are more narrow, rooted not in systemic organizational weakness but instead in design flaws (Marcus & Goodman, 1991). Just as their causes are more limited, so too are potential explanations. This is the type of apologetic response most likely to be dictated by legal counsel.

Scandals and illegalities represent the third type of accusations leveled against organizations. In scandals and illegalities, a company's image is damaged due to disclosures that the company "doesn't play by the rules," which results in public shame. Here, a company or corporate officials have engaged in controversial or illegal activities that are likely to bring social sanction, such as when the chief executive of the United Way was criticized for enriching himself by misusing donor gifts (Shepard, 1992), or when E.F. Hutton developed a complex scheme to defraud depositors of interest (Thackaberry, 1996). In scandals and illegalities, victims are less identifiable and typically less innocent (i.e., competitors). Apologetic responses in such cases are manifold, and tend to be limited only by the imagination of corporate officers, although scapegoating key employees figures prominently in this calculus.

Finally, the last context in which crises can be classified is a form of social irresponsibility. In this context, an organization has done nothing illegal but rather is accused of having committed acts that are incongruent with current social values (Huxman & Bruce, 1995). One such example of this form of crisis is when an organization follows the flow of capital and relocates from one site to a location in which costs are cheaper, resulting in tremendous displacement in the lives of employees. Such was the allegation that brought a crisis for the Chrysler Corporation when it chose to close its aging Kenosha, Wisconsin, plant (Schultz & Seeger, 1991).

No matter what type of crises an organization faces—be they allegations of accidents, scandals and illegalities, product safety incidents, or social irresponsibility—the fact of the matter is that apologiae have common ritualistic foundations. These ritualistic underpinnings present an occasion in which organizations must come to grips with their wrongdoing, publicly address their guilt, and then request a return back into the social community. No matter how guilty an organization might be, it must nonetheless face the public criticism in a public context and deal with the public sanction that comes with its guilt. By offering an apology, organizations show their contrition and, coupled with corrective action, find themselves restored into the community.

## Stances

Although organizations typically draw on common image-repair strategies, they tend to organize these strategies in a limited number of ways (Benoit, 1995; Coombs, 2004; Coombs & Holladay, 2002; Coombs & Schmidt, 2002; Hearit, 2001). Specifically, Hearit argued that organizations utilize one of five overall stances by which to deal with allegations of guilt. In other words, although organizations tend to use a multiplicity of strategies, their approach tends to feature one overall strategic stance. These stances include denial, counterattack, differentiation, apology, and a legal stance.

In the denial stance, an organization maintains that it has done nothing wrong. In such an instance, the organization regularly relies on a strategy of denial to, in effect, claim "We're not guilty." Such was the stance taken by the makers of Tylenol in 1982, in response to the seven deaths that occurred in the greater Chicago area due to product tampering (Benoit & Lindsey, 1987; Fearn-Banks, 1996). A variant of this strategy is used by organizations that cannot deny committing the act but nevertheless find themselves in a position in which they can deny intent. Denial strategies often rely heavily on an opinion/knowledge dissociation.

In counterattack, a second stance that is really an offshoot of denial, an organization seeks to deal with the problem of its guilt by first denying the act and then directly attacking its accuser, claiming that the charges are false or come from malicious intent. The use of such a strategy reverses the direction of the exchange in that the accused takes the moral high ground position of the accuser, and seeks to put the interrogator on the defensive (Hearit, 1996). Such was the tactic that GM used in defense of its C/K pickups, which *Dateline NBC* accused of being unsafe. GM challenged the newmagazine's credibility by calling into question the ethics of its reporting and its use of a staged explosion of the trucks in order to make its point.

A third approach is that of differentiation. This stance probably accounts for the bulk of apologia. Here, organizations seek to distance themselves from their wrongdoing by attempting to redefine it, explain it, account for it, or justify it. The idea in doing so is that once key publics *understand* what happened, they will be less likely to condemn the organization and its actions. Such a strategy usually acknowledges some guilt, but often seeks to explain it away using an individual/group dissociation. This stance is illustrated by the Toshiba Corporation after it was disclosed in 1987 that the Toshiba Machine Company sold top-secret milling equipment to the then-Soviet Union, which enabled the USSR to engineer quieter submarines, thus altering the strategic balance between the United States and the Soviet Union. Toshiba quickly apologized and then dissociated the Toshiba name from the wrongdoing; it defined the wrong as having been perpetrated by the Toshiba Machine Company, which from then on it referenced only as TMC (Hearit, 1994).

A fourth strategy is that of apology, whereby organizations deal with their misconduct by acknowledging it and confessing responsibility. This often is coupled with a strategy of corrective action. Although some companies honestly and forthrightly issue a direct apology for their wrongdoing, most tend to release a statement of regret whereby they apologize for the harm that resulted but are careful not to assume responsibility (Hearit, 1995a). AT&T directly apologized for a service interruption, for instance, and offered compensation, claiming that "apologies are not enough" (Benoit & Brinson, 1994, p. 82). In this context, organizations use an act/essence dissociation to acknowledge that although an act did occur, it does not reflect the essence of an organization.

Finally, research has shown that a preferred method for many organizations accused of wrongdoing is to say nothing publicly, but instead to take a private, legal strategy, whereby they seek legal absolution of their guilt and ignore public concerns (Fitzpatrick & Rubin, 1995). In this situation, due to liability costs an organization might incur, it instead seeks to avoid any public comment on its wrongdoing out of fear that words of conciliation or regret used to mitigate concerns in a public relations context could be turned against the organization in a legal one. In describing the particulars of this stance, Fitzpatrick and Rubin (1995) described the philosophy of communication of companies that (unfortunately) take this approach:

> (1) say nothing; (2) say as little as possible and release it as quietly as possible; (3) say as little as possible, citing privacy laws, company policy or sensitivity; (4) deny guilt and/or act indignant that such charges could possibly have been made; or (5) shift or, if necessary, share the blame with the plaintiff …. [N]ever admit blame. (p. 22)

Perhaps the most famous example of this type of strategy was that taken by Ford Motor Company in defense of its Pinto in the 1970s. The company hunkered down for a long legal battle and made its defense primarily in the courtroom (Kaufmann et al., 1994).

Although there are many stances available to corporate apologists, the next section, which seeks to examine specific case studies of corporate wrongdoing, shows that a company's response to allegations of wrongdoing is highly situation based; that is, the choices that apologists tend to make are highly contingent on the nature of the allegations. These organizations then choose a stance that is most likely to result in absolution of their guilt. This is shown in analyses of the clothing retailer Abercrombie & Fitch, manufacturers Firestone and Ford, and the not-for-profit organization the American Red Cross.

## CASE STUDIES OF CORPORATE APOLOGETIC DISCOURSE

## Abercrombie & Fitch

It is well known that clothiers push the envelope in their advertising in an effort to distinguish their products from others. The preternatural example of such a technique is that of Calvin Klein, whose 2 decades of advertising has constantly and consistently pushed the boundaries of public acceptability. It doing so, of course, such moves generate media coverage and considerable free exposure for the product line even as they promote a rebellious image (Hearit, 1998). One company that perhaps has learned too well from Calvin Klein is Abercrombie & Fitch, the Reynoldsburg, Ohio, clothing company (formerly a part of the ubiquitous line of the Limited Stores that have come to dominate American Mall retail) that is popular with teenagers and college students alike, which has a reputation for pushing the limits. Indeed, in 1998, critics forced the company to recall a catalog that featured a two-page article entitled "Drinking 101," which gave tips for "creative drinking," a move objected to by alcohol advocacy groups. The controversy led to exposure and increased sales of 70% for the quarter (Pickler, 1999a). The controversy was small, however, when compared to the one that came the following year.

*The Allegations.*    In December 1999, Abercrombie & Fitch published its Christmas catalog edition of *A & F Quarterly,* entitled "Naughty or Nice" (1999). Starting with a cover that featured a shirtless male model with his jeans unbuttoned, the catalog displayed a variety of different elements that pushed the limits of acceptable taste. Recognizing that the catalog would likely be offensive to some, the editors began with a letter to Santa imploring him that although he might "encounter something in the following pages that reeks of irresponsibility and recklessness" not to "punish us too harshly" ("Naughty or Nice," 1999, p. 10). The letter was accompanied by a cartoon showing Santa being whipped by Mrs. Claus in a corseted dominatrix outfit, elves in various states of undress, as well as Christmas gifts such as rubber vomit, fake boobs, and a shot glass set.

Other low points to the catalog included an interview with drag queen Candice Cayne, a piece by comedian Andy Dick on the pleasures of fellatio, and—in what caught the eyes beyond those of Abercrombie & Fitch editors' intended audience—images of male and female nudity as well as sex tips from porn star Jenna Jameson ("Naughty or Nice," 1999). Responsible for the catalog was Sam Shahid, a former creative director for Calvin Klein, who hired photographer Bruce Weber, noted for his Calvin Klein's Obsession advertisements (Wells, 2000).

In response to the offensive catalogue, Abercrombie & Fitch faced a crisis in which it was charged with an illegality, although in reality the guilt was more in the area of social irresponsibility. On November 17, 1999, Michigan Attorney General Jennifer Granholm sent a "Notice of Intended Action" letter to Abercrombie & Fitch, informing it that due to the catalog's graphic sexual nature, it could not legally be distributed to minors (Granholm, 1999). Specifically, the letter provided notice to A & F that "it must immediately cease and desist in disseminating this material to Michigan minors"(Granholm, 1999, p. 1). Furthermore, the letter "demand[ed] that A & F specify, adopt and implement reasonable policies, procedures and controls at its Michigan retail outlets to ensure that such materials are not disseminated to Michigan minors in the future"(Granholm, 1999, p. 1). If the company failed to make changes in its policy, under the Michigan Consumer Protection Act it faced possible civil penalties of up to $25,000 per transaction (Granholm, 1999).

In an interview, Granholm charged: "It's fine to push the envelope for adults or for college students over 18, but not when a large part of your market are 10- to 18-year-olds. This is off the charts. This is unacceptable" (Pickler, 1999a, November 18, n.p.). Later, in an interview with *Forbes* magazine, she observed, "They say they're marketing a lifestyle, but it's not a lifestyle I would want my kids to emulate" (Wells, 2000, p. 58). In effect, Granholm attempted to increase Abercrombie & Fitch's guilt by drawing from society's universal desire to protect children. In addition, the fact that the company appeared to intend to offend also functioned to amplify the clothier's guilt.

Of primary concern was the fact that the attorney general's office sent three underage children to Abercrombie & Fitch stores to attempt to purchase the catalog. Even though no adult was present, all three children—aged 10, 13, and 14, respectively—were able to successfully purchase the shrinkwrapped catalog, which came with the label "mature content" (Pickler, 1999a).

*The Response.* Abercrombie & Fitch took a two-pronged approach to deal with the tumult created by the catalog. Taking a page from Calvin Klein, the company's public stance was to follow a predictable script: claim innocence, proclaim that the catalog was never intended for anyone other than college students, and profess surprise that people found the issue the least bit offensive (Hearit, 1998). Abercrombie & Fitch spokesperson Hampton Carney used a strategy of denial of intent to claim that the catalog never was meant for anyone other than college students. He claimed, "It's never been intended for anyone under 18. We're very sensitive to that matter" (Pickler, 1999a, n.p.). Yet, Carney later admitted that although employees were told not to sell the catalog to minors, such employees "are not in the practice of carding people who want to buy it" (Pickler, 1999a, n.p.).

The company's more private stance was to deal quickly and efficiently with the legal issues raised by the case. By early afternoon on November 18, Michael Stevenson, vice president of finance, faxed the following response to the Attorney General's office: "In response to the concerns raised in your recent inquiry, Abercrombie & Fitch agrees to immediately implement procedures designed to validate that purchasers of its in-store magazines are 18 years of age or over" (Abercrombie & Fitch, 1999, p. 1). The one-paragraph announcement in effect complied with the legal requirements set down by the attorney general, but it offered no statement of regret or apology for the content of the catalog.

The very next day, Carney publicized that Abercrombie & Fitch, in a response to the formal complaint filed by Michigan Attorney General Jennifer Granholm, had put in place a policy that would confirm the age of the purchaser. In his statement, Carney used a strategy of corrective action in which he intoned, "We always wrapped it in plastic and put the advisory label on it, but we are now going to be carding to make sure the purchaser is 18 or over unless accompanied by a parent" (Pickler, 1999b, n.p.).

Apparently not chastised by the kategoria/apologia exchange, Carney acknowledged that the controversy had not hurt sales of the $6 catalog; in fact, he asserted, "It's flying out of the stores. We're actually considering going back to the press to run more copies" (Pickler, 1999b, n.p.).

Granholm admitted that the company had probably planned all along to have the offensive nature of the catalog generate publicity, and that she and parents were also playing a role in following A & F's script: "I would hate to see bad behavior rewarded, so I think parents should be very conscious of where they [their children] were spending their dollars. Do they want to support a company that promotes casual sex?" (Pickler, 1999, November 19, n.p.).

Hampton Carney spoke on behalf of Abercrombie & Fitch in order to explain the company's actions in the marketing and sale of the catalog to young people. In the opinion of this analysis, Carney's statements ethically failed, in terms of both the manner as well as the content of the apology. As it related to the manner in which the apologia was delivered, it fell short on multiple accounts. First was the issue of truthfulness. To claim that a company, whose target market included high school students, did not intend for teenagers under the age of 18 to get a copy of the *Quarterly* strained credulity, particularly when Carney admitted that there were no measures in place to keep young people from purchasing the book.

One also has to question the sincerity of the apology, in that although Carney acknowledged that new procedures had been put in place, he seemed to express more than a little enthusiasm that the controversy had helped to boost sales of the book, and one suspects of clothes in the store. In this way, it was poorly performed. Based on this fact, it is no small leap to conclude the crisis was created strategically by Abercrombie & Fitch to manipulate press attention in order to facilitate free publicity for the company. Although the company was quick to respond, this likely was an involuntary reply; the actions of the attorney general of Michigan, not the process of moral reflection, were probably what prompted a quick reply.

Finally, the apology did not address all stakeholders in that parents were left out of the discussion, although not on account of Attorney General Granholm, who regularly referenced parents in her remarks. Abercrombie & Fitch simply never mentioned parental concern in its statements.

As to the content of the apology, Abercrombie & Fitch's apology fails on these accounts as well. First, it did not acknowledge the presence of wrongdoing, in that it denied the presence of any intent. When Carney admitted that catalogs had been sold to minors, he acknowledged that the company did not go out of its way to keep the catalogs out of the hands of minors. No regret was communicated; at most, the only emotion demonstrated was feigned surprise. As to identifying with injured stakeholders, Abercrombie & Fitch never acknowledged that the content of the catalog was harmful to minors, nor did it seek any forgiveness for offending public sensibilities. The explanation that the company intended that only college students would purchase the catalogue was insufficient. Finally, Abercrombie & Fitch did perform corrective action when a policy to card minors was implemented; but the company did so only after it faced potential legal sanction from the attorney general of Michigan.

*Continuing Controversy.* The controversy did not die down after Abercrombie & Fitch reached an agreement with the Michigan attorney general. In Springfield, Missouri, Michelle Finch filed a legal complaint against Abercrombie & Fitch after a store employee sold the catalog to Finch's 15-year-old daughter. Finch exclaimed, "I may not be able to get the filthy catalog out of the store, but I can hurt them in other ways. I'm horrified that they would sell my daughter pornography" ("Mother Files Complaint," 1999, n.p.).

Finch's purpose for taking legal action was so that other parents would learn about the catalog's content. Following her complaint, Green County prosecutor Darrell Moore said he would likely follow up on the complaint by urging the store to pull the catalog and by forwarding the state's pornography statute to the store. He argued, "It may be in the best interest of the store to just pull the catalog. I'm shocked they would even do this. Why do you need this to sell clothes?" ("Mother Files Complaint," 1999, n.p.).

These problems continued to afflict Abercrombie & Fitch across the country. Similarly, Arkansas Governor Mike Huckabee described the catalog as "inappropriate" for a company that markets and sells clothes to teens, while Washington County Republican Women protested the catalog at a local mall ("Criticism of A & F Catalog Spreads," 1999, n.p.). In Illinois, Lieutenant Governor Corinne Wood wrote to newspapers in an effort to encourage shoppers to boycott the company's stores; she claimed the company was a purveyor of "soft porn" ("Criticism of A & F Catalog Spreads," 1999, n.p.). Wood explained, "I don't know if we can stop the Abercrombie & Fitches of the world from manipulating our teens. But I do know as parents we can try to send the right message" ("Criticism of A & F Catalog Spreads," 1999, n.p.).

Abercrombie & Fitch spokesperson Hampton Carney continued to plead innocent to the charges, never deviating from the set script. Incredulously, he continued to argue a strategy of denial of intent and differentiation; that, in the words of an Associated Press writer, the "photos were not meant to be provocative nor for preteens" ("Criticism of A & F Catalog Spreads," 1999, n.p.). Instead, Carney responded, "We're targeting only the 18- to 22-year-old college student" ("Criticism of A & F Catalog Spreads," 1999, n.p.).

Abercrombie & Fitch's long-term strategy was much more mixed. Initially, its strategy seemed to be to play down the racier elements of its catalogs. In "Wild & Willing" (2000), A & F's spring break issue, noticeably absent was the more direct nudity of the Christmas catalog; instead, the issue featured wet t-shirts, slightly pulled-down swim trunks, and some strategically covered nudity. Yet, the issue did propose Costa Rica as a spring break destination due to the fact that there is no law there against underage drinking and that "prostitution is legal." The issue also featured a "Naked News Wire" that, among other things, described famous people who were photographed in the nude, and listed locations to watch all forms of nudist activities, among them running, volleyball, and, of all things, cross-country skiing ("Wild & Willing," 2000). Once the public scrutiny was over, the catalog returned to its full old form. The summer issue, in addition to recommending an internship at Vivid Video (a porn outfit) or encouraging students to "Enjoy a cigar with the President" as a White House intern ("Go Play," 2000, p. 71), included graphic displays of nudity: One depicted three men chasing a topless woman; another one showed three women working to rid a man of his boxers. Clearly, it appears that Abercrombie & Fitch will continue to push the envelope in such a way so as to generate the outrage of parents while successfully selling clothes to their teenagers.

Although the drama of the case of Abercrombie & Fitch largely was a media-flap in which there was no real or tangible harm done, the next case discussed here, that of Ford versus Firestone, was one in which the damage done to victims was all too real. Indeed, it resulted in hundreds of deaths and injuries to consumers.

## Ford Versus Firestone

The Ford versus Firestone case is a difficult and complex one to analyze, because it is rooted in an environment in which there was an ongoing conflict—unlike most apologetic exchanges, which last a short period of time, this kategoria/apologia exchange lasted for more than a year (Blaney, Benoit, & Brazeal, 2002). Consequently, this section is organized around the initial allegations and response that characterized the crisis, the first round of government investigations, the initial legal settlements, Firestone's attempts at image repair, a second round of allegations followed by a second round of governmental investigations, and then the final legal settlements. Subsequently, this case analysis presents assessments of the ethical nature of the communication offered by the major participants at appropriate sections in which major apologetic statements were made by the key players of the exchange.

Additionally, it should be noted that the assessment of Ford's response is more complex than that of Firestone's, because it is clear that the primary problem in the entire crisis was rooted in a failure of tires (Blaney et al., 2002), although there were enough allegations on the part of opinion leaders and third-party participants to raise questions as to the Ford Explorer's contribution to the situation. Indeed, only after a determination of whether or not the Explorer had a design flaw can one judge the ethical quality of the company's communication. It is the opinion of this author, after examining the public data available in the case, that at root the problem was with the poorly constructed tires (built most likely during a strike, with replacement workers), although due to reasons of weight distribution the tire failures appeared to be higher on the Explorer than on other sport utility vehicles. Nonetheless, if the tires had been built correctly, any weight distribution issues on the Explorer would have been mitigated. This is further supported by the fact that National Highway Traffic Safety Administration (NHTSA) issued multiple recalls of the Firestone tires but did not open an investigation of the Ford Explorer, as well as the fact that Firestone's own independent expert came to the conclusion that under normal conditions tires did not deteriorate faster on the Explorer than on other vehicles (Bradsher, 2000q).

*Initial Allegations and Apologies.*    In 2000, Firestone was poised to celebrate the 100th anniversary of its founding; indeed, the tire company had begun to make sales gains at the expense of Goodyear and Michelin, as a result of the successful marketing of its connection with automobile racing (Bradsher, 2000e). Yet, in February, Houston television station KHOU ran a dramatic story that alleged problems with Firestone tires mounted on Ford Explorers (Deutsch, 2000). As complaints grew following the story, the National Highway Traffic Safety Administration opened an investigation on May 2, with 90 complaints filed (Deutsch, 2000). By the last day of July, *USA Today* broke the story nationally (Nathan, 2000), publishing allegations that government regulators had attributed first 62 and then 88 U.S. deaths (as well as 47 additional deaths in Venezuela) to tread separation on Firestone's 15-inch ATX and ATX II tires and on 15-inch Wilderness model tires made in its Decatur, Illinois, plant; with the disclosures, the company was plunged into a product safety incident tailspin (Bradsher, 2000e; Mayer & Swoboda, 2000).

At first, Firestone acted slowly in its response. The company initially made statements of denial that argued the tires had no flaws; yet, evidence began to mount against the tire manufacturer, owned and managed by the Japanese company Bridgestone. By August 9, Firestone admitted it faced a product safety crisis and used a corrective action strategy to announce the recall and replacement of 14.4 million tires, 6.5 million of which were believed to still be on the road (installed on light trucks). This recall included all 15-inch Wilderness tires made at the Decatur plant since 1996 (Bradsher, 2000l; Bradsher & Wald, 2000; Sims, 2000a). Two thirds of these tires came as standard equipment on Ford Explorer sport utility vehicles (Bradsher, 2000l). The cost of the recall was expected to be $350 million for Firestone (Sims, 2000b). The facts that the crisis would be highly mediated, was a simple script for consumers to follow, and resulted in harm to a sizable number of victims all functioned to increase Firestone's perceived guilt.

By August 11, people had become increasingly frustrated with the pace and the order of the recall. The nature of the recall was to focus initially on those areas that presented the most risk; hence, Firestone's decision to replace first those tires in the South and in the West, which had a disproportionate share of the tire separations due to the added heat of those regions (Blair, 2000). Such a plan caused an outcry in other parts of the country, where consumer advocates threatened lawsuits. Firestone defended its policy; spokeswoman Cynthia McCafserty said, "We will do everything we can to get them replaced, but we are focusing our efforts on parts of the country where there have been most of the incidents"(Blair, 2000, p. C1).

A particular dynamic of the problem with the Firestone ATX, ATX II, and Wilderness tires was that they appeared more prone to separate on Ford Explorers than on other vehicles, particularly in climates with high heat. Firestone at first took a cautious stance; it issued a recall but was careful not to directly blame the Ford Explorer, an option it chose due to the fact that Ford was Firestone's largest customer. The relationship between the two companies began in 1906, when Henry Ford signed a contract to purchase tires from his friend Harvey Firestone. Such a fact, however, does not address just how personal the relationship was; current Ford President and Board Chairman William C. Ford, Jr., is a scion of both families; he is the great-grandson of Henry Ford, and his mother is the granddaughter of Harvey S. Firestone (Bradsher, 2000h). Particularly emblematic was a statement by then-Firestone Vice President John Lampe that tried indirectly to point out that the problems with the tires only occurred on the Ford Explorer, without actually referencing the Explorer by name: "This situation is somewhat unprecedented in itself, because the incidents that we've seen and the problems that we've seen have been primarily on one size tire on one application. We've got the same size tire on a number of other applications, and we're not seeing the same sort of circumstances" (Bradsher, 2000e, p. C5).

On August 13, in an effort to reassure customers with tires waiting to be recalled (although instead of reassuring it had the effect of exacerbating the issue), Ford released information based on its own analysis of data supplied by Firestone. This information suggested Firestone had had knowledge of the problems with the tires as early as 1997; it also noted that the recalled tires had an injury and damage rate that was approximately 100 times greater than did those tires not recalled (Bradsher, 2000a). The report additionally suggested that Firestone's Decatur, Illinois, plant was the primary source of the faulty tires, particularly those tires made from 1994 to 1996 (Barboza, 2000a). Firestone countered that it had been unaware of the problem until Ford's analysis, according to Bob Wyant, Bridgestone vice president of quality assurance.

Pressure on Firestone and Ford increased even more dramatically when lawyers and safety critics held a news conference in Washington, D.C., urging Firestone to broaden its recall and claiming that Ford had produced a defective vehicle in the Explorer (Bradsher, 2000b). Legal advocates took aim at the decision to begin the recall in the states where a full 85% of the accidents had taken place (Arizona, California, Florida, and Texas); they argued that the companies needed to replace all the faulty tires nationwide (Bradsher, 2000b).

Advocates then took aim at Ford's and Firestone's explanations, and argued that the cause of the tire separations was due not to overloaded tires, warm weather climates, or poor manufacturing processes, but instead to design flaws in the Ford Explorer's suspension coupled with the technical specifications for the tires (Bradsher, 2000b). Allegations by consumer groups often serve policymaking functions; the case of Ford and Firestone was no different (Hearit, 1996). Joan Claybrook, noted president of Public Citizen, led the charge; she intoned, "I think it's a design defect" (Bradsher, 2000b, p.

C6). Ford countered with a strategy of denial: "We've built Explorers with brands of tires other than Firestones and had absolutely no problems" (Bradsher, 2000b, p. C6).

By August 15, government data revealed the number of complaints regarding Firestone tires had risen to 750, which included 62 deaths. This made the recall the most deadly automotive product safety incident ever (Bradsher, 2000c). Ford countered that even when the deaths by Firestone tires were included in the data, consumers who drove the Ford Explorer still faced a 22% lower death-rate risk in rollover crashes than did drivers of competitors' sport utility vehicles, and when all types of accidents were taken into account, a 24% less rate overall (Bradsher, 2000c).

In an effort to communicate with its customers, on August 21 Ford Chairman Jacques Nasser appeared on an advertisement aired during *Monday Night Football*. In the spot, he informed Explorer owners about the recall by Firestone and articulated the company position that the tire troubles were a tread issue, not a vehicle design issue.

Finally, on August 23, Firestone responded with a carefully-crafted print campaign that followed a ritualistic form as it attempted to communicate to the American public. Entitled "Firestone's Update on the Voluntary Safety Recall," the advertisement took the form of a letter that Chief Executive Officer Masatoshi Ono wrote to Firestone customers ("Firestone's Update," 2000). Ono began by noting the ongoing problems with a statement of concern, then followed with a corrective action strategy. He wrote:

> We are deeply committed to the safety of all our customers riding on our tires. Some of them are our own children, wives, husbands, friends and employees.
>
> Out of great concern for your safety, Firestone initiated the Voluntary Safety Recall of the P235/75R15ATX and ATXII tires produced in North America, and P235/75R15 Wilderness AT tires produced at our Decatur, Illinois plant. ("Firestone's Update," 2000, p. 9A)

The letter continued that the company had hoped to complete the recall by spring, but decided to race to finish it more quickly. To this end, Firestone announced that it would increase its worldwide production of replacement tires, ask competitors to increase their production, and offer a reimbursement to those who replaced their faulty tires with competitors' tires ("Firestone's Update," 2000).

As for an explanation of the tire problems, Ono first was careful not to imply that Firestone was fully to blame, leaving room in his description to suggest that blame might lay elsewhere. He wrote, "We are also working with the National Highway Traffic Safety Administration and Ford, and we are conducting an intensive investigation to find the root cause or causes of the problem. We are working around the clock, utilizing all of our resources to determine the cause of these failures" ("Firestone's Update," 2000, p. 9A). He then explained the difficulty in determining the cause of problem due to the complexity of tire manufacturing and other variables.

> It may take time to scientifically determine the cause of the problem. Tires are highly complex engineered products. A typical tire can have more than 26 components, 14 different rubber compounds, and require 29 separate steps to manufacture. In addition, there are many other forces that affect tire performance such as weather, temperature, vehicle loads, driving styles, vehicle dynamics, inflation pressure and road conditions. ("Firestone's Update," 2000, p. 9A)

Again, the nature of his statement indicated that Firestone had no intention to accept full blame for the problems. Furthermore, the appeal to complexity often is used by organizations to privilege their positions by moving the discussion from a public sphere to a technical one (Hearit, 1995a). In this way, complexity inverts the traditional organizational communication dictum to speak clearly; when dealing with problems of wrongdoing, complexity is the apologist's friend (Boorstin, 1961; Eisenberg, 1984).

On August 24, Ford officials went on the offensive, attacking the lawyers representing plaintiffs who had filed suit against Ford (Bradsher, 2000d). Specifically, Ford argued against calls for a broader recall, based on safety concerns. Helen Petrauskas, Ford vice president for safety and environmental engineering, argued, "A broader recall is wrong. It's wrong because many good tires will be delivered and used to replace good tires—and people who have tires which should be replaced will have to stand in line and wait" (Bradsher, 2000d, p. C6).

The other shoe appeared to drop on Firestone when, on September 1, the NHTSA offered a consumer alert on an additional 1.4 million tires, claiming that their failure rate was even higher than that of the already recalled tires. At first, Firestone refused to launch an additional recall (Bradsher, 2000f). However, recognizing that it had little choice, the company eventually agreed to recall the tires, all the while asserting that it disagreed with the NHTSA's conclusions (Mayer & Swoboda, 2000).

Given the amount of money involved in the recall, cracks began to develop in the Ford and Firestone relationship. Surprisingly, they came not from Firestone but from Ford. On September 1, 2000, the businesses began to part company when Ford's Jacques Nasser, in an attempt to protect the reputation of the Ford Explorer—Ford's top-selling sport utility vehicle and one of the most profitable vehicles in the Ford lineup—publicly spoke the line that would be the company's standard script throughout the entire crisis: "This is a tire issue without question; it is not a vehicle issue" (Bradsher, 2000e, p. C5).

As to the question as to whether an apology was necessary, Nasser intoned: "I'm sorry that these defective tires are on our vehicles" (Bradsher, 2000e, p. C5). As to whether to continue the relationship with Firestone, Nasser said, "This has been an extremely difficult and disappointing period in our relationship, and we'll take this a day at a time" (Bradsher, 2000e, p. C5).

The appearance of Jacques Nasser in the advertisement on *Monday Night Football* was coupled with a print campaign that ran during the first week of September. In it, Nasser attempted to reassure Ford's customers who had concerns about the recall. He began the advertisement with the valuative statement:

Your safety is our top priority.

"You have my personal guarantee that no one at Ford will rest until every re-called tire is replaced."

Jacques Nasser,
President and CEO Ford Motor Company
("Your Safety," 2000, p. 21)

Noting that there had been a "whirlwind of information" and that some customers might be justifiably "confused," the advertisement then proceeded to give customers a four-step guide as to how to get their tires replaced ("Your Safety," 2000, p. 21).

In assessing Firestone's early response, this case, unlike the others examined in the book, most directly features the problem of liability as a complicating circumstance. The financial costs to Firestone, in terms of the recall and potential legal judgments, show liability concerns to be paramount in terms of Firestone's response to the crisis. Similar costs and concerns, likewise, proved to be paramount in Ford's response.

Nonetheless, Firestone's initial communication must be assessed as ethically unacceptable, due to its slow and incomplete reaction. As to the manner of the response, the company failed to meet the standards of the ethically ideal, because it began with a strategy of denial, and only when faced with new and dramatic evidence did it begin to become more truthful in its responses and actually publish an open letter from Chief Executive Ono. In addition, although the company appeared sincere in its communication, it must be faulted for its slowness of response and for the involuntary nature of that response. When the crisis broke, Firestone did not even have a Web site, and only recalled the tires after pressure from consumers and the prospect of governmental intervention became all too real. To the company's credit, it did address all relevant stakeholders, seeking to communicate with customers as to how to get their tires replaced quickly as well as exercising great pains in its explanations not to directly criticize the Ford Motor Company, with whom it had a supplier relationship.

As to the content of its apologia, Firestone must be faulted for its lack of accommodative response. The company announced it would replace the tires and its intention to do so in a systematic way, but offered no acknowledgment of wrongdoing, statement of regret, or full acceptance of responsibility. Instead, the best the company could do was express "great concern" for its customers. Indeed, although Firestone was careful in how it did so, it began to subtly counterattack Ford, blaming the tire problems on a design flaw in the Ford Explorer and suggesting that people's driving habits or lack of tire care also could be contributing factors. With no acknowledgment of responsibility, it follows then that Firestone did not ask for forgiveness. The act of the recall, its plan to replace the tires of those consumers with the greatest need, and its willingness to pay customers to replace the tires with competitors' tires, did demonstrate a desire for reconciliation, thus meeting the legitimate expectations of stakeholders. Combined together, Firestone's actions were a form of appropriate corrective action. However, it appears in hindsight that Firestone did not fully disclose all that it knew relating to the problem tires, although there is some evidence that the company was slow in developing an understanding as to the extent of the problems with its tires.

Conversely, Ford's initial response to the crisis met the criteria of being ethically acceptable, although it was not ideal. Like Firestone, Ford was just as concerned with issues of liability and yet, at least initially, was much more proactive in its management of the crisis. Ford's initial responses were ones that were characterized by denial and differentiation. Although the company strategically named the problem as a "tire issue" as opposed to a "vehicle issue," such naming is within the bounds of acceptability. Led by Chief Executive Jacques Nasser, the performed response was one of sincerity. Furthermore, Nasser's response must be credited for its timeliness; evidence suggests that Ford had a much better initial understanding of the problems with the tires than did Firestone. Indeed, Nasser appeared to relish the opportunity to defend the integrity of the Ford Explorer. His appearance in an advertisement aired during *Monday Night Football* and the subsequent print campaign was an appropriate context by which to address all relevant stakeholders.

As to the content of Nasser's initial defense, although he denied that the Ford Explorer was responsible for the problems (and, hence, there was no acknowledgment of wrongdoing or asking for forgiveness), he did accept responsibility, in that the Firestone tires were on the Ford vehicles. He subsequently offered a statement of regret and concern, as well as promised not to rest until all the tires were replaced. In pushing so hard for Firestone to replace the tires quickly, and communicating in clear steps how customers could get their tires replaced, he was seen to perform an appropriate corrective action, even as he disclosed what Ford knew about the problem.

*Governmental Investigation and Action: Round I.*   The deteriorating relationship between Ford and Firestone, coupled with the growing number of deaths attributable to the tire crisis, soon caught the attention of Congress, which injected itself into the drama in early September. Predictably, members of Congress saw an opportunity to criticize Ford and Firestone for their failure to act quickly, as the death rate from the tires reached 88 (Wald & Bradsher, 2000). Senator Richard C. Shelby of Alabama, chairman of the Senate Appropriations Subcommittee for Transportation, took aim and issued a kategoria against both companies, giving their performances a negative review: "Ford and Firestone had at a minimum a moral obligation to make sure that the products they sell to the American public and other people in other countries are safe. And yet they both failed to bring this issue to consumers' and the federal government's attention, at the cost of dozens of lives, I am afraid" (Bradsher & Wald, 2000, p. A1).

First to testify was Masatoshi Ono, the chairman and chief executive of Bridgestone/Firestone. Although he offered an apology to the House committee, he also offered a carefully veiled counterattack against the Ford Explorer: "I come before you to apologize to you, the American people and especially to the families who have lost loved ones in these terrible rollover accidents. I also come to accept full and personal responsibility on behalf of Bridgestone/Firestone …" (Mayer & Swoboda, 2000, p. A1). Note that Ono did not admit to any tread separation; furthermore, his reference to the "rollover accidents" was an attempt to shift the blame to the Ford Explorer.

Ono also took the rhetorically dangerous tactic of blaming the accident victims. Under questioning from Representative W. J. "Billy" Tauzin of Louisiana, the chairman of the House Commerce Subcommittee, when asked what accounted for the problems with the tires, Ono responded that the failures resulted largely from a "lack of care [by consumers] for the tires. That would be my conclusion"(Mayer & Swoboda, 2000, p. A1).

Later, at 8:30 P.M. that evening, when he finally had an opportunity to begin his testimony, Ford CEO Nasser responded to the allegations with a strategy of differentiation that separated the Explorer from the problem. He said, "This is a tire issue, not a vehicle issue" (Bradsher & Wald, 2000, p. A1). Furthermore, he put Ford in the position of a protagonist and designated Firestone as the antagonist when he argued that Ford had not known there was a problem (presumably in the U.S. market) until that summer, when "we virtually pried the data from Firestone's hands and analyzed it ourselves" (Mayer & Swoboda, 2000, p. A1). When that occurred, Nasser continued, "Ford engineers discovered conclusive evidence that the tires were defective" (Mayer & Swoboda, 2000, p. A1). Finally, Nasser testified that in every instance in which Ford suspected a problem, the company asked Firestone to investigate and was told by Firestone that there was no problem other than that the tire owners had failed to properly maintain their tires. To this he added, "My purpose is not to finger point, but to show that Ford proactively took the initiative" (Mayer & Swoboda, 2000, p. A1).

The core issue of the hearings, according to Bradsher and Wald (2000), was not the display of contrition but *when* the companies realized there were problems with the tires. Firestone safety officials maintained that they did not learn of the seriousness of the problem until August 2000, when Ford informed the company of problems with Firestone quality data; yet, House investigators produced a memorandum dated January 2000 from company accountants that suggested the company knew that approximately two thirds of the claims regarding tread separation were from its Decatur, Illinois, plant, which had cost the company approximately $3 million (Bradsher & Wald, 2000; Mayer & Swoboda, 2000). Furthermore, it was revealed that Firestone had moved tire production for the Explorer from the Decatur plant that January, although the company did not explain why (Bradsher & Wald, 2000).

Some at Ford, conversely, appeared to know about the problems even earlier. According to a company memorandum, Ford struggled with how to replace faulty tires on Explorers in Saudi Arabia in March 1999, for fear of having to alert the U.S. Department of Transportation (Bradsher & Wald, 2000). As a result of what occurred in Saudi Arabia and additionally in Venezuela (which also claimed problems with Firestone tires installed on Explorers), Nasser responded with a strategy of corrective action that promised changes in how Ford would report such data in the future: "When we know it, so will the world"(Mayer & Swoboda, 2000, p. A1). Nasser also pledged to set up an "early warning" system to prevent future problems from going undetected (Bradsher & Wald, 2000, p. A1).

By September 11, the president of Bridgestone (the parent company of Firestone), Yoichiro Kaizaki, made his first public statements on the issue (Tanikawa, 2000). As to how the company had handled the tire problems, he responded with a conciliatory strategy in which the headquarters took the blame: "The way we have managed it was wrong. The responsibility for the problem lies with Tokyo" (Tanikawa, 2000, p. C12). This was a reference to the disclosure that the company had two different quality control standards between the Bridgestone and the Firestone brands. Kaizaki continued with a strategy of differentiation: "We managed subsidiaries located in Japan quite carefully but have not applied the same attention to managing overseas subsidiaries. We let the U.S. unit use its own culture. There was an element of mistake in that" (Tanikawa, 2000, p. C12).

In subsequent statements, Kaizaki gave more context to the managerial problem: "If there was a problem with a Bridgestone tire, our technology staff in Tokyo would rush to the site [overseas]. But if a problem arose with a Firestone tire, they wouldn't do anything" (Barboza, 2000b, p. C5).

The heart of the problem appeared to be in the company's Decatur plant, a site with a history of labor problems. In his response to the tire troubles, Firestone Vice President John Lampe was even more direct when he scapegoated the work done there: "It's very, very evident that there was something going on in Decatur that caused this. When we do something in the plant we want to do it the same exact way every time. We don't want to see a variance" (Barboza, 2000b, p. C5).

September 14 marked the first public statements by William Clay Ford, Jr., the chairman of the board of Ford Motor Company, the great-grandson of Henry Ford, and whose mother is the granddaughter of Harvey S. Firestone, Sr. (Bradsher, 2000h). In a news conference via conference call only, he denied that his family ties had been the reason he had held off commenting about the recall. Instead, he stated, "It hurts to see a family name and a family heritage tarnished so badly" (Bradsher, 2000h, p. C5). Following the company script, which differentiated the tires from the vehicle, Ford remarked, "We believe this is very much a tire issue, not a Ford issue" (Bradsher, 2000h, p. C5).

The apologetic statements by William Clay Ford, Jr., known to friends as Billy, mirrored Nasser's initial strategy. Ford's statement, as a chairman of the board, was not as full as Nasser's but supported it. Although expressing more concern for the difficult situation that the Firestone company was in, due to the fact that his family had once owned the business, Ford nevertheless followed the Ford Motor Company script and defined the issue as one involving tires, not vehicles. Some did observe that Ford made his statement in the form of a conference call, which did not permit questioning. Issues might be raised as to the appropriateness of that format, but all in all Ford's statement met the acceptable ethical standards that Nasser's response also had.

Nearing the end of September, with deaths now up to 103 and over 400 injuries reported, at the second round of Congressional testimony the gloves were completely off (Bradsher, 2000k). Part of the issue was the recommended tire pressure ratings used by Ford for the Explorer. Helen Petrauskas, vice president of environmental and safety engineering, argued that a 26 psi rating was optimal for vehicle performance and ride, and maintained that the Tire and Rim Association's guidelines supported such a claim (Wald, 2000b, p. C1). At this, Firestone Vice President John Lampe interrupted her testimony and replied, "26 is the minimum for a speed-rated tire" (Wald, 2000b, p. C1). Also at issue was the disclosure that Ford had not actually tested the Firestone tires on the Explorer but had instead done so on the F-150 pickup, which the company argued mimicked the characteristics of the Explorer (Wald, 2000a, 2000b). Ford announced the next evening that it had raised the recommended tire pressure from 26 psi to 30 psi (Bradsher, 2000l).

The gap in the relationship widened when, as Firestone announced that it would serve as the sole supplier for tires for the redesigned Explorer that was to go on sale in January 2001, Ford spokesperson Della DiPietro revealed instead that Michelin would be one of the tire suppliers for the redesigned Explorer—a move suggestive of a future separation of the two companies (Bradsher, 2000m).

Events for Firestone went from bad to worse on September 29, when federal regulators initiated another investigation of Firestone's Steeltex tires, which were used on larger trucks, vans, and sport utility vehicles such as the Chevrolet Suburban and the Ford Excursion (these were different tires than the Wilderness line; Bradsher, 2000n). Although there were only two problems raised from 1998 through the summer of 2000, it appears that with the increase in profile of the recall, customers were more quick to report problems. Accordingly, the NHTSA received 169 complaints, which included 8 crashes, 12 injuries, and 2 deaths due to tire problems.

All of the deaths and injuries, exacerbated by the constant sniping between the two companies, led Congress to begin to consider approval of new federal ratings on vehicle rollover. Up until this time, due to the constant opposition of the automotive industry, there had been no federal standard on rollovers in the 27 years the government had studied them, even though rollovers accounted for 9,500 of the 41,000 automotive-related deaths in that period (Bradsher, 2000j). Due to the controversy, the industry, in the form of the Alliance of Automobile Manufacturers, argued that the regulations were a bad idea but decided against challenging them. The new rating system, which ranked vehicles based on a five-star rating scale, finally passed Congress the second week of October (Bradsher, 2000o; Wald, 2000d).

In addition to the federal scrutiny, Firestone also faced a separate concern—being legally culpable for the production of the tires, as a result of the Congressional testimony. Subsequently, as part of a class-action lawsuit filed in a federal court in East St. Louis, Illinois, executives from Firestone were forced to provide depositions regarding their behavior (Grimaldi, 2000).

Most notably, CEO Masatoshi Ono, when deposed, changed his position completely. He claimed that his apology before Congress was not an admission of responsibility but rather a show of concern for those who had had accidents while using Firestone products. He differentiated: "This [apology before Congress] was a sympathy expressed for those individuals who operated vehicles using our products and got into accidents. So it's not as you [Gordon Ball, the plaintiff's attorney] state in your question an issue of a defect" (Grimaldi, 2000, p. E2). To which Ball replied, "Are you denying that Bridgestone/Firestone is at fault for the property damage and/or personal injury of the people who have used the tires that are subject to your voluntary recall?" (Grimaldi, 2000, p. E2). Continuing the doublespeak, Ono said, "If we are deemed responsible for the accidents, that is another matter. However, there are maybe outside causes that had caused the accidents. Then I wouldn't say we're responsible for those accidents" (Grimaldi, 2000, p. E2).

Ono also contradicted the testimony of fellow executive John Lampe, who acknowledged before Congress that a small number of tires "could pose a safety problem" (Grimaldi, 2000, p. E2). In referencing Lampe's admission, Ono said, "I do not know on what basis Mr. Lampe stated there were defects. Right now what I can say is we have not discovered defects" (Grimaldi, 2000, p. E2).

When pressed on the differences in Ono's present testimony from the one he had given before Congress, Firestone spokesperson Dan Adomitis continued the attempts to redefine reality when he claimed that Ono was simply restating what the company had been saying all along:

> Mr. Ono again expressed his sympathy for the families and Firestone's commitment to finding the root cause of the problem. As you know, we are still looking for answers. To this end, we have called in an independent investigator and we continue to work closely with [the National Highway Traffic Safety Administration] and Congress. (Grimaldi, 2000, p. E2)

Ono's deposition also revealed that he had offered to resign after the recall was announced, but that Bridgestone Corporation President Yoichiro Kaizaki asked him to stay on (Grimaldi, 2000, p. E2).

Yet, Ono resigned the day after his testimony had concluded (Wald, 2000c). He cited his age and health as justifications—"I don't feel too good in my stomach and my blood sugar is also high"—and said that because he had been on the job for 7 years, "I thought it's about time for me to retire" (Wald, 2000c, p. C2). John Lampe, a 27-year employee who had served as the vice president of Firestone, succeeded Ono. This move was seen as a signal by some that Firestone was becoming much more of an independent American subsidiary (Tanikawa, 2001d).

By October 11, Congress had finally passed a bill that was designed to punish more forcefully those who failed to disclose automobile safety defects. Specifically, the bill strengthened both civil and criminal liability for those who failed to report tire and auto safety defects, required notification to U.S. regulators of any safety-related problems in foreign countries, and mandated the disclosure of warranty data to government regulators (Wald, 2000d). It also included requirements that would eventually lead to a system that would display tire pressure within the instrument panel (Wald, 2000e).

By December 6, 2000, federal regulators announced that the number of deaths attributed to the Firestone tread separation had increased to 148 (Stout, 2000). Of those numbers, four deaths had occurred after the announced tire recall, although regulators were uncertain as to whether the people had neglected to get their tires replaced or were simply unaware of the recall (Stout, 2000).

The recall, congressional investigations, and the concomitant lawsuits had taken their toll. By December 14, Bridgestone forecasted that its 2000 profits were likely to fall 81%. This included a charge of $750 million against earnings to cover the costs of the recall and the lawsuits ("Bridgestone Cuts," 2000).

The controversy reemerged into the public eye in mid-December, when both Ford and Firestone presented the findings of their investigations to federal investigators, although they did so on separate occasions. Ford's major finding centered on placing the blame with the Decatur plant where most of the faulty tires were made. Specifically, Ford investigators discovered that the plant used different processes for handling the raw materials used in the construction of tires, processes that likely contributed to the breakdown of some of the materials (Bradsher, 2000q). This, of course, bolstered Ford's contention that the Firestone tires were faulty and that the investigation should be limited to the tires.

Firestone also released the results of its independent investigation led by University of California–Berkeley engineering professor Sanjay Govindjee, a tire expert. Govindjee contradicted previous Firestone accounts by concluding that, in normal driving conditions, tires did not deteriorate faster on the Explorer than on other vehicles (Bradsher, 2000q). He did discover, however, that the Ford Explorer does have an uneven weight distribution, with more weight on the left rear tire (the location of a lopsided number of tire separations that resulted in fatalities), although Govindjee was careful to announce that he had yet to conclude that this was a cause in the tire failures (Bradsher, 2000q). Govindjee's report gave some support to Firestone's position that the investigation should be broadened beyond the tires, given the large number of fatal tread separations that occurred primarily on Explorers.

However, the blame could not be placed solely on the Explorer. Rather, Firestone investigators concluded a dangerous cocktail was at work that, although it did include the design of the Explorer (including a rapidly growing weight), also was the result of faulty tire design and manufacturing along with poor tire care on the part of consumers (Bradsher, 2000r). This marked the first time that Firestone actually admitted to specific mistakes in the manufacturing process, although the company was careful not to pin the blame on workers. In response to concerns with regards to vehicle weight, Ford argued that early in the 1990s Explorers had been equipped with Firestone tires that had a lower weight load rating but had not experienced failures at the rate of the current tires (Bradsher, 2000r).

The primary defense of the Ford Explorer during this difficult fall came from Chief Executive Jacques Nasser. Like his initial apologia, Nasser's defense met standards of ethical acceptability. As to the manner of Nasser's defense of the Ford brand, it was effective in both manner and content, although, as the crisis went on, Nasser was faulted by some for coming across as too aggressive toward Firestone, to the point of bullying. As to the manner of Nasser's apologia, his response was an attempt to get at the truth of what was happening with Firestone tires. Although his testimony before Congress was part of an investigation and, in a way, was involuntary, he seemed to take pleasure in having the opportunity to tell Ford's side of the story—that the problem was a tire issue and not a vehicle one—and for this reason, it was an appropriate context by which to get the message out. His messages also were timely, in that it was the Ford Motor Company that seemed to be the driving force in the recall early on, presenting the most data. Nasser also came across as intent on reaching all stakeholders in an attempt to release information that could help them most, both in the fall and again in late spring, when Ford concluded there were problems on more Firestone tires.

As to the content of Nasser's apologia, he did not acknowledge wrongdoing other than the fact that Ford was slow to communicate to government regulators the problems with tires on Ford Explorers overseas. He did promise corrective action on this, stating that in the future the world would learn of any problem as soon as Ford did. Nasser also did express regret in his statements, but it was regret that Ford Explorers came equipped with unsafe tires. Nasser has to be commended in that although the problem was not seen initially to be the fault of the Ford Explorer, he did identify and seek reconciliation with injured stakeholders by actively working to get the tires replaced.

Conversely, whereas Nasser's statements constituted ethical communication, the probable low point in the exchange came from Firestone CEO Masatoshi Ono, who testified before Congress and then provided a deposition in which he contradicted his Congressional testimony. In his testimony before Congress, Ono began by offering an apology to those who had lost loved ones in crashes involving Firestone products—an exemplary move, but this apology must be taken in the context of his deposition in the following weeks. Subsequently, as to the manner of his apology, it was an inconsistent performance in that at first Ono seemed to suggest he was sorry for the defective products and then later he changed tack and would only admit to conveying sympathy on the loss of a family member. His manner was such that he did seem to convey emotion that he was genuinely sorry for what had happened. His apology before Congress was timely, in the sense that it was his first major opportunity to provide a public apology, although neither of the statements that he issued were voluntary but instead were compelled—the first before Congress and the second in a deposition. As to the contexts, they were both legal contexts as opposed to social ones, but given the problems they would clearly be seen as acceptable. Finally, the claims did address relevant stakeholders, but in a manner that was careful not to assume any responsibility.

As to the content of Mr. Ono's apologies, it is here where they become even more troublesome, for in neither one did he explicitly acknowledge wrongdoing, fully accept responsibility for what had happened, nor explicitly ask for forgiveness. To his credit, he did express regret that the accidents occurred while consumers used Firestone products, and he identified with those who had been injured or died. As to fully disclosing information related to the wrongdoing, he was careful in his public statements not to release any information that might incriminate the company. As head of the company that did conduct the tire recall, he led an appropriate corrective action, but did so in a way that avoided statements offering full compensation to victims.

Conversely, John Lampe, who replaced Masatoshi Ono as the head of Firestone in America, was much more forthright and met a higher ethical standard in his apologiae than did Ono. However, this analysis concludes that, at its best, Lampe's apologiae only met standards of ethical acceptability—and then not always. As to the manner of his communication overall, it has to be recognized as both truthful and sincere. Although they were a reaction to events, his statements certainly did appear to be more voluntary than had Mr. Ono's, and Lampe's testimony before Congress was an acceptable venue by which to address both regulators and consumers.

As to the content of Lampe's apology, it is here where he distinguished himself, at least at first. Although he never fully accepted responsibility, due to legal concerns, he did nonetheless offer statements acknowledging that the company had a problem; in particular, he was the first to admit that something was awry in the Decatur plant. In addition, he accepted much responsibility by not offering a scapegoating strategy initially, as evidenced by the careful way he argued that an unnamed vehicle (the Explorer) contributed to the problem. It was under his watch that the company more fully accepted responsibility for what had happened, as shown in its December report to congressional investigators. Lampe sought reconciliation with injured stakeholders in terms of how he conducted the recall. Nonetheless, he received mixed marks in the disclosure of information, because most of the major information revealed in the case seemed to come from Ford rather than Firestone. As to the corrective action performed, it was done throughout the case in the form of the tire recalls.

*Initial Legal Settlements.* On a separate front, both Ford and Firestone legal teams worked to settle the 200 suits filed by victims of tread separation on the Ford Explorer (Winerip, 2001). By January 2001, one of the more dramatic and high-profile cases involved 43-year-old Donna Bailey, a physical trainer who in March 2000 had been paralyzed from the neck down in an accident in Corpus Christi, Texas (Winerip, 2001). Led by superlawyer Tab Turner, the financial details of her settlement were not disclosed but the settlement did include a ritualistically performed apology to Ms. Bailey by three Ford officials, which was allowed to be videotaped, albeit with no sound. The videotape, which later was released to the news services by the attorneys involved, showed the three attorneys carrying briefcases as they approached Ms. Bailey's hospital room, and then a 15-second section of them speaking to her while she was lying in her hospital bed on a ventilator at the Institute for Rehabilitation and Research in Houston (Winerip, 2001).

After the videotape was made available to media, Susan Krusel, a Ford spokesperson, said, "We're pleased to have resolved the case informally with Ms. Bailey. Once again, we offer our deepest sympathies to her and her family" (Winerip, 2001, p. C11). Firestone Chairman John Lampe also sent Ms. Bailey a handwritten note that said, "There is nothing any of us at Firestone can say or do to return what you and your family have lost" (Winerip, 2001, p. C11). These efforts occurred in what was reported to be a concentrated effort by both Ford and Firestone to settle as many of the lawsuits as quickly as possible, although they attempted to do so in as private a way as possible in order to avoid providing evidence to other legal initiatives (Winerip, 2001).

Based on newspaper accounts of the initial settlements, both Ford and Firestone must be credited with making an ethically ideal response, particularly in the case of Ms. Bailey. Although details of the communication between the Bailey family and Ford and Firestone are scant (and, as a result, both are analyzed here together), it nonetheless appears as if both Firestone and Ford communicated ethically as it concerns both the manner and the content of the communication after the settlement. Specifically, the companies' statements were truthful, and they did not attempt to strategically name what happened. Given that the apologies were personally delivered to an individual stakeholder in the environment of compensation negotiations, the context is highly appropriate and avoids a media circus, and both companies come across as sincere. Although they appear to be less than timely and voluntary, coming after a settlement, Cohen (1999) did acknowledge that such statements still can function to reduce anger.

The content of the apologies, even if incomplete, also do seem to meet the requirements of ethical communication. Both expressed regret and sadness for the harms, and in doing so identified with the injured stakeholder. Although a statement of responsibility was not released publicly, it follows that because the companies settled with Ms. Bailey and provided her with compensation, the standards of ethical acceptability were met.

If Ford and Firestone are to be faulted in this case, it must be for the fact that, although they came clean and offered reconciliation to Ms. Bailey, the companies did not, as part of their settlement, fully disclose their communications to all, especially in the area of publicly accepting responsibility and offering an explanation that would meet the expectations of their consumers. (However, in Ford's case, it should be noted that, in keeping with the company's long-standing position, Ford did not acknowledge a design flaw with the Explorer; Ford shared responsibility with Firestone only because it was Firestone's faulty tires that were on Ford's products.) Again, fear of liability was present as a mitigating circumstance that prevented the companies from taking full responsibility. In this way, one can often read a settlement in which no wrongdoing or responsibility is admitted as a form of apology in which the responsibility assumed is not in the statement of accountability but instead in the payment of compensation.

*Firestone Image Repair.* The controversy captured another victim when on January 11, 2001, Yoichiro Kaizaki resigned as president and chief executive officer of the Bridgestone Corporation. This was a move that many saw as an attempt to take responsibility for the problems at Firestone and give the company an opportunity to rebuild its image (Tanikawa, 2001a). In addition to Kaizaki's resignation, Masatoshi Ono, who previously had served as chairman of Firestone, also resigned his position on the board of directors, along with three others (Tanikawa, 2001a).

As the recall was coming to a close, and with Firestone facing a 15%–20% drop in sales and a stock price down more than 40%, the beleaguered tiremaker began an advertising campaign in April 2001 that was the largest campaign in its history (Bradsher, 2001a; Bradsher, 2001b). In an effort to ritualistically reassure customers by praising the very values the company had broken (that its tires were safe), Firestone CEO John Lampe appeared in the advertisements arguing that the company was "Making It Right. You have our word on that" ("Making It Right," 2001, p. 11A). The advertisement, written by John Lampe, specifically recognized the value of trust:

> When you buy tires, you're not just buying rubber and steel … you want the confidence that your tires will get you to your destination—safely. Your safety is our primary concern. We want you to have confidence in the way Firestone tires are made and the way they perform. We'll do whatever it takes, however long it takes, to gain your trust. ("Making It Right," 2001, p. 11A)

In addition to pledging improvements in manufacturing techniques, Lampe then detailed how the company would keep the problem from ever happening again: "In the role of watchdogs, a new team of top technical and quality control managers has been assembled to continuously analyze tire and safety data. They'll act to uncover issues before they become problems" ("Making It Right," 2001, p. 11A).

The advertisement was accompanied by the launch of a brochure entitled "Inflate. Rotate. Evaluate. How to maintain your tires." This was created to help Firestone customers properly care for their tires.

As it announced the campaign, the company also used a corrective action strategy when it revealed that it had made a series of important policy changes: in the future, all quality-control problems would be reported directly to the chief executive. Additionally, the company announced it would improve its tracking of vehicles shipped overseas as well as pay closer attention to tire-related auto crash data (Bradsher, 2001a).

The advertisements featuring Lampe were then followed the next month with a campaign that featured Michael and Mario Andretti, famous racecar drivers, on the need for consumers to take proper care of their tires.

The advertising campaign led by Lampe was laudable and met high ethical standards. This can be seen in the manner in which it was done, because the company developed a campaign in which Lampe spoke directly to the company's primary stakeholders (its customers) in an appropriate context (a print campaign), and in which he straightforwardly addressed the company's past problems with its tires. As to the content of the campaign, although he did not apologize, Lampe did make a tacit acknowledgment of wrongdoing and accepted responsibility, as evidenced by his promise of "making it right." In this campaign, he identified with injured stakeholders and told of the changes in policy that Firestone had made to keep the problem from happening again. The emphasis on carefully caring for tires is laudable, although the company had to be careful not to implicitly blame customers for causing the problems due to poor tire care (as Ono had done before Congress).

With the presentation of investigation findings to regulators, the completion of the tire recall, the introduction of the redesigned 2002 Model Explorer, and the increased efforts to settle lawsuits, it appeared that the drama was coming to a close for both companies. As such, it was a shock that Ford wrote a whole new act when it announced in May 2001 that it would seek an even larger recall of Firestone tires.

*New Attacks and Counterattacks.*    Ford presented the results of its testing of the Explorer to federal regulators in April, without informing Firestone of its analysis or its plans to share it with federal regulators. This analysis prompted the need for another recall (Bradsher, 2001b, 2001d). Specifically, Ford argued that it had discovered problems with the tires, some from previously recalled models and others from tires not on the recalled models (15-inch Wilderness tires made at factories other than the Decatur plant, and the 16-inch Wilderness tires). These tires were alleged to fail at double the typical rate; yet, given the relative newness of the tires, their failure rate had yet to show up in crashes (Bradsher, 2001b). If Ford's claims were true, the data would result in an even larger recall than that initiated that previous August.

Firestone responded quickly and vociferously. Chairman and Chief Executive John Lampe made a strong denial: "Let me state categorically: tires supplied to Ford Motor Company, and other customers, are safe, and the tires are not defective" (Bradsher, 2001c, p. C2). Furthermore, he took direct aim at Ford and its Explorer with the counterattack: "As we have said since last August, the role of the vehicle must be taken into account" (Bradsher, 2001c, p. C2). Furthermore, in a letter to Ford CEO Jacques Nasser, Lampe wrote, "Prior to making any final decision to take action with respect to our tires, you owe it to Bridgestone/Firestone to share the findings and analysis which brought Ford to its conclusion" (Bradsher, 2001c, p. C2).

Firestone then went one step further: It made data available to personal injury lawyers that asserted design flaws on the Explorer were responsible for the deaths linked to their tires. Specifically, it revealed comparative data on the Ford Ranger pickup and the Explorer, and argued that failure rates of the same tire on the vehicles were 7 to 10 times higher on the Explorer ("Firestone Adds Data," 2001). Ford did not publicly respond, but a surrogate suggested that the Explorer's incidence rate was due to its higher center of gravity.

In a carefully scripted preemptive move—designed to take the argumentative landscape away from an anticipated announcement the following day by Ford to replace 13 million tires—Firestone declared on May 21 that it would cut all supplier ties to Ford (Firestone provided 41% of Ford's tires; Bradsher, 2001d). In a letter from John Lampe to Jacques Nasser, the Firestone chairman wrote:

> Business relationships, like personal ones, are built upon trust and mutual respect. We have come to the conclusion that we can no longer supply tires to Ford since the basic foundation of our relationship has been seriously eroded. This is not a decision we make lightly after almost 100 years of history. But we must look to the future and the best interests of our company, our employees and our other customers. ("Text of Letter to Ford," 2001, p. C4)

Lampe continued, adding that the fault did not lay with Firestone tires, but instead with the Explorer: "Our analysis suggests that there are significant safety issues with a substantial segment of Ford Explorers. We have made your staff aware of our concerns. They have steadfastly refused to acknowledge those issues" ("Text of Letter to Ford," 2001, p. C4).

Lampe concluded with a defense of the tires: "We believe you are attempting to divert scrutiny of your vehicle by casting doubt on the quality of Firestone tires. These tires are safe, and as we have said before, when we have a problem, we will acknowledge that problem and fix it. We expect you to do the same" ("Text of Letter to Ford," 2001, p. C4).

The letter was given to Carlos Mazzorin, group vice president for purchasing at Ford. Mazzorin and Ford officials had provided data suggesting that the need for the larger recall was again the result of flaws in Firestone tires. Lampe later described the release of the data by Ford as an attempt to make "the data to say what they wanted the data to say (Bradsher, 2001d, p. C4). Firestone then countered with a request that Ford share with Firestone a request for safety data on the Explorer. When Mazzorin declined to share said data with Firestone, he was presented with the letter to sever the relationship (Bradsher, 2001d). Firestone did agree to honor its current contracts with Ford, which would expire in less than a year.

As expected, Ford went ahead the next day with its announcement that it had decided to recall 13 million additional Firestone tires (Bradsher, 2001e). In his statement at a news conference, Jacques Nasser announced, "We simply do not have enough confidence in the future performance of these tires' keeping our customers safe" (Bradsher, 2001e, p. C1). Specific to the 13 million tires in the recall were all 15-inch tires not included in the August recall (among these were tires not made at the Decatur plant), and all 16- and 17-inch Wilderness AT tires (Bradsher, 2001e). Also included in the recall were 1.5 million replacement tires that had already been placed on Explorers during the August recall (Bradsher, 2001e).

In his explanation for the decision, Ford Chief of Staff John Rintamaki announced that the tires had a failure rate of 15 per million tires, compared with the 60–200 per million failure rate of the tires replaced in the fall (Bradsher, 2001e). Tires from other companies typically have failure rates of 5 per million. The recall was expected to cost Ford approximately $3 billion (Bradsher, 2001e), a figure later reduced to $2.1 billion after taxes (Gilpin, 2001).

Although some may see this new call for a recall a form of harassment on the part of Ford and Nasser, it should be noted that the decision was made at great cost to Ford. When one considers the content of Nasser's apologetic statements in May—that Ford wanted all Firestone tires off their Explorers even at great expense to the company—such an act demonstrates a great deal. It showed, for instance, that Nasser identified with those who had the defective products on their vehicles, and sought to reconcile with them by a strategy of corrective action whereby he fixed the problem by replacing their tires, even though this compensation offer was a great expense to the company. In so doing, it also shows that Ford was more liberal and forthcoming with revealing data that described the extent of the problems than was Firestone.

In response to Ford's actions, Firestone's Lampe replied by continuing to defend the integrity of its tires as well as its actions: "Our tires are safe. When we have a problem, we admit it and we fix it. We've proven that. The real is-sue here is the safety of the Explorer" (Bradsher, 2001e, p. C1).

In an unheard-of move by a tire manufacturer, Firestone announced on May 31 that it had asked the National Highway Traffic Safety Administra-tion to open an investigation of the Ford Explorer. Part of its justification was an alleged problem in the steering of the vehicle that made the Explorer harder to control during a tire blowout. In announcing his company's re-quest, Lampe leveled the counterattack: "When tires fail, either from a tread separation or a road hazard or other causes, drivers should be able to pull over, not roll over. The Explorer does not appear to give the driver that margin of safety to make it to the side of the road and change the tire" (Bradsher, 2001f, p. C1).

Ford Chief of Staff John Rintamaki responded with a denial that the Ex-plorer was unsafe, and continued to shift the blame to the tires: "You can talk about testing data endlessly. We are replacing Firestone Wilderness AT tires because they have elevated rates of tread separation in the real world" (Bradsher, 2001f, p. C8).

The move by Firestone appeared to be part of a concerted effort to rebuild its brand identity. It attempted to do so by acknowledging some responsibil-ity, by "Making It Right" for the tire problems, while it counterattacked the safety and integrity of the Ford Explorer (Barboza, 2001c, p. C2). In an inter-view with *The New York Times*, Lampe showed both an acknowledgment of some responsibility and at the same time leveled a countercharge:

> It's not just a tire issue, as Mr. Nasser would have liked everyone to believe
> during the Congressional hearings. This is an issue that concerns the tire
> and the vehicle. We've spent nine exhaustive months looking at the issue,
> sharing the information with Ford. But when we ask Ford: "What have
> you been doing on the vehicle side? What information will you share with
> us from the vehicle standpoint?" It's like butting your head against a brick
> wall. (Barboza, 2001c, p. C2)

The decision to go on the counterattack was supported by Bridgestone Chief Executive Shigeo Watanabe: "We have argued that it was not just the problem of the tire but the system, the combination of the tire and the vehi-cle. Ford does not provide information on their vehicles, and N.H.T.S.A. had not launched a probe, so we decided that we must do something our-selves" (Tanikawa, 2001b, p. C2).

Firestone's decision to go after the Explorer so directly was probably two-fold. One factor was the perception that Firestone was being browbeaten by Ford as led by Nasser. The second and probably more compelling factor was the fear of liability. If the tires were seen as the sole culprit, damage to Firestone could be severe; but if the Explorer were shown to be partially culpable, then there would be the potential to create some doubt in the minds of potential juries. This was borne out by fears that with hundreds of deaths and injuries, potential jury awards were expected to reduce the equity value of Firestone stock by one third (Tanikawa, 2001b).

Firestone's efforts appeared to meet with some success. On June 3, lawyers who represented those killed or injured by Explorers marched into a federal courthouse and sought the recall of all the Explorers made from 1990 to 2001, approximately 4 million vehicles ("Recall of 4 Million Explorers," 2001). In explaining their justification for the suit, Irwin Levin, a spokesperson for the lawyers who represented over 200 suits against the companies, remarked, "Ford and Firestone have chosen to point their guns at each other, and now they're confirming what we thought all along—that there are problems with both the tires and the Explorer" ("Recall of 4 Million Explorers," 2001, p. C2). Ford spokesperson Jason Vines described the request as "frivolous" ("Recall of 4 Million Explorers," 2001, p. C2).

As to the manner of Lampe's apology, with this second round of attacks and counterattacks he now placed the blame directly on the Ford Explorer and argued that Firestone had made good on its promise to replace the tires but Ford had done nothing to address concerns about the Explorer. As to timeliness, this apologia—like the other apologetic statements of the exchange—largely was compelled by the major actions of the case. His statement here seems less carefully designed to address all stakeholders, but instead a no-holds-barred defense of the company and its tires in an attempt to move culpability from the tires to the vehicle. Finally, the interview with *The New York Times*, the "nation's newspaper," was an appropriate context in which to defend the integrity of the tires.

One has to criticize Lampe, however, for the substantial use of denial as more problems came to the fore with the Firestone tires, first pointed out by Ford (and then, as discussed shortly, verified by the NHTSA). This can be thought of as a complicating circumstance, in that the considerable use of denial was an attempt to avoid making Firestone the sole liability target by consumers. Another factor was that Firestone faced catastrophic financial losses with the advent of this new recall. To Firestone's credit, Lampe, as well as Bridgestone Chief Executive Shigeo Watanabe, acknowledged that there were problems with the Firestone tires, but argued that they had been addressed. The heavy use of counterattack, however, limited the degree to which Firestone accepted responsibility. Furthermore, there is evidence to suggest that the company was trying to position itself for a final round of legal settlements with consumers, and had concluded it would fare better if blame could be spread to Ford.

*Governmental Investigation and Action: Round II.*    All the sniping by the two companies again raised the attention of Congressional investigators. In an effort to regain some of the moral high ground immediately preceding the next round of investigations, Ford released new data on June 14 alleging that the tires of the second recall had a much higher rate of failure than initially thought (Bradsher, 2001g). In particular, Ford said that the failure rates of 5-year-old Firestone tires was at 450 tires per million. In an unusual move, Ford even released images of a Firestone tire coming apart in some of its laboratory tests. Representative Billy Tauzin's spokesperson was not impressed by Ford's attempts: "While Ford's busy spinning its story in the press, our investigators are left spinning their wheels. Ford has still not answered a truckload of questions" (Bradsher, 2001g, p. C4).

In the second round of Congressional hearings, on June 18, federal regulators announced that the death toll was now at 203, up from an earlier figure of 174 ("Panel Says Replacement Tires," 2001). Furthermore, committee spokesperson Ken Johnson revealed that investigators had found that Ford was replacing Firestone tires in its latest "recall" with tires that failed at a higher rate than did some of the Wilderness AT tires ("Panel Says Replacement Tires," 2001, p. C4). Johnson charged, "After carefully analyzing thousands of pages of documents, it's now clear to us that Ford in some cases is replacing Firestone tires with brands that actually have higher claim rates. Why? Frankly, we don't have a good answer" ("Panel Says Replacement Tires," 2001, p. C4).

The next day, Representative Tauzin released the actual data; he asserted that seven of the models of tires that Ford had used as replacement tires had higher rates of failure than did the Wilderness ATs. But rather than clarifying the issue, Tauzin actually muddied the matter further. Only willing to identify the Goodyear Wrangler HT and the General Grabber APXL, he acknowledged that he was not sure as to the validity of the data, and appealed for the NHTSA to sort the issue out or there would be a recall on the replacement tires.

The second half of the hearings took place with more back and forth between Nasser and Lampe. Lampe accused Ford of comparing old Firestone tires with competitors' new tires in an effort to have higher negative data against Firestone. Additionally, he pointed to the Explorer's continued rollover problems in Venezuela, although there were no longer any Firestone tires installed on vehicles there, and that the separation of tread should not render a vehicle uncontrollable. Nasser replied that Ford had compared tires of similar age, that most of the accidents in Venezuela were "fender benders," and that "a tread separation is a catastrophic event. It is virtually impossible to design a vehicle around a catastrophic event" (Wald, 2001, p. C4).

In an interesting sidebar to the story, Firestone announced on June 27 that it would close its Decatur, Illinois, plant due to the overcapacity the company now was experiencing as a result of the flat demand in the industry and the lingering doubts that customers had about the safety of Firestone's tires. Although everyone believed otherwise, the company denied that its decision to close the Decatur plant was a result of the faulty tires emanating from the site. John McQuade, vice president for manufacturing operations, announced, "This is about balancing supply and demand. This has nothing to do with the quality or professionalism of our Decatur employees" (Barboza, 2001d, p. C1).

*An Additional Recall.*   By July 19, Firestone had faced another serious blow. This time, the NHTSA asked Firestone to issue a recall for all 15- and 16-inch Wilderness AT tires from the 235/75R15 and 255/70R16 lines (Bradsher, 2001i). Firestone responded that it would not issue a recall: "We don't believe the action that the agency perhaps is contemplating is warranted. Our customers can drive with confidence on our tires. We're 100 percent committed to doing everything for the safety of our driving public" (Bradsher, 2001i, p. A9).

The problem for Firestone was that if the company did issue a recall on the tires currently replaced by Ford, then Ford would have a solid legal basis on which to ask Firestone to pay for the recall. The NHTSA responded to Firestone's decision that "Firestone was asked to recall some of the tires, and they refused to do so. Therefore N.H.T.S.A. will issue an initial defect decision, the next step toward a forced recall" (Bradsher, 2001i, p. A9). This action did indeed lead to a forced recall, announced the week of October 3, that concluded that the 3.5 million Wilderness AT tires were defective ("Ford Settles More Explorer Lawsuits," 2001).

*The Legal Battle.*   In the first legal battle to come to trial against Firestone of the 500 already filed (Ford had already settled for $6 million), jurors deliberated the case of Marisa Rodriguez, who was paralyzed and suffered brain damage when, in March 2000, the 1998 Ford Explorer in which she was a passenger had a blowout in the right rear tire, causing the vehicle to roll over (Oppel, 2001a, 2001b). Her husband, Dr. Joel Rodriguez (also represented by superlawyer Tab Tuner, who continued to play his role smoothly), sought in closing arguments to have the jury send a message about safety: "This is your opportunity to communicate with these people. If you are in corporate America and you're dealing with people like that, you talk money" (Oppel, 2001a, p. C3). The plaintiff's attorneys alleged that Firestone knew it had quality problem in the Decatur plant as early as the mid-1990s, and that by 1997 it was working with Ford to address tread separation problems in Venezuela (Oppel, 2001a). Ford had already settled and, fearing a negative trial outcome, Bridgestone/Firestone also chose to settle the case with the Rodriguez family for $7.5 million (Oppel, 2001b). The following week, Bridgestone/Firestone announced that it had settled a second lawsuit that had been set to begin in Brownsville, Texas. ("Firestone Settles Suit," 2001).

By mid-October, efforts to settle lawsuits regarding the Explorer and Firestone tires had gone into high gear, and the drama began to disappear from media accounts. Ford made it known that it had settled suits related to 11 more rollover accidents; this meant that a total of over 100 lawsuits had been resolved ("Ford Settles More Explorer Lawsuits," 2001).

The Ford and Firestone example, of course, shows how difficult it is to assess blame, in that there were multiple apologies from multiple actors. As noted by Hearit (1995a), due to the polyarchic context of the battle, "corporate" blame has numerous places to go in the diffusing of guilt; this was especially true in the apologetic exchange that constituted Ford versus Firestone: Ford blamed Firestone; Firestone blamed the Explorer; Firestone union workers blamed replacement workers who had been on the job from 1994 to 1996; Republicans blamed the Clinton administration for not noticing the problem sooner; Democrats blamed President Reagan, who killed tire safety regulations in 1981 and cut the budget for regulation; and still others blamed the trial lawyers, who kept more than 20 deadly accidents from being entered into a federal database whose purpose was to track safety problems, while at the same time the lawyers were initiating lawsuits against Firestone and Ford (Bradsher, 2000i).

It is important to note that, when considering the problem of locating guilt, it is easy to think only in terms of the corporations that are alleged to commit errors. Yet, as the next case—that of the American Red Cross—shows, not-for-profits are not immune to allegations of unresponsiveness to the communities in which they operate.

## The American Red Cross

On September 11, 2001, terrorists commandeered jets; flew them as bombs into both towers of the World Trade Center, the Pentagon, and the Pennsylvania countryside; and, in the process, killed almost 3,000 people. In the aftermath of this tragedy, the American Red Cross, as it has in so many previous disasters, sprang into action: It collected blood for use to aid the victims, and quickly created the Liberty Fund, which would be used to assist the families of those who were victims of the attacks.

*A Difficult Season.*   Given the scope and weight of the disaster, public scrutiny of the U.S. government as well as other public institutions was high. Concomitantly, the Red Cross also faced a tremendous amount of attention. In one instance, critics complained that the Red Cross had collected more blood in the aftermath of the disaster than it could use, and some of it had to be destroyed. Yet, much more damaging for the Red Cross and its 2-year president, Dr. Bernadine Healy (a former cardiologist who had previously spent an 8-year term as the head of a cardiac intensive-care unit; Seelye & Henriques, 2001), were allegations that she had administered the Liberty Fund, which had collected donations of over $500 million, in a manner that was incongruent with the expectations of donors as well as those of local Red Cross chapters. These allegations set off a drama that lasted 3 months. Specifically, critics and public officials took issue with Healy's decision to redirect some of the Liberty Fund's monies for other strategic purposes of the Red Cross, such as to prepare the organization for potential bioterrorist attacks. Instead, they insisted that all monies donated to the Liberty Fund should go to victims and their survivors, as donors had believed would happen when they made their contributions (Seelye & Henriques, 2001). In this way, Healy and the American Red Cross were accused of social irresponsibility, and the subsequent level of media scrutiny and criticism functioned to increase the problems that the aid agency faced.

As a result of these criticisms and ongoing dissatisfaction with her autocratic decision-making style, Dr. Healy resigned on October 26, 2001, in a hastily called meeting with 200 staff members at Red Cross Headquarters in Washington, DC. She then met with reporters and announced her decision to resign, claiming that "I had no choice" (Seelye & Henriques, 2001, p. B9). Her resignation was due to take effect at the end of the year.

In addition to criticism for how she managed the Liberty Fund, two other subplots were undercurrents in Healy's decision to resign. First, she had supported the right of Israel to join the International Committee of the Red Cross. At issue was whether Israel would be forced to use a cross or a crescent as its emblem. Healy had stood boldly in support of Israel's membership, even to the point of withholding U.S. dues as part of a protest. She defended her decision to do so: "We are a major international force, a major international player ... but I think perhaps more importantly, we are a country that doesn't exclude. You don't belong to a country club that excludes blacks or Jews" (Seelye & Henriques, 2001, p. B9).

Second was her decision on behalf of the Red Cross not to join a central database created to distribute funds fairly and evenly to victims of the 9/11 terrorist attacks. The Red Cross had concerns about privacy matters, and was concerned that victims might not come forward out of fear. Twice she appeared to privately agree with New York Attorney General Eliot Spitzer (who would discretely threaten legal action) to join the database, and then subsequently make public remarks to the contrary (Henriques & Barstow, 2001; Seelye & Henriques, 2001). Both of these problems strained Healy's relationships with members of the board of directors who oversaw the American Red Cross.

When asked about her relationship with the board at her resignation press conference, Dr. Healy replied, "I think the board felt that perhaps I was out ahead of them in some ways, making policy that they felt they should be making" (Seelye & Henriques, 2001, p. B9). Her normally steely demeanor showed cracks at the press conference. When asked if her leaving in the middle of a major crisis was good for the country, Healy could not speak and started to walk out of the conference, with tears in her eyes. A number of reporters followed her. As she exited, Healy said, "They [the board] didn't have any more confidence in me" (Seelye & Henriques, 2001, p. B9). She stayed on in her position until the end of the year, when she was replaced with Harold J. Decker, a former Pharmacia executive, who was appointed interim president.

***Problems With the Liberty Fund.*** Given the stinging criticism that the Red Cross faced from families of victims who were in need of assistance, the aid organization announced on October 30, 2001, that its Liberty Fund now totaled more than $547 million. As a result, the Red Cross would stop collecting more funds for the victims of the 9/11 attacks. Instead, the organization would turn its attention to how to best distribute those funds (Barstow & Seelye, 2001). In doing so, new President Decker acknowledged, "Is it always perfect? No it can't be perfect. That's what disasters are all about" (Barstow & Seelye, 2001, p. B11). He pointed out just how much knowledge the Red Cross has gained as a result the attacks: "We have learned an incredible amount about what we would have to do if this were to happen again" (Barstow & Seelye, 2001, p. B11).

Although it appeared that the resignation of Dr. Healy would stem the tide of criticism by offering her as a scapegoat, the Red Cross only found itself under more scrutiny and exacerbated its problems dramatically more when it announced that it planned to distribute only $300 million to victims' families. Its plan was to hold back over $200 million for yet unforeseen 9/11 needs, as well as to prepare for future potential terrorist attacks and to fund a $50 million blood reserve program (Henriques & Barstow, 2001). Decker announced that the decision to do so was based on warnings from the Bush administration of future attacks, as well as the then-ongoing anthrax poisonings. In a justification for the decision, he said, "Usually a disaster has a starting point and an ending point. We're not sure there's an ending point" (Barstow & Seelye, 2001, p. B11).

The decision to hold a significant amount of the funds in reserve and not disperse them to victims of the attacks drew immediate and pointed criticism. The attorney general of the state of New York, Eliot Spitzer, took issue with the script the Red Cross had chosen to follow: "I'm of the belief that most individuals, if not all individuals, who made contributions in the aftermath of Sept. 11 fully expect those contributions to benefit those affected by Sept. 11. It is my strong belief that charities should honor that donative intent" (Barstow & Seelye, 2001, p. B11). When questioned further about the decision, Spitzer said, "It doesn't yet raise a red flag or a red cross, but it does raise a question" (Barstow & Seelye, 2001, p. B11).

The Red Cross continued to defend its decision; it argued that it had placed the money in reserve for future terrorist attacks and not for victims of floods or hurricanes. Red Cross spokesperson Bill Blaul justified the decision: "We think the clear distinction here is between acts of terrorism and acts of God. I can't see a guy who gave us $100 saying, 'I don't want that money helping those three families of anthrax victims'" (Barstow & Seelye, 2001, p. B11). Yet, criticism of the Red Cross did not end with Blaul's justification. Instead, the Red Cross came under even more intense criticism from members of Congress, who accused the not-for-profit agency of having misled donors, held back on the distribution of funds, and sought to further its own institutional goals rather that the needs of the victims (Barstow, 2001). In response to the Red Cross's decision to hold $264 million of the $564 million in reserve, Representative Billy Tauzin of Louisiana, chairman of the House Committee on Energy and Commerce, complained that "Something's wrong" (Barstow, 2001, p. B1). Representative Bart Stupak of Michigan was even more direct; he leveled a stinging accusation against the aid organization: "I think you took advantage of a very tragic situation" (Barstow, 2001, p. B7).

Dr. Bernadine Healy responded in characteristic fashion; she refused to back down and instead ritualistically reaffirmed that "This is a new war" (Barstow, 2001, p. B1). Healy explained that just as the Red Cross did not distribute funds collected after Pearl Harbor solely to victims and their families, so the not-for-profit would continue to make strategic decisions in this case as well. The Red Cross, Healy contended, would not simply divide $564 million by the total number of victims and then cut a check for each family member (Barstow, 2001, p. B1).

Healy continued that those who donated money to the Red Cross were made well aware that not every dollar collected would go directly to the victims and their families. Members of Congress took exception, and an analysis in *The New York Times* showed that television advertisements for the Liberty Fund made no reference to such a position (Barstow, 2001). Print advertisements, however, did give some indication, albeit not pronounced, urging people to "help save lives" and in small print at the end of the advertisement was the line "for this tragedy and the emerging needs from this event" (Barstow, 2001, p. B7).

Dr. Healy continued to defend the decision and argued that the phrase "emerging needs" was a clear allusion to the decision not to distribute funds solely to victims of 9/11, and that Congress was missing the whole point of the Red Cross, which was to be an agency designed to respond to all disasters. As a result, Healy counterattacked and claimed that Congress had used the Red Cross for its own political purposes; she explained, "I don't know why they didn't get it; I think they went in with their own spin." (Barstow, 2001, p. B7).

In an effort to stall some of the scathing criticism, by November 11, the American Red Cross felt compelled to announce that it would return a donation to any contributor who requested it, but still continued to defend the policy to withhold $200 million for future terrorist-related disasters (Kilgannon, 2001). Furthermore, in response to concerns about the pace of aid distribution, the Red Cross made known that it had dispersed approximately $150 million to nearly 2,300 victims and their families—approximately $30,000 each—and already had distributed money to those affected by the anthrax poisonings (Barstow, 2001).

The statements of Dr. Bernadine Healy, spokesperson Bill Blaul, and Interim President Harold Decker, in the aftermath of the September 11 terrorist attacks and the subsequent testimony before Congress, are difficult to judge (and, given the fact that they spoke from a common script, they are assessed together here). As to complicating factors, one does get the sense, as acknowledged by the Red Cross, that this was a new kind of disaster and the organization learned a great deal as it went through the process. As a result, although overall their apologetic statements certainly were not ideal, they did meet standards of acceptableness in both the manner and the form of the apologia, especially when one takes into account the complicating circumstances that surrounded the problem. Clearly, the organization was in a position in which it had to defend a difficult policy choice.

As it relates to the manner of their apologiae, they were truthful; to their credit, they did not shrink from tough questioning nor massage their responses. Instead, especially in the case of Healy, she performed her role well in that she directly and forthrightly answered the queries of self-interested members of Congress. Neither can one fault her for being insincere in her manner. Furthermore, although the organization of which she was president was subject to a hearing before Congress—a more than appropriate context—she responded with the attitude and tone of one who has an opportunity to tell her side of the story; in this way, Healy met standards of timeliness and voluntariness. Additionally, she did not shy away from speaking to the needs of all constituencies.

As to the content of the apologiae, although Healy did not acknowledge any wrongdoing for what had happened, Decker admitted that some mistakes had been made and offered regret. He agreed that the response of the Red Cross had been "less than perfect," but that was not at all usual because they were in the business of disaster management. He also noted that all the institution had learned would prepare it for future similar disasters. All of the parties went out of their way to identify with the injured stakeholders, and pointed out the many people that the current policy already had helped. In continuing on with a strategy of denial, Red Cross officials used multiple arguments; specifically, they argued that they were not sure the disaster was over, that this was a different kind of disaster—a terrorist one, rather than the acts of God they typically deal with—and that, as a result, the organization intended to follow past precedent, as with Pearl Harbor, and keep some of the funds for future disasters. Whether or not that was true depended on the perception of donors, who appeared to believe that they were making donations to 9/11 victims and not to the Red Cross's institutional objectives. This is evident in the fact that the Liberty Fund's advertisements displayed some ambiguity as to where donations would go, and in this way it did not meet the full expectations of stakeholders.

In not initially changing the policy, there does appear to be a complicating circumstance. It seems that the problem of discretion was very real, and used as a justification by Healy not to join the central databases proposed by others.

*Policy Changes.*    Given the ongoing bad review that the Red Cross continued to receive from Congress, victims, Eliot Spitzer, and others, they had no choice but to change course and follow a new script. On November 14, the Red Cross board finally publicized that it would distribute the full $543 million of the Liberty Fund to the victims of the 9/11 attacks and had canceled its original plans to withhold upward of $200 million to prepare for future terrorist acts (Henriques & Barstow, 2001). In its announcement of the decision, David T. McLaughlin, chairman of the American Red Cross board of governors, said, "The people of this country have given the Red Cross their hard-earned dollars, their trust and very clear direction for our Sept. 11 relief efforts. Regrettably, it took us too long to hear their message. Now we must change course to restore the faith of our donors and the trust of Americans" (Henriques & Barstow, 2001, pp. A1–B10).

Interim President Harold Decker was even more direct and offered a mea culpa: "We deeply regret that our activities over the past eight weeks have not been as sharply focused as America wants, nor as focused as the victims of this tragedy deserve" (Henriques & Barstow, 2001, p. B10). Decker also announced that the Red Cross would finally participate in the charitable database set up by New York Attorney General Eliot Spitzer, which most other charities had already joined. Spitzer responded to the news that the Red Cross' decision was "a monumental step forward. What had been a misstep of some magnitude has now been corrected" (Henriques & Barstow, 2001, p. B10). Members of Congress also voiced their approval. Representative Charles Bass of New Hampshire applauded the Red Cross decision for moving "to respond to, clearly, what was the American will" (Henriques & Barstow, 2001, p. B10). Liz McLaughlin, the wife of one of the victims, acknowledged what a help the decision was, saying, "Now at least we know we're O.K. for a year" (Henriques & Barstow, 2001, p. B10).

In announcing the decision, the Red Cross revealed that it intended to disperse about one half of the funds—approximately $275 million—by the end of the year, and would announce in January 2002 how it would disperse the remainder of the funds (Henriques & Barstow, 2001). Details of the decision were explicitly described. The Red Cross would extend its 3-month aid program—its "family gift" cash grant—to a year for the victims of the terrorist activities. This would add $111 million to the $47 million already distributed (Henriques & Barstow, 2001). The Red Cross also intended to hire an additional 200 caseworkers to aid in speeding the assistance to victims' families. Finally, the not-for-profit would use only the interest earned on the Liberty Fund to pay for the administrative costs of the fund and its disbursement. At the end of the day, Red Cross officers projected that administrative costs would be fewer than 10 cents to the dollar (Henriques & Barstow, 2001). This appeared to put the issue to rest.

On the last day of January, the Red Cross, as promised, released details of how it would disperse the remainder of the Liberty Fund monies (Saulny, 2002). By now, the "residual" amount left in the fund had swelled to $360 million. Although fundraising efforts had ceased, the Red Cross announced that it had received approximately $540 million in total donations, with the amount expected to reach $850 million (Saulny, 2002). As he announced the totals, board of governors chairman David McLaughlin said that the volume of donations "sends a clear and unmistakable message—the American people want the victims of this disaster taken care of" (Saulny, 2002, p. B3).

Making the announcement that would bring the drama to the close was former senator and international mediator George Mitchell, whom the Red Cross hired to oversee the management and develop a plan for the dispersion of the funds (Saulny, 2002). Mitchell announced that $240 million more would be given directly to the families of victims; $80 million would be directed to mental health services related to the terrorist attacks; $25 million would be distributed to maintain support centers and other forms of direct disaster assistance; and, finally, the remaining $15 million would go to support those who were from "non-traditional families" who nonetheless had suffered loss in the attacks (Saulny, 2002, p. B3). Mitchell also lamented that the missteps taken by the Red Cross had hidden the not-for-profit's "tremendous amount of good work" (Saulny, 2002, p. B3), and then offered a defense of sorts for the organization: "To its credit, the Red Cross acknowledged its mistakes and changed some of its policies that were mistaken" (Saulny, 2002, p. B3).

Also participating in the announcement was Board Chairman David McLaughlin, who said, "No matter what the Red Cross does, it is inevitable and understandable that not everyone will be fully satisfied. Therefore, the objective of this or any other plan must be to distribute the available funds in a way that is most fair and best meets the needs of those who suffered loss.

This plan does that" (Saulny, 2002, p. B3). In addition, McLaughlin announced that the Red Cross expected that 90% of the fund would be dispersed by the anniversary of the attacks, with approximately 4% of donations spent on operating expenses.

In his meetings with the victims of the attacks, George Mitchell said that two themes stood out in how the funds should be distributed. First, they should be dispersed in such a way so as to be seen as "prompt and fair" (Saulny, 2002, p. B3). Second, those who suffered loss revealed a "strong sentiment that victims themselves are in the best position to assess their own needs and to choose how best to use the funds in meeting those needs" (Saulny, 2002, p. B3).

A critic of the initial decisions made by the Red Cross, Eliot Spitzer strongly supported the announcement: "I think this is a very affirmative step by the Red Cross, and it demonstrates that there were some missteps early but the Red Cross has righted the course and is fulfilling the mission the Red Cross has historically filled and the intention of the donors" (Saulny, 2002, p. B3). Lisa Friedman, who lost her husband Andrew in the attacks, worked as a representative of the victims' families and especially desired that the plan would quickly distribute funds to families of all the victims: "I believe this plan does that, or I wouldn't be here" (Saulny, 2002, p. B3).

By February 2002, the Liberty Fund had raised $917 million. It had provided $552 million to 53,457 individuals and families (Purnick, 2002). The goal was to disperse the remaining $365 million in the next 7 months—by the one-year anniversary of the attacks.

In the second round of apologetic statements, the officials of the American Red Cross, in effect, finally "got it right" by taking a more conciliatory approach toward its critics and the victims of the attacks. In this way, they offered exemplary apologies. As to the manner of the apologies, they were delivered in a series of news conferences, an appropriate public forum. Furthermore, although the apologies were late in being made, they came across as sincere, in that the organization seemed to finally "get it," and arrived at voluntarily. They addressed the criticism and needs that came from all stakeholders, and contentwise appeared to be truthful.

As to the content of the apologies, it is here where the Red Cross truly made things right with its multiple stakeholders: victims, governments, and donors. First, there were multiple apologies from a number of officials at the Red Cross, who assumed responsibility for what had taken place and expressed regret for the institution's slowness in responding to concerns. Apologies came from Board Chairman David McLaughlin, from Interim President Harold Decker, and even George Mitchell acknowledged that the institution had made some mistakes.

The apologies, of course, were only the half of it. The Red Cross then announced a number of policy changes that it would make: It would return any donation to any donor who requested it; it would speed its efforts to disburse monies; it would no longer withhold $200 million for future disasters; and it would join Spitzer's database. Additionally, it would hire more workers; it would lengthen its aid program to a year; and, finally, it would provide more money for mental health needs, develop support centers, and help to meet the needs of nontraditional families. In this way, the Red Cross performed an appropriate, if not extensive, level of corrective action. By changing policies as dramatically as it did, the not-for-profit sought to bring about reconciliation with injured parties—an objective it reached with approval from victims' families and Spitzer's endorsement—thus bringing the difficult chapter to a close.

## CONCLUSION

All three apologia demonstrate some interesting factors as to the nature of corporate apologetic address. First, they show the eponymous nature of corporate apologetic speech. All of the cases here show individuals speaking in a corporate voice by which they give precedent to the corporate position and subjugate their own (Namenwirth et al., 1981). As a result, it is possible to see organizational officials who take multiple positions throughout an apologetic exchange until they find one that best serves organizational interests.

Second, the apologiae analyzed here all reveal that organizations, like individuals, tend to "slouch toward success" or toward "doing the right thing." Most seem to start with a denial strategy—or at least a denial of intention strategy—and only when such an approach no longer works do they seem willing and likely to try an alternative approach. The alternative approach, of course, tends to be more conciliatory and accommodative. This trend should be represented in future models that seek to account for how crisis communication tends to evolve (Coombs, 1999; Sturges, 1994).

Third, wrongdoing by a person at an institution is an easier problem to deal with rhetorically than is institutional wrongdoing that is related to the complex intersection of humanity with technology. Firestone, and to a lesser degree Ford, were caught up in complex discussions of tire technology; production methods; the intersection among speed, heat, and weight; weight distribution; and vehicle design. Conversely, an organization such as the Red Cross, which can locate the bulk of its policy problems in the management decisions of individuals such as Dr. Bernadine Healy, faces a less difficult rhetorical terrain to navigate, because once the offending individual is removed, guilt is absolved.

Finally, this analysis has shown that although apologetic statements can have some "success" in the argumentative marketplace, it is only when organizations respond with an apology that they are likely to meet the expectations of their constituents and news media, who will then be satisfied enough to move on. In this way, apologies are very effective at completing the guilt, apology, and forgiveness cycle, and thus depriving journalists of an ongoing and continual story.

# 7

# Institutional Apologies

## *Institutional, Religious, and Governmental*

This is how Aaron is to enter the sanctuary area: with a young bull for a sin offering and a ram for a burnt offering.

From the Israelite community he is to take two male goats for a sin offering and a ram for a burnt offering.

Aaron shall bring the bull for his own sin offering to make atonement for himself and his household, and he is to slaughter the bull for his own sin offering. He is to take a censer full of burning coals from the altar before the Lord and two handfuls of finely ground fragrant incense and take them behind the curtain. He is to put the incense of the fire before the Lord, and the smoke of the incense will conceal the atonement cover above the Testimony, so that he will not die. He is to take some of the bull's blood and with his finger sprinkle it on the front of the atonement cover; then he shall sprinkle some of it with his finger seven times before the atonement cover.

He shall then slaughter the goat for the sin offering for the people and take its blood behind the curtain and do with it as he did with the bull's blood: He shall sprinkle it on the atonement cover and in front of it. In this way he will make atonement for the Most Holy Place because of the uncleanness and rebellion of the Israelites, whatever their sins have been. He is to do the same for the Tent of Meeting, which is among them in the midst of their uncleanness.

No one is to be in the Tent of Meeting from the time Aaron goes in to make atonement in the Most Holy Place until he comes out, having made atonement for himself, his household and the whole community of Israel.

Leviticus 16: 3, 5, 11–17 (*The Holy Bible*, 1973/1984)

Although a scapegoat was a powerful instrument by which to deal with the problem of sin in the camp, it did not repair the relationship between the offender and the Transcendent. For that, the Hebrew Scriptures required the ritualistic sacrifice of a bull, a lamb, or (for especially poor families) 2 turtledoves (the Christian counterpart of this ritual presents Jesus Christ as the Perfect Lamb). Likewise, for an institution accused of acting incongruent with public values, a ritualistic sacrifice is necessary to purge that guilt. This often requires organizations and institutions to utilize a mortification strategy in which guilt is accepted.

The form of justificatory discourse about which the least is known is that of institutional apologia; that is, apologiae that emanate from governments, religious groups, or educational organizations. As chapter 5 demonstrated, the work on individual apologia is well developed; a majority of the scholarship on apologia addresses the subject of individuals caught in a wrongdoing. Also thoroughly documented is that of organizational or corporate apologia, which comprise a growing number of analyses. Comparatively undeveloped, however, is knowledge of the substance, style, and situation that inhere in institutional apologia. Indeed, to date only a few analyses have examined the apologetic discourse of institutions as institutions (Brown, 1990; Courtright & Hearit, 2002; Harter et al., 2000; Sellnow & Seeger, 2001; Tavuchis, 1991; Thackaberry, 2004). This chapter, consequently, lays the groundwork for the study of institutional apologia through an examination of three cases in which institutions caught in a crisis have attempted to resituate their actions. Such efforts to repair their damaged images probably can be more precisely described as institutions that try to fully address the less than honorable chapters in their past, chapters that bespeak of transgressions inconsistent with the institutions' values and identity (Cheney & Vibbert, 1987).

## INSTITUTIONAL APOLOGETIC THEORY

To be sure, much present-day apologetic discourse does originate from public organizations. A recent example of such discourse is President Clinton's May 16, 1997, apology for the Tuskegee experiments, which sought to account for the federal government's syphilis experiments on African-American men that resulted in considerable harm (Harter et al., 2000). Other examples of institutional apologiae include President Reagan's defense of his administration's actions in the Iran-Contra affair (Benoit et al., 1991), the Canadian government's apology to the Inuits ("Canada Says Sorry," 1998), as well as the Australian government's apology to the Aborigines, to name but a few (Corder, 1999).

### Contexts

Institutions face criticism when their behaviors are perceived to demonstrate an incongruence with the values of the larger social system in which they operate (Dowling & Pfeffer, 1975). Like corporations, institutions may face criticism for accidents that have occurred and resulted in tragedy and death. Concomitantly, institutions also face scandals and illegalities in which their officers are guilty of wrongdoing and face civil or criminal liability. Other potential causes of institutional crises may be inadequate responses to natural disasters, terrorism, economic crises, or public health failures (Seeger et al., 2003). The largest context of actions for which institutions are likely to face criticism, however, concerns the area of public irresponsibility, or what Seeger et al. (2003) described as "crises of public perception" (p. 54), because public institutions are uniquely vulnerable to allegations that their conduct has violated the values that reflect their stated charter or mission.

One unique feature of the context of institutional apologia is the notion of a nondenial apologia (Kruse, 1977). As earlier demonstrated, individual and corporate apologiae almost invariably start with strategies of denial that the apologist has done nothing wrong whatsoever. It is only when the facts become clear, or challenges are made to an apologist's claims, that such apologists tend to adopt a more conciliatory stance that features nondenial strategies. Conversely, when institutions respond to allegations (as discussed in the following section), it is likely that the negative judgment is based on strong or incontrovertible evidence and, as a result, the charge cannot be denied. Because of this, such institutions avoid a whole host of issues that characteristically are featured in the apologetic exchange: countercharges, minimizations, and the whole back-and-forth nature of the drama. Instead, institutions tend to be much more concerned with how posterity will judge their actions and, as a result, try to frame their response in such a way that historians will record that the organization in question dealt with the less than honorable chapter in an admirable manner.

## Substantive Characteristics

Although institutions do rely on well-documented justificatory strategies, their apologetic discourse appears to feature a distinct set of factors. In particular, there are five strategies that tend to be highlighted in institutional apologetic address. The first is confession or mortification (Benoit, 1995; Hearit, 1995a). In this way, institutions are likely to take a conciliatory strategy and come clean as to the nature, extent, and duration of their wrongdoing. The mortification strategy is one of ritual suicide whereby institutions accept guilt rather than deny it (Burke, 1970).

The second strategy, corrective action, tends to accompany mortification (Courtright & Hearit, 2002). This is the case because institutions must show what they propose to do in order to prevent a recurrence of the problem that precipitated the wrongdoing in the first place. In this way, a corrective action strategy is an effective tool of suasion, in that it puts an institution in a position to show that it has learned from its wrongdoing, and draws on the well-instantiated myth that institutions are led by rational managers capable of making wise decisions because they have learned from their mistakes (Hearit, 1995a).

Another strategy accompanying mortification is that of compensation. When used in regard to institutions, compensation becomes much more important; otherwise, an apology is no more than empty and hollow words. Compensation, in effect, is a form of restitution whereby an institution makes good on the wrong that it has perpetrated; by doing so, it adds weight to the mortification strategy (Courtright & Hearit, 2002). This occurs for two reasons: First, institutions are large, and their size tends to be accompanied by considerable economic resources; second, and more important, institutions are beholden to their publicly stated values.

A corporation, for instance, might attempt to clothe its outputs in a mission statement in order to legitimize its profit-making activities (Levy, 1986), yet almost everyone recognizes that a corporation's fiduciary obligation before the law is to return a profit for its stockholders. An institution, conversely, has a purpose larger than profit, be it a government that exists to ensure the safety and well-being of its citizens as well as promote the common good; a religious institution, whose purpose is to promote its gospel and perform a social good; or an educational institution, whose purpose is to promote inquiry and instruction. Because of this, it is much easier to demonstrate that an institution has acted in a manner that violates the spirit of its mission and, consequently, calls for an apology become much more compelling. (For more on compensation and restitution, particularly as it relates to the guilt of nations, see Barkan, 2000; Brooks, 1999; Minow, 1998; Torpey, 2003; Wallace, 1998; Wiesenthal, 1998.)

In addition to mortification and the accompanying strategies of corrective action and compensation, institutions also tend to emphasize a transcendent stance. Such an approach deals with the problem of guilt through a redefinition of a situation by translating it into another context (Burke, 1973). In such an instance, misconduct is redefined through a process Burke described as "debunking," whereby guilt is lessened by showing its similarity to familiar human emotions (Burke, 1961, p. 338). In this way, institutional apologists are able to defend an act by referencing altruistic or high-level motives (Burke, 1961, 1970). Other forms of transcendence include underscoring common characteristics or motives, or using common symbols by which people who previously disagreed can come together (Burke, 1969).

Transcendence is powerful rhetorically in that not only is it able to restore order in order to remove guilt, but it is also uniquely suited to corporate or institutional use. Burke noted:

> One may "transcendentally" organize his interpretation of human motives by the following broad emphases: a human act is done for God, for an ideal (humanity, culture, justice, truth), for a corporate grouping (political or otherwise), for oneself. Historical-collectivistic emphases generally play about an intermingling of ideal and corporate grouping. (Burke, 1984, p. 338)

A final characteristic of institutional discourse is that there is considerable sensitivity to the ritualistic components of apologetic speech due to the often moral, ethical, or religious vocabularies that surround public institutions. The guilt that organizations face through their negligence is not just symbolic, but substantive as well. Because of this, institutions restore their damaged image through scrupulously animated and dramatic means. Here their institutionalism works in their favor, because they are able to call on the ceremonial aspects that inhere in their mission, be they a church or temple with all their religious rituals by which they enact their values, or a government with its inherent collection of ceremonies and pageants (Goffman, 1971). The quality of the performance, then, can be evaluated in order for observers to judge the sincerity of the effort, be it in a personal letter, a public apology, or a moving service or official state event.

This emphasis on the ritual and symbolic can be seen quite clearly in the first case study of this chapter—the apologetic efforts on the part of the U.S. government in its explanations for the tragic sinking of a Japanese fishing boat due to a collision with a nuclear submarine.

## CASE STUDIES OF INSTITUTIONAL APOLOGETIC ADDRESS

### U.S.S. Greeneville

*The Accident.* On February 9th, at 1:45 P.M. Hawaii time, approximately 9 miles from Diamond Head, the *U.S.S. Greeneville*, a nuclear-powered Navy attack-class submarine that was conducting an emergency surfacing drill known as a "main-ballast blow," collided with the Japanese fishing boat, the *Ehime Maru*, which was carrying, in addition to its crew of 20, 13 students and 2 teachers from the Uwajima Fisheries High School, a vocational high school program in southwestern Japan (Cushman, 2001; Marquis, 2001). The collision tore through the Japanese vessel's hull into the engine rooms and caused the trawler to sink within 5 minutes (Cushman, 2001). Twenty-six people on board were able to be rescued, with nine reported missing—among them four high school children, two teachers, and three crew members.

What appeared to be a tragic accident took on a troubling tone the very next day. The Navy acknowledged that the submarine was performing an emergency drill when the accident occurred. It also revealed that 16 civilians had been on board the *U.S.S. Greeneville* as "observers," as part of the Navy's Distinguished Visitors (DVs) program, although the Navy refused to identify them (Cushman, 2001; Jehl, 2001; Myers & Dao, 2001). This revelation, added to the fact that the victims were predominantly students and the apparent negligence on the part of the crew, functioned to dramatically increase the level of guilt, and plunged the U.S. Navy into a social responsibility crisis. Although the Navy would conduct its own investigation, the National Transportation Safety Board (NTSB) was assigned the role of lead investigator due to the fact that the accident involved a civilian vessel in American waters (Jehl, 2001).

The Navy has a very specific procedure for how a submarine is to surface. First, it rises to periscope depth (approximately 45–55 feet) and then raises its periscope. Passive sonar monitors then are deployed to detect noise and, in particular, propellers from surface craft. A 180-degree periscope search, which allows a submarine crew to see 6–8 miles, is then performed to confirm that the area is clear. The sub then surfaces after an internal alarm is sounded (Marquis, 2001).

*Initial Accusations and Apologies.*   The day after the accident, Admiral Thomas Fargo, commander in chief of the United States Pacific Fleet, quickly apologized for the incident and said the focus of the investigation would be to determine if proper procedures had been followed in the surfacing drill. In addition to the admiral's apology, the U.S. Secretary of State, Colin Powell, apologized to his Japanese counterpart, Foreign Minister Yohei Kono, and conveyed condolences from President George Bush (Cushman, 2001). The captain of the *Greeneville,* Commander Scott Waddle, was "relieved of his post pending the results of the inquiries" (Jehl, 2001, p. A1).

The early handling of the incident only exacerbated political tensions between the United States and Japan. Already in a bit of disrepair due to U.S. plans for a missile defense shield and the continual issue of the 47,000 U.S. troops stationed at Okinawa, the accident escalated the political problems for the new Bush administration. Family members in particular were incensed when news accounts revealed that although the *U.S.S. Greeneville* surfaced and opened it hatch after the accident, submarine personnel did not aid in the rescue efforts (Jehl, 2001).

On February 11, Japanese Prime Minister Yoshiri Mori met with the U.S. Ambassador Thomas Foley and lodged an official protest over the accident (Jehl, 2001). In an interview, Secretary of State Powell continued the apology coupled with a bolstering strategy: "We're doing everything we can to express our regret and also to make sure this doesn't affect the very strong relationship that we have with Japan" (Jehl, 2001, p. A18). In interviews throughout the weekend, both Powell and Secretary of Defense Donald Rumsfeld described the accident as a "tragedy" (Jehl, 2001, p. A18).

The number of apologies offered by senior governmental and naval officials was staggering. Apologies came from elected officials and their appointees—President George W. Bush, Secretary of State Colin Powell, Secretary of Defense Donald Rumsfeld, and U.S. Ambassador Thomas Foley—as well as from senior naval officials—Admiral Thomas Fargo, the commander in chief of the United States Pacific Fleet, and Admiral William J. Fallon, the vice chief of naval operations. Perhaps the concerted effort was best summed up by Colin Powell, who said the U.S. government was apologizing "every way we know how" (Jehl, 2001, p. A18).

Given that these apologetic statements were brief public remarks regarding private governmental negotiations, they are treated here as a group, in that they functioned as part of an integrated campaign, drawing on a common script that was followed by senior governmental and military negotiations. In these statements, the apologies were exemplary in that they are ethical in both the manner and form in which they were delivered. As it concerns the manner of the apologies, the multiple apologies met all of the criteria for an ethical apologia. They were truthful; none tried to "spin" the accident in any way; rather, they referred to what happened as a "tragedy." They also were offered sincerely; there was no question raised as to whether the governmental or naval officials meant the comments. Senior officials were quick to apologize and seemed to do so voluntarily, in order to keep a breech from opening in the U.S./Japanese relationship. If any fault could be found it would be that officials apologized too quickly, instead of waiting for more facts to come out. The apologies effectively reached all stakeholders, in that they were addressed to the Japanese government, the people of Japan, the victims, and their family members. Finally, as to the appropriate context, apologies were delivered on television by President Bush, Colin Powell, and Donald Rumsfeld, as well as by hand-delivered letter.

As to the content of the apologies, they met exemplary standards as well. The apologies from senior officials all went out of their way to acknowledge that the U.S.S. Greenville was the cause of the accident, fully accepted responsibility, and sincerely expressed condolences for what had happened, describing it as a tragic accident. The apologies used a tone of conciliation, which asked for forgiveness. The apologies also identified with those injured in a number of ways, in that care was taken to apologize in a manner congruent with Japanese social custom as well as the eventual offer to raise the sunken vessel (which cost $60 million) in order to retrieve the remains—an idea consistent with Buddhist tradition. As far as disclosing information related to the offense, that was initially slow, although this was because the facts only became known from the investigation. None of the apologies offered to end the Distinguished Visitors program, and in this way may be

faulted in the area of corrective action, but Commander Waddle was removed from his command. Finally, the U.S. government eventually did pay
compensation, via the costs of raising the trawler as well as the monies paid
to the families of the victims ($11 million to the Ehime Prefecture, to pay for
the cost of the craft, for counseling, and to build a monument, and another
$13 million directly to the families of the victims; French, 2002).

*Legal and Investigative Developments.*    The story took an ominous turn
on February 13th when Lieutenant Commander Conrad Chun, a Navy
spokesperson, revealed that two participants of the Navy's Distinguished
Visitor's program had been seated at the controls of two of the submarine's
watch stations during the drill (Sterngold & Myers, 2001). Chun defended
the presence of the civilians, stating, "It is not uncommon for guests on this
type of visit to participate" (Sterngold & Myers, 2001, p. A1). The program
was in place to build support for the submarine program and to show politicians, celebrities, journalists, and businesspeople the consequences to the
Navy of continued budget cuts. Retired submarine captains defended the
program and denied that it was in any way dangerous; Captain John Peters
said, "You put them in a seat and let them feel like they are really doing
something but you always keep the control in experienced hands"
(Sterngold & Myers, p. A20).

Early indications were that one of the "observers" was at the "helmsman's
seat," which controlled the vessel's angle in the water, and the other pulled
the "chicken switches" that injected pressurized air into the ballast tanks in
order to begin the maneuver—two locations that, although critical to controlling the submarine, had unlikely been contributing factors to the accident. As one officer put it, "The question is not how they surfaced the
submarine. The question is why they didn't know a ship was up there"
(Sterngold & Myers, 2001, p. A20).

George W. Bush, in his role as president, called the Japanese prime minister on February 13th and apologized for the accident. He said, "I apologized
on behalf of our nation for the accident that took place and the lives that are
missing" (Sterngold & Myers, 2001, p. A20). Relatedly, the Navy announced it would send a submersible to the ocean's bottom in order to
survey the vessel.

Part of the problem, which caused the issue to escalate, was the revelation
that Japanese Prime Minister Yoshiro Mori was playing golf when reporters
informed him of the incident; allegedly, he complained about the interruption and then proceeded to play for 2 more hours (Strom, 2001). Given that
his initial response was tepid, observers concluded that his need to look involved in the situation was behind the Japanese government's request that
the U.S. Navy raise the *Ehime Maru*. Bunmei Ibuki, a Japanese minister, issued the request: "There is a great possibility that the missing people are

trapped in the hull of the ship. If it is technically possible to raise the sunken training ship, the government should continue calling on the U.S. side to ascertain the location and state of the vessel and raise it as soon as possible" (French, 2001a, p. A20).

Cultural observers suggested that the call to raise the trawler had less to do with political pressures and was more about cultural sensitivities—the importance in a predominately Buddhist culture to retrieve physical remains after death. French (2001a) noted:

> According to Japan's funerary customs, inspired by Buddhism, death is almost impossible to acknowledge without seeing the physical remains of the deceased, or at least one of his or her possessions. Without such direct contact with the dead, many here believe, neither the souls of the deceased nor the bereaved can ever achieve a state of rest. (p. A20)

Although the Navy was not talking, one of the civilian observers was. A colorful character in the drama, Texas oilman, John Hall, acknowledged that he was the civilian who tripped the "chicken switch" that began the main-ballast blow, and said in an interview that Commander Waddle and another officer did 360-degree periscope sweeps at least six times—one time to order the submarine to be raised 2 feet to get a better view (Drew, 2001). When asked what he saw on the periscope monitors, Hall replied, "Nothing but gray" (Drew, 2001, p. A13). Hall also took issue with Japanese reports that the *Greeneville* did nothing to aid in the rescue; he noted that the submarine readied a diver to be sent to the scene but could not release him out of the hatch due to heavy seas that could have put the submarine at risk (Drew, 2001).

Such a public acknowledge of a civilian "at the controls" only contributed to Japan's outrage. The Japanese Defense Minister, Toshitsugu Saito, declared it "outrageous" (Drew, 2001, p. A13). Relatedly, Japan's Foreign Minister Yohei Kono phoned Colin Powell to demand more information about the part the civilians had played in the accident. The Navy also announced on February 16th that it would no longer conduct such drills with civilians on board.

After undergoing a week's worth of criticism for its stonewalling, and an increasing amount of criticism from the Japanese ("Navy Stonewalling," 2001; Strom, 2001), the U.S. Navy finally came to the realization that it had to take action and do so quickly, because its lack of response was exacerbating tensions between the United States and Japan. To this end, on February 17th the Navy began to take direct steps to resolve the crisis: It would assemble a Court of Inquiry, the Navy's highest form of administrative investigation, to examine the causes of the collision (Myers, 2001a). Such a Court of Inquiry is not a criminal one, but more like a grand jury trial whereby the top three officers of the submarine—Commander Scott Waddle, Executive Officer Lieutenant Commander Gerald K. Pfeiffer, and Officer of the Deck, Lieutenant j.g. Michael J. Coen—were put on trial for their actions to determine if there was enough evidence to warrant a criminal trial ("Look at Sunken Ship," 2001). The Court of Inquiry would be convened by three admirals (a fourth, a Japanese admiral, was later added; Sciolino, 2001a). In announcing the decision, Admiral Thomas B. Fargo said, "The seriousness in which I view this tragic accident is reflected in the level of investigation and the seniority of the court members. It will provide a full and open accounting for the American and Japanese people" (Myers, 2001a, p. 1). The outcome of the case had the potential to lead to criminal prosecution, and, if necessary, a court martial would have been convened.

The Navy also announced on February 17 the identities of the 16 civilians who had been onboard (Myers, 2001a). Navy officials acknowledged that although it was unlikely that the civilians at the controls had caused the accident, there certainly was the sentiment that the presence of so many people distracted the crew in its performance of the drill (Myers, 2001a). The Navy also announced that its deep-sea submersible, the *Scorpio II*, had found the wreckage of the *Ehime Maru* at a depth of 2,003 feet, sitting largely upright, approximately 1,000 yards from where the collision had occurred. This disclosure raised hopes that the vessel would be able to be raised (Myers, 2001a).

Tensions between the United States and Japan were strained again on February 19 when Commander Scott Waddle communicated to National Transportation Safety Board (NTSB) that, on the advice of his lawyer, he would only respond to its questions in writing, pending the outcome of the Court of Inquiry. Additionally, he would limit the questions only to those regarding his actions and those of the submarine crew after the accident ("Submarine Commander," 2001).

Finally, as a result of the ongoing investigation by the NTSB, on February 21 more details of the collision began to emerge. According to NTSB spokesperson John Hammerschmidt, one crewmember of the *U.S.S. Greeneville* acknowledged that the presence of so many guests was indeed a distraction that prevented the fire control technician, whose job it was to plot the presence of other vessels in the water through the use of sonar, from plotting the position of vessels in the area on a chart before the captain and the officer of the deck (Sciolino, 2001a). Hammerschmidt reported that the crewman had "ceased this updating because of the number of civilians present" (Sciolino, 2001a, p. A1). The NTSB also revealed that the *Greeneville* initially identified the presence of the *Ehime Maru*, plotted as *Sierra 13*, approximately 71 minutes before the accident, and that the *Greeneville* had also known that two other ships had been present in the area. NBC News reported that the crewman who used the sonar re-discovered the fishing trawler moments before the accident but did not alert the captain to its presence ("New Clues from the *Greeneville*," 2001).

Fallout from the new revelations was swift. Japanese Chief Cabinet Secretary Yasuo Fukuda claimed the revelation that the *Greeneville* knew of the presence of the *Ehime Maru* for over an hour indicated "grave negligence" on the part of the American crew, and that the Japanese would demand "strict disciplinary steps on the U.S. side" (French, 2001b, p. A3).

Most frustrating to the Japanese, however, in light of the apologies from President Bush, Secretary of State Powell, Secretary of Defense Rumsfeld, and Ambassador Foley, was the absence of a response from the main character in the drama, Commander Waddle, the captain of the *Greeneville*. This all changed on February 25, when Waddle sent a letter to the people of Japan. He wrote:

> It is with a heavy heart that I express my most sincere regret to the Japanese people and most importantly, to the families of those lost and injured in the collision between the *U.S.S. Greeneville* and the *Ehime Maru*. No words can adequately express my condolences and concern for those who have lost their loved ones. I too grieve for the families and the catastrophic losses that the families have endured. (Sciolino, 2001b, p. A10)

The letter, which was not made known to Navy officials before it was sent, also stated that Waddle hoped that the soon-to-begin Court of Inquiry would "resolve the questions and uncertainties surrounding this tragedy" (Sciolino, 2001b, p. A10).

Overall, Waddle's apology did not meet a minimum ethical standard, because it was delivered in the shadow of civil and criminal liability concerns. As a result, Waddle chose to privilege his immediate legal context over that of reconciliation with the victims. As to the manner of the apology, his first apology did come across as truthful in that it did not attempt to strategically name the act. He described what happened as a "collision," and nothing more and nothing less. It is in the area of sincerity where he was faulted, because, in writing a letter, his apology was impersonal and left no manner for the recipients to judge the genuineness of his performance. News accounts revealed that many Japanese questioned Waddle's sincerity (French, 2001c; Sciolino, 2001b). Furthermore, his timing was already late, in that in spite of the many apologies offered, it was only Waddle's that the Japanese seemed to be interested in hearing. He is to be credited on the criterion of voluntariness, not because he did not feel pressure from the Japanese people, but rather because he did not apologize at the direction of the U.S. Navy. Waddle did address all relevant stakeholders—the victims' families, as well as the Japanese people—although its fair to fault him for doing so in the form of a letter.

Concerning the content of his apology, it is here where Waddle's statements truly did not measure up. First, he never acknowledged wrongdoing; he described the accident in matter-of-fact terms. Although he did express regret for the occurrence and identified with the tremendous loss faced by the families, he never accepted responsibility for the accident, nor did he ask for forgiveness. As a result, all the other dimensions of an ethical apology were absent as well: There was no stated desire for reconciliation, no full disclosure as to the facts of the collision, no offer of corrective action or compensation. In many ways, Waddle's apology should be faulted most in the sense that he did not address the legitimate expectations of the Japanese, because the apology was weak and inconsequential.

**Additional Apologetic Efforts.**   In order to head off further damage to U.S./Japanese relations, Admiral William J. Fallon, the vice chief of naval operations, was sent to Japan the following week, on February 27, with details of the accident and to deliver a formal letter of apology from President Bush (French, 2001c; Sciolino, 2001b). In a statement released on his arrival in Japan, Fallon said:

> I sincerely and humbly request—on behalf of the United States government,
> the United States Navy and the American people—that the government
> and people of Japan accept our apology for the tragic loss of the *Ehime Maru*.
> I know my words cannot express the profound sorrow and regret that the
> American people feel over this tragic event. (French, 2001c, p. A4)

Later in the day, Fallon met with Prime Minister Yoshiro Mori and hand delivered an apology from President Bush. The response from Mori was tepid: "It is important that the two countries continue to make efforts in the U.S.–Japan alliance" (French, 2001c, p. A4).

More progress at repairing the damaged relationship appeared to be made the following day, when Commander Waddle, dressed in a business suit, appeared at the Japanese consulate in Hawaii and delivered personal letters of apology to the visiting vice minister in the foreign ministry, Yoshio Mochizuki (Sciolino, 2001c). Waddle approached the vice minister, bowed deeply, and spoke a few words in Japanese. (Waddle had been born in Japan when his father was stationed there in the Air Force.) He also communicated his willingness to travel to Japan, at the proper time, in order to apologize to the families of the victims face to face. Mochizuki told reporters later, "When Waddle handed the letters to me tears fell from his eyes. He repeated over and over to me his words of apology" (Sciolino, 2001c, p. A12). He acknowledged that Waddle had used the word *apology*, so "I accepted it as an apology" (Sciolino, 2001c, p. A12).

It was in this apology that Waddle began to make up for the insufficiency of his first attempt. Although many of the details of this apology were kept private and not revealed to media, there are enough details known by which to offer an assessment. Because Waddle appeared less concerned with the legal implications of his actions, his apology was much more ethical. Concerning the manner of his apology, whereas his sincerity was faulted after the first one, it appeared to be highly present in the second one, as evidenced by the report that Waddle shed tears, which demonstrated regret on his part. The unexpected act of showing up at the Japanese consulate also showed a willingness to make an effort to repair the breach and was an appropriate place by which to make an apology, in that he was now on the territory of the Japanese.

As to the content of his apology, it is evident that he finally began to meet Japanese expectations as to the nature of his apology in that he demonstrated regret and some acceptance of responsibility by using the word *apology*. The communication of his intention to come to Japan to meet with the families of the Japanese also demonstrated a desire to seek reconciliation and functioned as an attempt at corrective action, in that it showed he was willing to work to repair the damaged relationship.

The act of contrition appeared to have its desired effect. Chihoko Nishida, the wife of a missing member of the crew, said, "I wish he had expressed his feelings to the families sooner. But at least I would like to accept his intention to apologize" (Sciolino, 2001c, p. A12).

*New Developments.* On the same day in Japan, Admiral William Fallon met directly with the families of the victims. He communicated to them, "I'm here to request in the most humble and sincere manner that you accept the apology of the people of the United States and the U.S. Navy, as a personal representative of President Bush" (Sciolino, 2001c, p. A12). Furthermore, Fallon promised that the inquiry would "provide a full and open accounting" (Sciolino, 2001c, p. A12). He concluded his remarks with the plea: "I humbly request your acceptance of my apology" (Sciolino, 2001c, p. A12). He then promptly bowed deeply. Ryosuke Terata, a representative of the families and the father of a missing student, responded, "I felt the envoy was sincere, and it was the most satisfying meeting we have had yet. We thank you for meeting with us" (Sciolino, 2001c, p. A12). Fallon returned to the United States on March 2 and issued the following statement: "The families of the victims have graciously accepted our apology. They are appreciative of our intensive search and recovery efforts, and are reassured that we will do everything we can to prevent such a tragedy from happening again" (Myers, 2001b, p. A8).

Given that Fallon did not have liability concerns front and center, as Waddle did, he was able to be much more direct in his apology first to the people of Japan and then, in this instance, to the family members of the victims. As such, his apologies met high standards of ethical adequacy. As to the manner of his apologies, they were truthful; they spoke of the "tragic loss" faced by the Japanese people. Furthermore, they were sincere and voluntary, in that they were delivered in person with no perceived reticence. As to timeliness, although the apologies were not delivered quickly, in terms of the pace of nation-states, they were delivered in an appropriate timeframe. The fact that they were delivered in a public statement on arrival and then in a private meeting to families showed that they were well designed to reach all shareholders, as well as performed in the appropriate context.

Contentwise, the apologies also were exemplary. They identified with the victims in that they acknowledged the tragic loss that the families faced and took general responsibility for the accident as having an American cause. Although the apologies did not explicitly acknowledge the fault of the *Greenville*, it certainly was implied. Fallon went out of his way, however, to ask for forgiveness, and attempted to do so in a style that was consistent with Japanese social custom. In terms of seeking reconciliation, it is only on this criterion where he might have been faulted, in that he appeared a bit too eager to communicate to the United States on his return that the Japanese had graciously accepted his apology. As to the other dimensions (i.e., full explanation, corrective action, and compensation), all three were being developed in other contexts and, as such, did not need to be addressed in his public statements.

Meanwhile, the National Transportation Safety Board revealed that Commander Waddle had made only a brief check of the horizon—for approximately $1\frac{1}{2}$ minutes—first at approximately 65 feet and then again after rising 3 more feet, before he ordered the main ballast blow drill to proceed (Myers, 2001b). The *Ehime Maru* was behind the *Greeneville* in its "baffles"—in effect, a sonar blind spot 2,000 yards away; it was traveling at 11 knots directly toward the *Greeneville*, which resulted in the smallest possible profile. *The New York Times* reported on March 4 that the submarine's only purpose for going to sea that day was a public relations tour for the guests who were part of the Navy's Distinguished Visitors program; a multiple-day-training drill had been canceled (Myers & Dao, 2001).

*The Court of Inquiry.*    On March 5, the Navy convened its Court of Inquiry to examine the causes behind the collision between the *Greeneville* and the *Ehime Maru* (Myers, 2001c). More than 400 journalists, many from overseas, arrived to observe the trial, as did six relatives of the victims and three Japanese government officials. Primary testimony came from Rear Admiral Charles H. Griffiths, Jr., who had conducted the preliminary investigation of the accident for the Navy. He gave a powerful performance as he revealed a series of errors of judgment that contributed to the collision—chiefly the failure by sonar operators to communicate their tracking of the *Ehime Maru* and to adequately search the horizon for vessels before the *Greeneville* surfaced. Griffiths disclosed that there was a sonar operator at the controls who had yet to be certified and was not adequately supervised due to the presence of the 16 guests. Furthermore, he suggested that the guests did not just disrupt the surfacing maneuver but considerably affected the submarine's operations throughout the whole day, and caused the vessel to be 45 minutes late in executing its "plan of the day" (Myers, 2001c, p. A10). Griffiths also revealed that the waves and swells were 6–8 feet, with hazy weather, yet he thought the *Ehime Maru* should have been spotted; he observed that the periscope sweep only lasted 80 seconds (not the 90 seconds originally thought), although a standard sweep should last 3 minutes or more.

The second day of testimony resulted in even more damaging revelations by Griffiths. He noted that the chief of staff for the Pacific Fleet, Captain Robert L. Brandhuber, had been aboard the submarine and was in a position to caution Commander Waddle but did not. Griffiths testified, "I think he should have had a sense that corners were being cut" (Myers, 2001d, p. A17). He also faulted the executive officer, Lieutenant Commander Gerald Pfeifer, for not speaking up: "He was thinking these things, but did not articulate them to the commanding officer or the officer of the deck" (Myers, 2001d, p. A17). Griffiths' testimony also revealed that the ship had gone to sea with less than a full crew: only 106 of its 163 crew members were aboard that day. Critically, among those not present were a senior fire control technician and a senior sonar operator. Most serious was the fact that a fire control technician did spot the *Ehime Maru* within 2,500 yards but did not speak up to Captain Waddle because he felt "inhibited" by the presence of so many visitors (Myers, 2001d, p. A17). Griffiths contended, "It's a very disturbing thing in that one case that could have made such a difference" (Myers, 2001d, p. A17).

Day 3 of the Court of Inquiry resulted in cross-examination by Waddle's attorney, Charles Gittins (Myers, 2001e). Gittins got Griffiths to acknowledge that although the *Greeneville* had been behind schedule, there would have been no problem if it had been late in its return. Griffiths also conceded that although the periscope search was quick, it was within normal parameters. Finally, it was revealed that Lieutenant Coen had ordered a different fire control technician to give "forceful reports of contacts" (Myers, 2001e, p. A14).

As he completed his testimony on the fourth day, Griffiths addressed the issue of Waddle's culpability for the first time. Charles Gittins asked, "Did you find any evidence that Commander Waddle acted criminally, negligently in the operation of the vessel?" Griffiths responded, "In my opinion, he was not criminally negligent" (Myers, 2001f, p. A10). Additionally, evidence did come out that a fire control technician, Petty Officer First Class Patrick T. Seacrest, had plotted the *Ehime Maru* at 4,000 yards, which was within range of the *Greeneville*, but Seacrest did not inform the ship's executive officers. Griffiths stated, "He should have forcefully told the captain and the officer of the deck" (Myers, 2001f, p. A10); "this is one thing that could have changed history" (Myers, 2001h, p. A1).

The day also had a dramatic development, albeit outside of the Court of Inquiry. Prior to the inquiry's beginning, Waddle spoke to family members of some of the victims and used the word *apologize* ("Waddle Speaks," 2001, p. 1). The family members listened to Waddle, but informed him that they could not accept his apology until all of the family members were together in a group, which they were able to arrange later that afternoon. Kazuo Nakata, who lost a son, characterized the exchange in the following way: "Since this is an issue of communication between two hearts and two humans, I will accept his apology. Many words are not needed. What the sub commander said is sufficient. I think Waddle can bow his head in apology. I had hoped he would apologize earlier" ("Waddle Speaks," 2001, p. 1).

The final day of testimony from the first week focused on the use of computer simulations of the periscope sweeps conducted by members of the *Greeneville*. Testimony by Captain Thomas G. Kyle arrived at two conclusions. First, he faulted Waddle for not using the periscope extensively enough to check for surface vessels, noting "Three minutes is the benchmark" (Myers, 2001g, p. A6). He also argued that Waddle had not raised the submarine high enough, given the swelling seas of 6–8 feet, in order to adequately judge surface traffic (Myers, 2001g).

Testimony from the commander of the entire Pacific submarine fleet, Rear Admiral Albert H. Konetzni, Jr., occurred the following Monday, March 12. He acknowledged that he had initially authorized the voyage, writing across the memorandum, "Don't break china" (Myers, 2001i, p. A17), but said it had been wrong to cancel a training mission and simply proceed with a cruise for the visitors. When asked if the visitors contributed to the accident, he replied, "They had nothing to do with this. Forget about it" (Myers, 2001i, p. A17). Instead, he faulted the sub's captain, Scott Waddle (whom he described as "one of my best friends") for his failure to adequately ensure that the area was completely free of vessels: "He has the obligation, truly the obligation, to make sure the area above is clear" (Myers, 2001i, p. A17). Yet, Konetzni noted, "You couldn't replicate this [the conditions that led to the accident] in a million years" (Myers, 2001i, p. A17). In a related development, the Navy announced that it was considering salvaging the *Ehime Maru* in such a way that would not raise the vessel to the surface but would enable divers to retrieve the bodies—at a cost of approximately $40 million (Myers, 2001i, 2001j).

After 7 days of testimony by Navy personnel that focused on the actions Commander Waddle and his crew had taken, Hisao Onishi, the captain of the *Ehime Maru,* appeared before the Court of Inquiry (Myers, 2001j). Speaking through a translator, Onishi offered few new details in testimony that lasted less than an hour but certainly gave a human dimension to the tragedy. Describing the collision, he said, "There was a terrible sound of Bang! Bang!" that occurred and the ship came to a halt (Myers, 2001j, p. A18). He noted that the ship was quickly doomed: "I felt that the time was very short. I felt the ship went in about 5 minutes—not even 10 minutes" (Myers, 2001j, p. A18). Onishi said that the U.S.S. Greeneville first left the scene and then returned, but appeared to do nothing to aid in the rescue: "We were hoping they would lower their inflatable boats," but instead the Ehime Maru's crew had to wait an hour in their rubber lifeboats for the Coast Guard to arrive (Myers, 2001j, p. A18).

Navy personnel then returned to the stand. Petty Officer First Class Edward McGiboney shed some light on why the Greeneville did not know of the presence of the Ehime Maru. Part of the problem was that prior to the surfacing drill, the Greeneville did a number of high-speed drills; such maneuvers wreck havoc on sonar data and leave it looking like, in the words of McGiboney, "spaghetti" ("Just Minutes Might Have Sufficed," 2001, p. A9). When then asked why the crew did not subsequently discover the Ehime Maru during the periscope check, he replied, "I don't think we had enough time" ("Just Minutes Might Have Sufficed," 2001 p. A9), and noted that the crew was forced to do in 6 minutes what normally took 10 minutes.

Finally, on March 19, a number of important developments took place. First, the fire control technician who knew of the Ehime Maru's presence, Petty Officer First Class Patrick T. Seacrest, took the stand. He revealed that he did not focus on the Ehime Maru due to the fact that sonar had just identified the presence of another ship that had caught his attention (Sterngold, 2001a). He also disclosed that although the Greeneville's computers had shown the Ehime Maru as dangerously close, because the vessel failed to turn up on the periscope check he had assumed the computer was wrong and subsequently reprogrammed the Greeneville's computer to place the Ehime Maru out of the range of the Greeneville. When asked if such a decision to do so was "proper procedure," he replied, "No, it's not written down anywhere" (Sterngold, 2001a, p. A1). Seacrest also acknowledged that he had failed to plot the presence of vessels in the area on a paper wall chart that could be seen by all. When asked if he had gotten lazy, he responded, "Yes sir. A little bit" (Sterngold, 2001a, p. A17).

Second, Commander Waddle appeared before reporters for the first time and announced that although no decision to testify had yet been made, if he did do so "The first word I will say to the court will be the fact—that I'm accountable and I'm responsible for the accident that led to the tragic collision and sinking of the Ehime Maru." He added, "None of my crew members should be accountable or responsible for that accident" (Sterngold, 2001a, p. A17).

Third, the other senior officers of the Greeneville submitted their testimony. Lieutenant Commander Gerald K. Pfeifer, the Greeneville's executive officer, did not testify orally but instead submitted a formal written statement to the court. The officer of the deck, Lieutenant j. g., Michael J. Coen, spoke to the families of the victims who were at the Court of Inquiry: "I want you to know that you are in my thoughts and prayers at all times. And you will be for the rest of my life" (Sterngold, 2001a, p. A17). In an unusual twist, he did not take an oath, which meant that his testimony could not be cross-examined by Navy lawyers.

At last, on March 20, the final day of the trial, the Captain of the *Greeneville*, Commander Scott D. Waddle, took the stand to testify. He began by criticizing the Court's decision not to grant him immunity; he claimed that his testimony was critical to help the Navy respond to the sinking based on the facts rather than political pressure "at the highest levels" (Sterngold, 2001b, p. A1). He had decided to testify anyway, against the advice of his lawyer, because it was "the right thing to do" (Sterngold, 2001b, p. A1).

Although Waddle took responsibility for his command, he also seemed to spread the blame around; he maintained, "I did not micromanage my crew. I empowered them to do their jobs" (Sterngold, 2001b, p. A15). But in the questioning by the admirals in charge of the court, it became quite clear that they had reservations about the control and management of Waddle's crew. Waddle admitted that he had hurried his way through the periscope sweep but denied that he felt rushed. Waddle also revealed that 9 of 13 members of the crew had changed their watch positions without notifying him, and that he had not noticed. He also acknowledged that even though one third of his sailors did not go out on the special tour, he did not take any special precautions to ensure the safety of the ship or the ships in the area. Perhaps the most revealing moment came when it was revealed that even though the sonar monitor was broken, Waddle gave no special instructions to his crew members to pay extra-close attention to the sonar. Admiral Sullivan's response was incredulity: "I just don't believe it" (Sterngold, 2001b, p. A15). Admiral Nathman concurred, saying, "It makes me question the standards on *Greeneville*" (Sterngold, 2001b, p. A15).

The Court of Inquiry also revealed on that day that Waddle faced three charges: dereliction of duty, placing the submarine in a hazardous situation, and negligent homicide—the last of which could carry a maximum prison term of 10 years. Following Waddle's testimony, *The New York Times,* in an editorial, argued that the evidence revealed in the Court of Inquiry called for a court martial ("Taking the Greeneville Case," 2001).

The Navy finally ended its search for the missing crew members and passengers of the *Ehime Maru* on April 7, but only after receiving permission from the families of the victims ("Families OK End," 2001, p. 1). The permission came through the Ehime Prefecture Governor, Moriyuki Kato, whom the Navy had asked (through the Japanese Foreign Ministry) to help communicate the families' wishes to the Navy. The families also signaled a willingness to enter into negotiations with the Navy with regards to compensation. After meeting with the families, Kato said, "I felt that the acceptance of the briefing and the termination of the search indicated that the families and victims have come to terms with the incident" ("Families OK End," 2001, p. 1).

On April 13, the Court of Inquiry released its findings in a 2,000-page document to Admiral Thomas B. Fargo, the commander of the Pacific Fleet (Kifner, 2001a; Sciolino, 2001d). The report unanimously recommended that Captain Waddle not face a court martial. Based on the evidence submitted in the document, Fargo had 30 days to order courts martial or other forms of discipline against Waddle or other members of the crew, although he was expected to act more quickly.

The decision by the court seemed to suggest that although Waddle's leadership and direction had been careless and sloppy, it had not failed to the point of being criminally negligent. As a result, he was much more likely to face some form of disciplinary letter of reprimand but not jail time (Sciolino, 2001d). Although such a decision would help to preserve morale in the submarine fleet, it was expected to set off a furor in Japan. On hearing from press reports that courts martial were unlikely, Kasuo Nakata, the father of a teacher who drowned in the collision, said, "I'll be very angry if I learn officially that the court-martial will not take place" (Sciolino, 2001d, p. 18). Takahiro Hosokawa, who represented the families of the rescued students, said, "It [the Navy] should definitely convene a court-martial and further clarify the cause of the accident and who was responsible for it" ("*Ehime Maru* Families," 2001, p. 2). Toshio Kamado, the father of one of the surviving students, was even more direct: "I suspect (Waddle) will be ordered to retire and that will be that. Disciplinary action without convening a court-martial looks like "punishment with honor" to me. He should be tried as a military officer" ("*Ehime Maru* Families," 2001, p. 2).

As expected, Admiral Thomas B. Fargo, commander of the Pacific Fleet, announced on April 19 that Waddle would not face a court martial. Instead, his fate would be decided by an admiral's mast: a nonjudicial administrative hearing. The admiral's mast, a form of punishment that harkened back to the days in which punishment would be meted out on the deck of a ship near the main mast by the boat's captain, would include a letter of reprimand that would end Waddle's naval career (Myers, 2001k). Surprisingly, as details came out after the report, it became clear that the Navy was unlikely to end the Distinguished Visitors program due to the strong support throughout the Navy for the program, which witnessed 7,836 visitors in the year 2000, including 307 on submarines like the *Greeneville* and 1,478 aboard aircraft carriers (Kifner, 2001b).

*The Admiral's Mast.*   The drama ended, at least in terms of the military chapter, on April 23 at Admiral Thomas Fargo's headquarters in Honolulu, where Waddle and other officers faced their future in an admiral's mast hearing (Kifner, 2001c). As expected, Waddle received a "punitive letter of reprimand" and was found guilty of two violations of Article 15 of the Uniform Code of Military Justice: "dereliction of duty" and "subjecting a vessel to hazard"(Kifner, 2001c, p. A16). He also agreed to resign from the Navy. Fargo decided that Waddle would be allowed to retire at full rank (by October 1)—meaning that he would receive his full pension. The admiral also "admonished" the others aboard the vessel, including the executive officer, Lieutenant Commander Gerald K. Pfeifer, the chief of staff of the submarine fleet, the chief of the boat, and the senior sonar operator (Kifner, 2001c, p. 16). In reprimanding Waddle, Fargo asserted that the *Greeneville* captain had "created an artificial sense of urgency in preparation for surfacing on 9 February when prudent seamanship, the safety of his submarine and good judgment dictated otherwise" (Kifner, 2001c, p. A1). He argued that "this tragic accident could and should have been avoided by simply following existing Navy standards and procedures in bringing submarines to the surface" (Kifner, 2001c, pp. A1, A16). He also spoke to the presence of the civilians on the *Greeneville*, noting that:

> [N]one of the embarked civilians onboard *Greeneville* on 9 February directly contributed to this collision …. They did, however, prove to be a distraction to the commanding officer, hindered the normal flow of contact information in the moments leading up to the collision and as such affect[ed] the performance of his control room watchstanders. It was Commander Waddle's responsibility to prevent this from occurring. ("From Statement By Admiral Fargo," 2001, p. A16)

When asked if the punishment was merely a "slap on the hand," the admiral replied, "[H]e was stripped of his command, and to a commanding officer who was served for 20 years, this is absolutely devastating." Fargo also opined, "He has paid dearly" (Kifner, 2001c, p. A16).

*Japanese Anger.*   Reaction from the Japanese government was not as angry as expected. Kazuhiko Koshikawa, spokesperson for Prime Minister Yoshiro Mori, seemed to accept the decision. He said, "With the measures taken against Waddle and others, their liability has been made clear. These decisions were made under U.S. rules and the Japanese government does not at this point plan to make any specific demand to the United States" (Kifner, 2001c, p. A16).

Outcry in Japan continued to be dramatic and to show cultural rifts between the two countries. Families of the victims were aghast at the penalty.

Ryosuke Terata, who lost his son Yusuke, complained, "If he were in Japan, he would be fired and indicted on charges such as professional negligence resulting in death" (Sims, 2001, p. A16). The father of a teacher, Kazuo Nakata, highlighted the unsatisfactory way—in a Burkean dramatistic sense—that the tragedy had ended: "I cannot help feeling that the way this has ended is a farce" (Sims, 2001, p. A16). Moriuki Kato, governor of the Ehime prefecture, rejected the decision: "The punishment is absolutely not one that the families can accept. I had hoped they would give him the utmost, strictest reprimand" (Kifner, 2001c, p. A16).

Uwajima City Mayor Hirohisa Ishibashi argued that even with the weak sentence, Waddle's obligations were not over: "Unfortunately, I cannot help but feel the punishment may be too light. Families and students are demanding that Waddle come to Uwajima and apologize. But I am too agitated at this point to say, please come" (Mogi, 2001, April 24, n. p.).

This call for Waddle to come to Japan was echoed by family members. Toshio Komado, for instance, whose son Atsushi was one of the survivors, made it clear that they were still expecting to hear directly from Captain Waddle: "The students are seeking a direct apology from him. We want him to come to Japan and apologize, not as a civilian but as a member of the United States Navy" (Sims, 2001, p. A16).

*Final Developments.*    With the conclusion of the Court of Inquiry, Commander Waddle then offered a final statement through his attorney, Charles W. Gittins:

> This hearing concludes a very difficult time for my family and I, and it has effectively ended my Navy career. It was not the end I had envisioned for my career when I took command of the Greeneville. [But] ... as the commanding officer I was and am responsible and accountable for my actions and the actions of my crew that led to the terrible accident at sea. (Kifner, 2001c, p. A16)

Waddle then offered another apology: "My heart aches for the losses suffered by the families of those killed. To those families, I again offer my most sincere apology and my hope that our government will promptly and fairly settle all claims made by the families against the United States" (Kifner, 2001c, p. A16).

It was only with the conclusion of the admiral's mast that Waddle was able to apologize in a fully satisfactory way. On that occasion, he finally seemed to believe he was in a position in which he could acknowledge the wrongdoing, apologize, and take full responsibility for the accident. He noted that he was "responsible and accountable," and defined what had happened as a "terrible accident." He also seemed to go out of his way to seek reconciliation, in that he purposefully apologized directly to the family members. It was only then, albeit quite late, that he was able to meet the expectations that the victims had for him. Waddle eventually did make a visit to Japan in December 2002; he laid a wreath of white lilies and prayed at a memorial to those lost on the *Ehime Maru* (Yamaguchi, 2002).

The sensitive nature of the accident meant that the situation was not fully resolved, even after the court decision. On a symbolic level, the Navy then proceeded to do an unprecedented act: raise the sunken *Ehime Maru* from its depth of 2,000 feet. The plan, which began in July, was to raise the vessel, using a variety of sophisticated underwater technology, to shallow waters and divers would then be able to recover any bodies that might still be in the vessel ("Navy to Raise *Ehime Maru*," 2001). By October, the Navy—in conjunction with the civilian marine contractors it had hired, two Japanese engineers, and a number of Japanese divers who would aid in retrieving remains—began to make progress, towing the vessel 16 miles underwater to a location 1 mile from Oahu's southern shore in 115 feet of water (Sterngold, 2001c). By October 17, the Navy had its first success, recovering one of the bodies lost in the accident ("Navy Divers Find First Body," 2001). Lieutenant Commander Neil Sheehan, liaison officer to the victims' families, said of the recovery effort, "The U.S. Navy is committed to treating the families respectfully and honorably. We're committed to an honorable closure for those families" ("Navy Divers Find First Body," 2001, p. A18).

The $60 million effort appeared to be helpful in healing the rift between Japan and the United States and bringing the drama to a close. Moriyuki Kato, governor of the Ehime district, said, "I pray that as many bodies as possible will be found, and am thankful for the U.S. Navy's thorough preparations leading up to this day" ("Navy Divers Find First Body," 2001, p. A18). By Friday, October 20, Navy divers had found and recovered five more bodies from the *Ehime Maru,* and acknowledged that it had not expected to find more than seven of the nine who had perished in the accident ("2 More Bodies Recovered," 2001).

Although the loss of life and the complexity of the crisis for the U.S. government and Commander Waddle made it difficult to resolve this tragedy, the decisions to raise the *Ehime Maru* and retrieve the bodies as well as to offer compensation appeared to mitigate much of the anger over the crisis. Conversely, the following case, that of a contested mascot at an academic institution of higher learning, was decided in such a way so as to make any long-term resolution difficult.

## The University of North Dakota

One of the issues that has come to vex academic institutions concerns the names chosen decades ago for their mascots. Indeed, the last 20 years have witnessed many institutions trying to resolve the problem that, as times have changed, some mascots have come to be perceived as less than ideal for an image-conscious college or university (e.g., the Beavers) or, in more serious cases, other mascots are seen by ethnic groups as insensitive at best or racist at worse. A perennial problem, of course, is that of the use of Native American nicknames by universities. Indeed, in a study by Franks (1982), he found that Native American terms were two of the ten most popular mascot names: *Warriors* ranked fifth and *Indians* ranked eighth. (The other eight were all animals.)

The sides in mascot controversies are well demarcated. Native Americans reference the negative connotation and stereotyping that occurs when Native American images like "Warriors" or "Braves" are used (often attended by mascots in sacred headdress or other costume, and accompanied by chants and tomahawks). Defenders conversely point to the tradition and history of the institution that the name has come to represent, and argue that by keeping their name they are preserving the memory of a particular tribe. (For more on mascots and their role in contemporary sports, see Banks, 1993; Connolly, 2000; Franks, 1982; King, 1998; King, Springwood, & Vine, 2001; Lessiter, 1989; Nuessel, 1994; Spindel, 2000; Vanderford, 1996.)

Given the controversy, institutions have dealt with the issue in a variety of ways. For example, Wheaton College (of Illinois) has made the change from the "Crusaders," which referenced a less than honorable chapter in the history of the Christian church, to the "Lightning," a benign name that still has a divine reference. Conversely, Eastern Michigan University changed its nickname from the "Hurons," a reference to a small tribe in Southeastern Michigan and Northern Ohio (otherwise known as the Wyandotte) to the ubiquitous and somewhat vacuous "Eagles." Both the small remaining band of Hurons, who now live in Oklahoma, as well as many members of university's alumni association objected to the change. In fact, the acrimony turned so severe that Eastern Michigan saw its donations drop $400,000 and had to threaten the "Huron Restoration, Inc." with legal action in order to get the splinter group to cease using the Huron nickname (Connolly, 2000). Conversely, Central Michigan University has chosen a middle route, keeping the name "Chippewas" but removing all Native images from its jerseys and helmets and instead using a block "C" for its logo.

Perhaps the mother of all nickname fights is still ongoing at the University of Illinois, whose athletic teams are known as the Fighting Illini, and are led on gameday by mascot Chief Illiniwek (portrayed by a U of I student in Native American headdress and costume). There have been resolutions, commissions, and even legislative action in an attempt to resolve the issue for the University of Illinois, but these have met with little success (King, 1998). However, this case, as do all of the mascot issue cases, illustrates the inherent tensions within universities in their need to balance the competing constituencies of their alumni and their traditions, their institutional identity and aspirations, and their responsiveness to cultural change and the representations of ethnic groups on which their mascot images are based.

*The Controversy.*  One institution that has faced this issue is the University of North Dakota, a state-funded institution with 11,000 students, located in the community of Grand Forks. Perhaps the University of North Dakota's greatest claim to fame is its hockey team, a Division I powerhouse that has been to the "Frozen Four"—collegiate hockey's version of the NCAA Final Four basketball tournament—numerous times. At issue in this case is the use of the nickname and its incarnations: the "Sioux" and the "Fighting Sioux."

The University of North Dakota adopted the Sioux as its nickname in 1930; the purpose of this was to "strike fear into the hearts of the Bison at rival North Dakota State University [NDSU], in Fargo" (Brownstein, 2001, p. A47). No serious objections to the name were voiced until Native American students began to arrive on campus in large numbers in the 1960s and 1970s. The presence of students who saw the nickname as an affront to their personal history and identity began to cause friction with other students. In 1972, for instance, a Native American student was jailed after he got into a fight with fraternity members, resulting in the hospitalization of three frat brothers. The fight broke out over an explicit sculpture of a nude Native American woman the frat brothers made during the King Kold Karnival, hung with the sign "Lick 'em Sioux" (Brownstein, 2001, p. A47). A similar type of incident occurred in 1992 at a homecoming parade, when spectators performed the tomahawk chop and told Native American students to "go back to the reservation" (Brownstein, 2001, p. A 47).

In addition to the problems on campus, the name is always an issue whenever the University of North Dakota plays the NDSU Bison. At these athletic contests, the chants come out—with the Bison yelling "Sioux suck" and other creative combinations. Other offenses have included a t-shirt worn by NDSU fans that showed a Native woman on her knees underneath a bison with the slogan: "Blow Us—We Saw. They Sucked. We Came" (Brownstein, 2001, p. A47). Another logo, sporting a Native American in headdress with bright red lips and crooked nose, was emblazoned with the caption: "A Century of Sucking, UND Sioux 1890–1990" (Brownstein, 2001, p. A46).

It is against this backdrop that the controversy over the Sioux name has played out. Many backers of the name have noted that it is only logical for the University of North Dakota to keep the nickname, because it is a vehi-

cle by which to honor and keep alive the memory of the Sioux and its traditions across the plains of North Dakota, as well as the fact that the
institution has enrolled 350 Native American students in what is arguably
one of the top institutions in the country for its role in educating Native
American students. Furthermore, the school has over 25 programs with
American Indian emphases, and it touts its role in having trained one fifth
of all Native American physicians in the country (Brownstein, 2001).
Such a position is summed up in the words of Earl Strinden, semi-retired
head of the alumni association: "This is Sioux territory, for crying out
loud!" (Brownstein, 2001, p. A47). Strinden continued, "When the
hockey team plays in Boston, the people will think, "Fighting Sioux, what's
that?" They'll want to find out about the Sioux. There are those on this
campus who want to make sure that Native Americans are always victims"
(Brownstein, 2001, p. A47).

Conversely, most Native American students see the nickname as an
affront to their identity. They view the name and the accompanying image to demean and to reinforce stereotypical perceptions of Native
Americans, and to appropriate an image that belongs not to the university but instead to the Sioux nation. Furthermore, they question how a
nickname they do not want can function to honor them. The fact that
Native American students argue that the nickname victimizes an entire
culture increases the guilt faced by the institution and raises the question
as to its social responsibility.

*Plans to Change.*    In 2000, the university appeared to be moving in the
direction of changing or retiring the Sioux nickname. President Charles E.
Kupchella, responding to protests from Native American students, created a
commission that investigated the use of the name and the controversy that
went along with it. Indeed, indications were that Kupchella was communicating according to a script, laying the groundwork to make the name
change in January 2001. In an e-mail to Board Chairman William Isaacson
on December 16, 2000, President Kupchella indicated that "I see no choice
but to respect the request of Sioux tribes that we quit using their name, because to do otherwise would be to put the university and its president in an
untenable position" (Brownstein, 2001, p. A48). He later claimed that the
e-mail was reflective of how he may have been leaning at the time but had
yet to make a decision (Brownstein, 2001).

*The Threat.*    The decision to change the name was derailed when a letter from an angry alumni arrived on December 20, 2000. The letter came
from Ralph Engelstad, a University of North Dakota alumni and former
hockey team goalie from 1945 to 1950. Engelstad was a successful Las Vegas
casino owner, and had made a $100 million pledge to donate money to build

a state-of-the-art hockey facility for the university. In his letter, Engelstad changed from friend to antagonist and threatened to cancel his gift and cease construction on the hockey arena unless the university made a decision to retain the Sioux logo and slogan. He wrote:

Dear Chuck:

I am sorry to write this letter but as a businessman I have no choice.

Commitments were made to me by others and yourself, regarding the Sioux logo and the Sioux slogan before I started the arena and after it had been started.

These promises have not been kept and I, as a businessman, cannot proceed while this cloud is still hanging above me ….

I understand that you are to make a decision sometime in the future but I do not understand where one person gets the authority to make this kind of a decision on behalf of all alumni, students, the City of Grand Forks and the State of North Dakota ….

Please be advised that if this logo and slogan are not approved by you no later than Friday, December 29, 2000, then you will leave me with no alternative but to take the action which I think is necessary.

If the logo and slogan are not approved by the above-mentioned date, I will then write a letter on December 30, 2000 to all contractors and to everybody associated with the arena canceling their construction contracts for the completion of the arena. I am a man of my word and I will see to it that a settlement is made with all subcontractors, with anyone who has purchased pre-paid advertising, I will refund money to all ticketholders and abandon the project. It would be then left up to you if you want to complete it with money from wherever you may be able to find it.

I have spent, as of this time, in excess of $35,000,000.00 which I will consider a bad investment but I will take my lumps and walk away.

As I'm sure you realize, the commitment I made to the University of North Dakota was, I believe, one of the 10 largest ever made to a school of higher education, but if it is not completed, I am sure it will be the number one building never brought to completion at a school of higher education due to your changing the logo and the slogan.

You need to think how changing this logo and slogan will effect [sic] not just the few that are urging the name change but also how it will effect [sic] the university as a whole, the students, the City of Grand Forks and the State of North Dakota.

If I walk away and abandon the project, please be advised that we will shut off all temporary heat going to this building and I am sure that nature, through its cold weather, will completely destroy any portion of the building through frost that you might be able to salvage. I surely hoped that it would never come to this but I guess it has.

It is a good thing that you are an educator because you are a man of in-decision and if you were a businessman, you would not succeed, you would be broke immediately.

Please do not consider this letter a threat in any manner as it is not intended to be. It is only a notification to you of exactly what I am going to do if you change this logo and this slogan.

In the event it is necessary to cancel the completion of this arena, I will then send notification to anyone who is interested in informing them of the same and laying out to them all of the facts and all of the figures from all of the meetings that led me to make this decision.

Your lack of making a decision has hung over our heads too long and we can't go on with it any further.

It is your choice if you want to put hundreds of construction workers out of a job and deprive the local businesses of Grand Forks of the income they are receiving from the construction of the arena ....

Yours truly,

Ralph Engelstad

("A $100-Million Donor's Ultimatum," 2001, p. A47)

**Board Action.**    Given President Kupchella's many signals of his inten-tion to change the name, the State Board of Higher Education (the final de-cision-making authority in the state on issues of higher education), in what appeared to be a hastily called meeting the day after the letter arrived (De-cember 21), took the issue out of the president's hands and voted 8–0 to re-tain the use of the nickname. In addition to making the president look weak, the decision caught the ire of the Faculty Senate, who overwhelmingly passed a resolution on January 11, 2001, whereby it argued "that the Board of Higher Education's intervention without prior notice or explanation was an unjustified interference with a pending deliberative campus process, and the Senate calls on the Board to reconsider and retract its decision" ("UND Senate Resolution," 2001, n.p.).

*The Story Behind the Story.* The University of North Dakota had a long-standing and rather complicated relationship with Engelstad, and this situation was not the first controversy it had encountered in its dealings with him. The university's hockey rink had been named after Engelstad following a $5 million gift from him. However, even that gift had been shrouded in controversy. Engelstad might be described as eccentric at best and racist at worst. In the 1980s, he was fined $1.5 million by the Nevada Gaming Control Board for damaging Nevada's image across the nation. Engelstad apparently had an affection for Nazi memorabilia and in his Imperial Palace hotel and casino he had one of the largest antique car collections in the country, among which were several Nazi vehicles, including Hitler's 1939 parade automobile (Brownstein, 2001). Engelstad also had a large collection of Nazi posters, uniforms, banners, and the like. He had come under fire and was subsequently investigated by the Nevada Gaming Control Board for two parties he had held in 1986 and 1988, on Hitler's birthday. The parties featured a birthday cake decorated with a swastika, German food, and a life-sized portrait of Hitler accompanied by a second portrait—that of Engelstad dressed in a Nazi uniform (Brownstein, 2001). Engelstad also was reputed to have sent out bumper stickers to his guests with the phrase "Hitler was Right" (Brownstein, 2001, p. A48).

Faced with all the scrutiny and negative media attention, Engelstad was forced to use a strategy of denial; he issued a statement that "I despise Hitler and everything he stood for" and instead claimed that the parties were "spoofs" designed to mark the growing collection of memorabilia (Brownstein, 2001, p. A48).

Embarrassed by this incident at the time, the university set a seven-member delegation to conclude whether Engelstad was indeed a racist and to determine whether the university should continue to have a formal affiliation with him. The university appeared appeased when, a few months later, Engelstad removed the memorabilia. The group concluded he was not a Nazi supporter, but instead had simply acted in "bad taste" (Brownstein, 2001, p. A48).

Elizabeth Hampsten, an English professor who was University Senate president at the time, recalls she had reservations and voiced objections, but not "loudly enough": "I felt that we didn't have enough information to make that determination. It was a whitewash" (Brownstein, 2001, p. A48). But the damage had been done to the institution's reputation: "We should have put a stop to it then. When I talk to people at other universities, they can't believe it. We've become a laughingstock" (Brownstein, 2001, p. A48).

David H. Vorland, director of university relations, took a different tact; although acknowledging Engelstad's faults, Vorland tended to see him as more of an eccentric:

> We have an alumnus who has demonstrated major support. Do you think we should destroy a relationship with an individual like that without serious consideration? It would be ideal if he had no warts. But there are not many people like that, particularly among those who have battled their way up from modest beginnings to positions of extraordinary wealth. (Brownstein, 2001, p. A48)

Indeed, the incident created a dangerous precedent in that it showed how powerfully beholden the university was to Engelstad's money, in that it was willing to overlook a benefactor with such embarrassing public "warts" in order to continue a relationship with him. This relationship was one that ultimately tied the university to its patron's wishes in a context in which the donor had control over far more than the dollar value of his major gift.

*President Kupchella's Apologia*    The action by the State Board of Higher Education to take out of President Kupchella's hands the decision about whether to change the Fighting Sioux nickname put him in a difficult situation, because it made him look weak and powerless. Perhaps trying to put the best spin on the issue, some have observed that the matter was really a question of poor timing, and that the board's quick action on the matter was designed to be a face-saving effort for the president in order to keep the state's Legislative Assembly from getting involved and creating a "public showdown" (Brownstein, 2001, p. A49).

Regardless, on December 21, 2000, President Kupchella released a statement in response to the board's efforts in order to repair the damage done to the university's reputation as well as his own. He started with the acknowledgment that he had been close to a decision when the board intervened: "As the board took up the issue of the Sioux nickname and made its decision today, I was in the final stage of considering several options and was prepared to take action to be announced during the first part of January" (Kupchella, 2000, n.p.).

Kupchella then used a strategy of defeasibility in which he conceded that the board's decision effectively took the issue out of his hands. He noted, "Instead, the decision has been made unanimously by the body that has ultimate authority in all matters related to this University and the other public institutions of higher education in North Dakota" (Kupchella, 2000, n.p.).

At this stage, all Kupchella could do was use a bolstering strategy by which he articulated his commitment to the University of North Dakota and his desire to respond to the decision by making the university even more effective in its delivery of Native American programs:

> The University of North Dakota is proud of its record in providing educational opportunities for our Native American citizens, and for attempting to generate understanding and appreciation of Native American culture. But much more needs to be done, and I pledge to lead UND in new efforts to accomplish this goal. It is especially important that we make sure that Native American leaders are invited to the campus to see what the University is doing to support Native American students and to learn more about the richness of their culture and to seek their insight into how UND can better serve their needs. (Kupchella, 2000, n.p.)

Finally, Kupchella concluded with a statement that seems to be its own form of corrective action, in that if he could not follow through on the Native American students' wishes, he would do all he could to enhance their educational opportunities: "I have made an unconditional commitment that the University of North Dakota will seek to become the leading institution in the United States of America in serving Native Americans, both as students and as citizens across the region. We will continue to pursue that objective" (Kupchella, 2000, n.p.).

What is noteworthy of Kupchella's statements is their failure to criticize the board for its decision or to express anger for the board taking the decision out of his hands. Indeed, his milquetoast response drew criticism from the group B.R.I.D.G.E.S. (Building Roads Into Diverse Groups Empowering Students), a Native American student organization on the University of North Dakota campus that expressed anger at Kupchella's unwillingness to confront the board.

Assessment of this apologia is a difficult one, in that it was Ralph Engelstad's challenge that put the University of North Dakota in a difficult position, and by doing so forced the university to defend itself. Yet, just as the institution—and in particular, President Kupchella—was about to make a difficult and risky decision to change its mascot, the decision to do so was taken out of Kupchella's hand, a complicating factor that directly affected his ability to resolve the problem. Hence, in his apologetic statement he put forth a great deal of defeasibility, but he attempted to make the best of a difficult situation. In this way, although the apologia was not exemplary, it was nonetheless well above the bar of being morally acceptable.

As to the manner of his apologia, Kupchella's action and word choice were such that he was truthful, in that he did not engage in politically charged rhetoric in which he tried to name the actions of the board. Rather, he was sincere, and appealed to all parties involved in the issue, both during the decision and after it, to characterize themselves by their civility. The issuing of a public statement was acceptable, although not as ideal as a news conference.

As to the content of his apologia, Kupchella should be faulted in that he recognized the finality of the board's decision, and did not, at that time, seek to undo it nor threaten to resign. In addition, he should have been more direct and offered his regret to Native American students and those who supported a mascot change. Instead he appeared to take a different tack, which was to identify directly with the injured parties—particularly those Native American students—and offer his own antidote to bring reconciliation with them as well as to seek to correct the wrongs done to the Sioux in another way: making the University of North Dakota the premier institution for Native American students and to serve Native American communities in the Upper Midwest. In this way, he was not able to fix the name, but instead articulated a laudable commitment to enhancing the material conditions of Native American peoples. Perhaps given the way that the board made Kupchella look powerless, the only satisfactory response would have been to resign in protest.

*Epilogue.*    As is often the case in apologetic situations, the response of the key player does not function to end the controversy. Such was the case with the mascot issue at the University of North Dakota. Rather than resolving the issue about the nickname, the actions of the board created even more conflict on campus the following winter, when tensions became so severe that President Kupchella had to issue a statement calling for more civility on campus. In it, he wrote:

> Again, I call on all—especially those who feel some passion about this issue on one side or the other—to tone down the rhetoric; such tactics advance no cause, no matter how righteous. The University must be a safe place from which to explore ideas. I care deeply about the welfare of all students and employees at the University of North Dakota. (Kupchella, 2001, n.p.)

He then reiterated his commitment to strengthening study offerings for Native American students as well as better serving the Native American community.

Forgotten in all of the activities were the lives of the Native American students on campus. Monique Vondall, a member of the Chippewa tribe and a student at the University of North Dakota, observed, "It's hard not to see history repeating itself in Ralph Engelstad's efforts" (Brownstein, 2001, p. A49), referring to the fact that in it there is "an echo of past defeats, when choices regarding their [Native Americans'] honor were made by others, and power and money won out over doing the right thing" (Brownstein, 2001, p. A49).

By October 2001, the hockey arena was completed and set for opening day festivities. It certainly was first class, with 11,400 padded seats, 48 luxury boxes, a $2 million scoreboard with four screens, an Olympic-sized practice rink, as well as an extravagant locker room and state-of-the-art exercise equipment (Sullivan, 2001).

By this time, both Engelstad and the university seemed to attempt to distance themselves from the controversy that surrounded "the letter." Noticeably absent from the festivities, Engelstad issued a statement in which he claimed his rationale for building the arena was to do something for the city of Grand Forks, which had been devastated by the extensive flooding and fire that damaged much of the downtown area in 1997 (Sullivan, 2001). The gift was to be $50 million for the arena and an additional $50 million for academic programs, but the decision to accelerate the pace of construction and complete the project, which employed 2,500 people over 22 months, proved much more costly. In his statement, Engelstad continued to defend his support of the "Fighting Sioux" logo and motto, which was used approximately 4,500 times in the new building: "I believe tradition is important. I am disappointed in the modern-day relentless demolition and ridicule of admirable tradition" (Sullivan, 2001, n.p.). Continuing, he argued, "the spirit of being a Fighting Sioux [is] of lasting value and immeasurable significance" (Sullivan, 2001, n.p.).

Even with Engelstad absent, the festivities were not without controversy. In the ceremony, the university unveiled a bronze statue of a Sioux warrior with an accompanying plaque dedicated to Sitting Bull, proclaiming him a "patriot, statesman, diplomat, warrior and prophet" (Sullivan, 2001, n.p.). Yet, one of Sitting Bull's descendants, Isaac Dog Eagle, wrote to President Kupchella and asked for the statue to be removed, claiming that the university was displaying a likeness without authorization to use the family name.

At the dedication, Erik Enno, a Lakota of the Turtle Mountain tribe, thanked Engelstad for the building, and described it as a "lasting tribute in the name of our people" (Sullivan, 2001, n.p.). President Kupchella added that the building was "first class" (Sullivan, 2001, n.p.).

In an unusual arrangement, however, Englestad owned the building—which sat on land owned by the university. However, he had plans to donate the building to the university at some point in the future, suggesting years of potential control and conflict to come (Sullivan, 2001).

Although Englestad, who passed away in November 2002, may appear to have won the battle, the issue is not going to go away anytime soon, and in the longer term is likely to be changed. Other third-party participants appear ready to enter the drama. Later that October, for instance, the St. Cloud State University asked the University of North Dakota to leave its logo home when the UND hockey team came to play ("St. Cloud State Asks North Dakota," 2001). Although it would not have canceled the game if UND had declined the request, St. Cloud nevertheless made the behest at the request of its students and faculty, with some arguing that the UND logo constituted "hate speech" ("St. Cloud State Asks North Dakota," 2001, n.p.). Relatedly, St. Cloud President Roy Saigo submitted a resolution that the National Collegiate Athletic Association ban all Native American nicknames from use. Morris Kurtz, St. Cloud athletic director, said, "President Saigo has taken this as a personal issue and taken it to the highest level" (St. Cloud State Asks North Dakota," 2001, n.p.).

Such a message was heard loud and clear at the University of North Dakota. Lucy Ganje, an associate professor of communication at the university and a frequent student supporter of the effort to eliminate the offensive nickname, said that it is becoming more clear that "change is going to come about from pressure from without" ("St. Cloud State Asks North Dakota," 2001, n.p.).

Although the University of North Dakota was in an intractable situation, with multiple constituent groups requiring different outcomes, the next case study is unique in that the apology came not as a result of calls for an explanation, but instead from a desire to clear the record and reputation of the Roman Catholic Church.

## Papal Apology

Few popes appear to have been more influential in their leadership of the billion-member Catholic Church than Pope John Paul II (Holmes, 1998). In his tenure, through his use of travel (over 500,000 miles to more than 100 countries) and his mastery of television, he has been able to lead as a moral force, as evidenced by his endorsement of the Solidarity movement in Poland that eventually led to the bloodless, full-scale collapse of communism in Eastern Europe. His subsequent successes were not all political, of course; he also has reshaped the Catholic Church with his imprimatur; by virtue of his longevity, he has been able to appoint nearly all of the College of Cardinals, as well as select more than half of the church's 4,200 bishops (Holmes, 1998). Personally, he was known as a warm and charming man, and as an intellectual with an impeccable moral character. Yet, he was also known as the Pope who unexpectedly delivered two major apologies during his leadership of the Catholic Church.

*The Shoah Apology.* The first apology, which occurred in 1998, was part of a larger attempt to heal a centuries-long rift between Christianity and Judaism. The apology took the form of a document entitled "We Remember: A Reflection on the Shoah," which sought to account for the Holocaust as well as acknowledge the conditions created by the Catholic Church that had allowed it to proceed without moral opposition. The idea of the apology was that, by remembering its horror, the possibility of a reoccurrence of the Holocaust would be lessened (for a copy of the document, see http://www.vatican.va/roman_curia/pontifical_councils/chrstuni/documents/rc_pc_chrstuni_doc_16031998_shoah_en.html). Although some commentators and Jewish leaders like Israeli Chief Rabbi Meir Lau wanted the Pope to be even more direct in his criticism of Pope Pius XII and the Catholic Church's silence and unwillingness to condemn Nazi atrocities, others were satisfied and recognized that the document was a major step forward ("Papal Apology," 1998; "Pope to Apologize," 2000).

Following the release of the Shoah document, John Paul II made a trip to Jerusalem in March 2000 (the first papal visit there since Pope Paul VI's trip in 1964), during which he visited holy sites of Christians, Muslims, and Jews, and prayed at the Western Wall. In the words of one Holocaust survivor, the visit, along with the apology, "marks a turning point for Jews and Christians" (Herring, 2000, p. 4-2).

*Apology for the Sins of the Second Millennium.* The second papal apology occurred in March 2000. As part of the apologetic process, the Catholic Church released a document entitled "Memory and Reconciliation: The Church and the Mistakes of the Past" (Stanley, 2000a). This document attempted to set the context for the apology that would be delivered by the Pope later in the month, noting that the goal was "purification of memory" (Stanley, 2000a, p. A10). Specifically, it distinguished between the sins of the "sons and daughters" of the Catholic Church as opposed to the Catholic Church itself, which was "holy and immaculate" (Stanley, 2000a, p. A10). It admitted to and decried the "intolerant methods and even violence in the service of the truth" and focused on historic as well as contemporary sins such as the disregard for the poor, apathy, and a failure to work strongly to defeat abortion (Stanley, 2000a, p. A10). The 31-page document did not attempt to account for all of the Catholic Church's past sins, and it tried to strike a balance and reassure Catholic leaders who were concerned that the emphasis on apologies had gone too far. It was unique in that it was an apology for which no critics or third-party experts were calling.

The ritualized apology was delivered in Rome on March 12, 2000, during a Lenten address that ended in a mass. It focused on forgiveness and reconciliation, a theme that had been woven into many of John Paul II's addresses during the preceding year. Such a theme is part of the Pontiff's overall legacy; there are references dating back to 1994 that acknowledged human rights abuses ("Pope Repeats an Apology," 1999).

The mass first began with a sermon in which the Pontiff made a number of apologies. Then, the heart of the mass took the form of a liturgy by which the

Cardinals of the Catholic Church offered a specific litany of sins, which was then followed by a papal response.

In his homily, the Holy Father situated the process of apologizing as part and parcel of everyday Christian confession:

> Before Christ, who for love bore our sins, we are all invited to a deep examination of conscience. One of the characteristic elements of the great jubilee lies in what I have described as purification of memory. As the successor of Peter, I ask that in this year of mercy, the church, strengthened by the holiness that she receives from her Lord, kneels before God and begs for forgiveness for past and present sins of her sons .... ("Excerpts From the Apology," 2000, p. A10)

Hence, although the act of the apology is on the surface dramatic and exceptional, the Holy Father argued that on another level it is representative of the self-examination required of all Christians. One dynamic, however, that made the act uncommon was the reference to the Jubilee. (The Pope had declared the year 2000 to be a Year of Jubilee.) The Jubilee, found in Leviticus 25 in the Hebrew Scriptures, was to be celebrated every 50 years. In it, the ancient Israelites were to celebrate a Sabbath of Sabbaths—after a period of seven Sabbaths. The point of the Jubilee was that all Israelites would return to their homeland, land would be returned to its original owners, slaves would be set free, and the poor would have their debts forgiven (hence, the Pope's emphasis during the year 2000 on debt relief for poor countries). The Catholic counterpart to this ritual occurs every 25 years and emphasizes repentance and the forgiveness of sins. In order to enter a new millennium with an emphasis on evangelization, the Pontiff concluded that this evangelism could be successful only if the Catholic Church confronted its sins and then offered an apology.

Because of this, the homily culminated with a stirring section that began with a direct strategy of mortification. John Paul II said, "We humbly ask forgiveness [because] we cannot not recognize the betrayal of the Gospel committed by some of our brothers, especially in the second millennium .... Recognizing the deviations of the past serves to reawaken our consciences to the compromises of the present" (Stanley, 2000b, p. 1). The Holy Father then apologized for the Catholic Church's social justice record, particularly as it concerned the poor, women, indigenous peoples, and specifically Jews.

The homily then addressed the sins committed during the Crusades and the Inquisition, although John Paul did not call them by name. He instead described the wrongdoing as sins committed during the "second millennium." He intoned:

> We forgive and we ask forgiveness! ... We cannot not recognize the betrayals
> of the Gospel committed by some of our brothers, especially during the sec-
> ond millennium. We ask forgiveness for the divisions between Christians, for
> the use of violence that some have resorted to in the service of truth and for
> the acts of dissidence and hostility sometimes taken towards followers of
> other religions. ("Excerpts From the Apology," 2000, p. A10)

He continued with a strategy of mortification, next drawing personal application: "For the part that each of us with our own behavior played in these
evils, contributing to stain the face of the church, we humbly ask for forgiveness" ("Excerpts From the Apology," p. A10). Then, in an allusion to the
Lord's Prayer (Matthew 6:9–13), he proclaimed forgiveness to others who
had sinned against Catholics, because forgiveness of one's sins compels
Christians to forgive the sins of others: "At the same time, as we confess our
sins, let us forgive the sins committed by others towards us" ("Excerpts From
the Apology," 2000, p. A10).

The homily culminated in a stirring liturgy delivered as part of the mass,
with the Pontiff flanked by seven cardinals and bishops who then recited a
litany of the sins of the church. One such category was sins that had been
committed against Jews. Cardinal Edward Cassidy confessed, "Let us pray
that, in recalling the sufferings endured by the people of Israel throughout
history, Christians will acknowledge the sins committed by not a few of their
number against the people of the Covenant and the blessings, and in this
way will purify their hearts" ("Excerpts From the Apology," 2000, p. A10).

The Holy Father responded:

> God of our fathers, you chose Abraham and his descendants to bring your
> name to the nations: We are deeply saddened by the behavior of those who
> in the course of history have caused these children of yours to suffer, and
> asking your forgiveness we wish to commit ourselves to genuine brotherhood
> with the people of the Covenant. We ask this though Christ our Lord. ("Ex-
> cerpts From the Apology," 2000, p. A10)

Cardinal Joseph Ratzinger continued with a confession for the methods
sometimes used by Catholics in their defense of the Catholic Church: "Let
us pray that each one of us, looking to the Lord Jesus, meek and humble of
heart, will recognize that even men of the church, in the name of faith and
morals, have sometimes used methods not in keeping with the Gospel in the
solemn duty of defending the truth" ("Excerpts From the Apology," 2000, p.
A10). John Paul II responded, "In certain periods of history, Christians have
at times given in to intolerance and have not been faithful to the great com-
mandment of love, sullying in this way the face of the Church ..." ("Excerpts
From the Apology," 2000, p. A10).

Cardinal Francis Arinze concluded the litany when he confessed that the Catholic Church's treatment of women has not always been ideal. He intoned, "Let us pray for women, who are all too often humiliated and marginalized, and let us acknowledge the forms of acquiescence in these sins of which Christians, too, have been guilty" ("Excerpts From the Apology," 2000, p. A10). To which the Pope replied, "Lord God ... at times the equality of your sons and daughters has not been acknowledged, and Christians have been guilty of attitudes of rejections and exclusion" ("Excerpts From the Apology," 2000, p. A10).

Overall, the reaction to the apology was positive. It marked another step in efforts to repair the Vatican's relationship with Israel. Others noted that the apology was unique among all religions, and there were few precedents for it, even in the Catholic Church (Steinfels, 2000). Because of this, one priest predicted it would "take years for the church to absorb it" (Stanley, 2000b, p. A10). Those who criticized the apology complained that it was disingenuous for the Catholic Church to acknowledge that its sons and daughters had sinned while it had not, although others faulted the apology for not being more explicit in naming its sins (Stanley, 2000b; Steinfels, 2000).

The apology delivered by Pope John Paul II was exemplary in almost every way. As such, it reached the highest standards of ethical communication. As it related to the manner of the apology, it was truthful. Although it did not go out of its way to name every particular sin committed by the Catholic Church over 2 millennia, as pointed out by its critics, it did nonetheless name some of those sins in such a way that it directly confronted its instances of major errors, thus addressing all stakeholders who have had a part in the Catholic Church's activities. The fact that the apology was integrated into an actual mass meant that it was performed in a highly appropriate and ritualized context, appropriate in that the central theme of any mass is one of reconciliation. Given the formality and gravity of the mass, the location also ensured that the apology came across as sincere. Particularly interesting, however, was the voluntary nature of the apology, in that no one had demanded nor expected one; this made the apology all the more compelling. In this way, it was an exemplary example of an institution that, through moral reflection, decided it must confront its guilt. Finally, the timeliness of the apologetic statements was noteworthy, in that they came in conjunction with a Year of Jubilee that had restoration as its fundamental theme.

As to the content of the apology, it is here where once again the apology met high ethical standards. The apology explicitly acknowledged wrongdoing perpetrated by Christians, and identified and sought reconciliation with injured stakeholders—Jews, women, and individuals injured in the spread of the Gospel. Although the apology and the larger apologetic context was exemplary, it must be pointed out that it did not disclose any new information related to the offenses, however much one might have reasonably expected it to, given the ongoing controversy concerning Pope Pius IX's actions during the Holocaust. Nor did the apology offer any form of corrective action to ensure that such abuses would not recur—although one might argue the apology itself would work to prevent abuses from reoccurring. Finally, the apology did not offer compensation to its victims, nor could it, because a unique feature of the apology was the fact that most of the victims of its wrongdoing had long since passed away.

## CONCLUSION

As demonstrated by the cases analyzed in this chapter, there are a number of important distinctions that differentiate institutional apologia from other forms of apologia, which, to reference Tavuchis (1991), is the many apologizing to the few. Time is different in institutional apologia in that it is much more structural than chronological—and appears to operate in a much larger frame. In dealing with institutional and governmental apologies, institutional apologists appear to be less likely to offer a quick apology to extricate themselves from a difficult situation; rather, they tend to apologize after the passage of time in which an institutionwide reflection and consensus is able to form, as well as the emergence of a constituency that will allow it. Whereas the *Greeneville* case resulted in a quick apology, the University of North Dakota case has taken decades of learning and reflection and is still unresolved, and the Roman Catholic Church took centuries to ask for forgiveness from Jews, women, and individuals injured in the spread of the gospel.

Another factor that distinguishes institutional apologia is that of source. Although it has been a truism from the beginnings of apologia studies that they can originate only from the one who committed the offense, a unique feature of institutional apologia is that they are more than likely to originate from sources other than those who committed the wrongdoing (Kruse, 1981a; Ryan, 1982). Said another way, the current head of an institution often apologizes for a sin committed on another head's watch.

A third factor particular to institutional apologia is that of constituency. Whereas in individual and corporate apologia the apology is directed to the victim or to the family of the victim, victims in institutional cases are much more broadly and imprecisely defined and, often, have long since passed away (Perrow, 1984). How does one, then, receive forgiveness for an abuse perpetrated centuries ago? If the victims are indeed dead, then the nature of the apology is indeed different and the institution that clothes its language in the discourse of forgiveness is actually seeking an outcome that is quite different. This again returns to one of the central claims of this book: Because the offense is in the territory of the social personae of an individual, organization, or institution, apologiae are secular remediation rituals that seek to alter the terms of the discourse. Institutional apologies, and most all apologies for that matter, have as their goal the public repair of a relationship not through forgiveness but instead via public acknowledgment. As a result, they end to be less driven by survival motives—to get out of an immediate jam—and much more driven by social motives—to be thought of positively by people or other groups (Kruse, 1977).

From these analyses, two additional conclusions are notable. First is the idea that *identity* is probably a more precise term than is *image* when it comes to institutions. This is because the term *image* suggests the flexible perceptions that publics hold about a particular company, whereas *identity* gets more at deeply rooted cultural themes that inhere within an organization or institution. In this way, *identity* more precisely arrives at what key publics and other observers believe an organization or institution to be in reality (Cheney & Vibbert, 1987).

Second, in the case of the Catholic Church apology, the fact that its victims had long since died raises the most interesting of questions relating to the nature of institutional apologies: How can an apology function in which those who perpetrated the abuse, as well as the victims on whom it was heaped, have long since passed away? In other words, the guilty are unable to offer an apology and there are no victims around to receive it. In effect, the real meaning of this sort of institutional apology is that the children, in effect, apologize for the sins of their fathers.

Such a move is reflective of the fact that, for an institution, the act of an apology is as much about the institution as it is about the victims, in that it goes directly to issues of organizational identity. It gives answers to such basic questions as to what does the organization *value*? Or what kind of culture should be present in an institution such as this? Indeed, in the case of the Papal apology, it is reflected in the earlier-noted statement that apology and reconciliation are among the most basic of Christian duties. In this way, perhaps even more than individual and corporate apologies, institutional apologies are responses to the needs and desires of constituencies to put it all on the public record—to take their private rituals of interpersonal communication and recast them as public and, indeed, secular remediation rituals.

# 8

## Conclusions

### Corporate Apologia, Ideology, and Ethical Responses to Criticism

> When the whole nation had finished crossing the Jordan, the LORD said to Joshua, "Choose twelve men from among the people, one from each tribe, and tell them to take up twelve stones from the middle of the Jordan from right where the priests stood and to carry them over with you and put them down at the place where you stay tonight."
>
> So Joshua called together the twelve men he had appointed from the Israelites, one from each tribe, and said to them, "Go over before the ark of the LORD your God into the middle of the Jordan. Each of you is to take up a stone on his shoulder, according to the number of the tribes of the Israelites, to serve as a sign among you. In the future, when your children ask you, 'What do these stones mean?' tell them that the flow of the Jordan was cut off before the ark of the covenant of the LORD. When it crossed the Jordan, the waters of the Jordan were cut off. These stones are to be a memorial to the people of Israel forever."
>
> Joshua 4:1–7 (*The Holy Bible*, 1973/1984)

Like this example from the book of Joshua, the text of the Hebrew Scriptures abounds with examples of the Children of Israel being required to remember, to write down the details of a critical event, or to make a memorial. Such an obligation is suggestive of a critical function of corporate apologia, which is the act of putting the details of the wrongdoing, and the subsequent organizational response, on the public record—making an organization's guilt and mortification a form of memorial for all to see (Phillips, 2004; Seeger et al., 2003).

## CORPORATE APOLOGIA
## AS COMPELLING MEMORIAL

The central purpose of this book has been to examine how individuals, organizations, and institutions seek to respond to criticism of an ethical nature. Consequently, it has argued that due to the multimediated environment in which we live and work, apologia, as a form of human exchange, has been critically transformed from a private matter to a public one, and from an exchange between individuals to a social matrix that includes companies and institutions. Such a transformation places a critical emphasis on the enactment of the apologia, in that an apologist must present a compelling performance, one that follows an acceptable public script and meets public expectations for an acceptable drama (Turner, 1982). This, of course, leads to the primary conclusion of this work: *Because a perceived offense is in the territory of the social identity of an individual or institution, apologiae are a form of secular remediation rituals—rituals that acknowledge wrongdoing and place it on the public record as a memorial. In so doing, they do not have as their desired outcome the forgiveness of the guilty party, but rather the exacting of a proportional humiliation by which to propitiate the wrongdoing. Socially, such acts function to restore faith in the social hierarchy by a discourse that praises the very values individuals and organizations are accused of having broken.*

Consider the examples surveyed here. The Catholic Church could not achieve forgiveness by issuing its apology, because the victims to whom it apologized had long since passed away. Similarly, Firestone and Ford as companies were unlikely to receive forgiveness for faulty products; instead, they sought a less hostile environment by which they might quickly and sufficiently settle liability claims against them. Nonetheless, by "being in the dock" and convincingly performing an apologia, corporate apologists reaffirm public social values, and the community can then move forward due to the recognition that such values have once again been affirmed as binding. Goffman (1971) made this same point when he wrote that the ritual of repair is such that the "virtual offender portrays his current relationship to rules, which his actions appear to have broken, and to persons present whose territories should have been protected by these rules" (p. 116). In other words, when companies or institutions engage in apologiae, they reaffirm the unceasing legitimacy of the standard they have violated.

The purpose of this final chapter, then, is to draw a number of interpretations that emanate from this position. In particular, this chapter is organized around five key conclusions that concern the characteristics of apologetic discourse in the 21st century: the implications of the increasingly corporate nature of apologia, the corrupting character of liability in the apologetic exchange, the critical role of ritual in completing a "successful" apologia, the value of an ethical approach to apologetic discourse, and, finally, the social function performed by contemporary apologiae.

## THE INCREASINGLY "CORPORATE" NATURE OF APOLOGIA

One of the troubling conclusions of this work is that discourse has become increasingly corporate in nature—with both meanings of the terms evident. Indeed, one of the tensions of this book has been to cover the full range of apologiae and apologies without featuring only corporate examples. Yet, even the noncorporate examples have been shown to reflect the shadow of organized persuasion.

### The Eponymous Nature of Discourse

Only modest amounts of the public discourse that is proffered is constructed by individuals (acting alone) anymore. Witness that from the three examples of individual apologiae analyzed: Bill Clinton, John Rocker, and Doris Kearns Goodwin (and there are countless other examples from which to draw). The idea of an individual apologist who tries to clear his or her name in a single speech has long since passed; the discourse from all three of these individuals constituted apologetic campaigns (Gold, 1978). Certainly in the case of President Clinton, he had a team of advisors and speechwriters who played a role in the crafting of his multiple apologiae and then his final apology. Yet, even in the other examples cited here, both were individuals who were surrounded by teams of advisors and lawyers who, in the case of John Rocker, had as their purpose the preservation of his image as well as that of the Atlanta Braves and major league baseball; or, in the case of Goodwin, produced a campaign that had as its objective the protection of the brand that Doris Kearns Goodwin has become. In this way, an apologia is a dramatic production that requires multiple players, is set on a mediated stage, with an actor who seeks to develop a compelling performance, and as a result follows a corporately written script that seeks to bring the drama to a compelling close. In some ways, apologetic address is the ultimate in reality programming.

### Economic Interests

But this "corporateness"—or acting together—has a second implication. In ways that William Whyte's (1956) famed "organizational man" could not have imagined, modern public discourse also has become increasingly corporate in the commercial sense (Crable, 1986; Sproule, 1988). It is embedded in institutions with large economic interests that traffic in advertisements and sound bites, and this corporate nature has inverted the public policy process to the point where public policy functions to serve corporate rather than human interests (Sproule, 1988). Subsequently, people have become increasingly eponymous; that is, they are defined by the institution of which they are members—witness the relative (lack of) success that an independent scholar achieves no matter how good his or her work is. Hence, "encouragement" for individuals and organizations to apologize is likely to come from the economic interests that individuals and institutions represent.

## Changing Ideas of Guilt and Responsibility

A third issue with the corporate nature of apologies is that it undercuts traditional conceptions of guilt and forgiveness. Corporations and institutions are sociopathic; they are incapable of emotion and feeling (Tavuchis, 1991). For them to then express remorse over their wrongdoing and subsequently issue an apology is a mockery of the idea. Furthermore, as this study has revealed, some of the guilt for which institutions are asking forgiveness are instances that occurred decades and even hundreds of years before. Such an apology cannot be meaningful for the victims. This means that public apologies no longer have as their goal forgiveness, but instead the repair of a public image through memorializing the wrong. These are but a few of the problematic implications of the progressively corporate nature of apologia.

## THE PROBLEM OF LIABILITY

## Managing Multiple Interests

The corporate nature of contemporary discourse is one that privileges economic interests. Hence, when an organization is criticized for its actions, the charge essentially claims that the organization's use of exchange power is unacceptable, because the institution—as evidenced by its acts, which are taken as representative of organizational attitudes—has not demonstrated congruence with public values. The difficulty in responding to such allegations, particularly if the criticisms are true, is that there are competing interests that must be served. In a phrase, an organization must manage multiple identities with publics that have incompatible interests (Cheney, 1991).

As noted earlier, in Marcus and Goodman' (1991) analysis of company statements after revelations of illegalities, accidents, and product safety incidents, the authors concluded that when corporations issued defensive statements (i.e., denials), the requisite effect on the price of its stock was positive; conversely, when they offered accommodative statements, investors tended to divest themselves of a company's stock out of liability concerns. Contrast this determination with the conclusions of Bradford and Garrett (1995), who discovered that consumers view responses that feature conciliation and compensation to be among the only ethical responses to allegations of wrongdoing. As such, the central tension in responding to criticism is the balance of stockholder and stakeholder interests. Said another way, a company that responds to criticism of its actions must maintain a careful balance between being socially responsive to its community and fiducially responsible to its investors (Epstein, 1972). The same is true of institutions—they must balance social with liability concerns; witness the recent splintered, insufficient response of the Catholic Church in America to the problem of clergy abuse. If any institution should respond out of concern and compassion, it is the Catholic Church, yet to respond too accommodatingly would bring with it almost incalculable liability costs. Because of this, the church leaders face a difficult, Hobson's choice.

## Tumultuous Legal Environment

Undeniably, the corporate nature of apologia has brought about huge concerns with liability. Chapter 3 addressed the turbulent nature of the contemporary legal environment and the poisonous role that liability concerns play in company strategy. Indeed, the case of Ford and Firestone highlights just how grave liability concerns, and the financial costs that surround them, can be.

Consider the following facts. First, with the emergence of "superlawyers" who specialize in large lawsuits against one company or industry, there has been the associated emergence of technical firms that appear on the surface to be oriented toward consumer advocacy (e.g., Safetyforum.com, Safetyresearch.net, Safetyfocus.net). Yet, on closer consideration, they are in actuality designed to locate injured parties who desire to sue as well as to assist attorneys in litigation against tire companies (Bradsher, 2000, 2000p; Hearit, 1996). Second, on the day after Firestone announced the recall of a large number of its truck tires, the American Trial Lawyers Association had formed a litigation unit in order to pursue lawsuits against the company (Deutsch, 2000).

Finally, and most chilling, according to Bradsher (2001h), trial attorneys knew earlier than governmental investigators that there was a problem with Firestone tires on Ford vehicles, yet they chose to do nothing about it. Indeed, evidence exists that attorneys discovered a problem with the tires as early as 1996 (Bradsher, 2001h). The motivation for not communicating the problem to federal officials was unabashedly financial, in that if federal investigators completed an investigation without finding a defect, attorneys would lose any chance to be successful in court (Bradsher, 2001h). Indeed, while trial attorneys were quietly initiating lawsuits against Ford and Firestone, at the same time they were able to keep "almost 2 dozen fatal crashes out of a federal database" (Bradsher, 2000i, p. 4-1). When pressed on this problem, Ralph Hoar, who owns Safetyforum.com, asserted that "lawyers had a responsibility to their clients, not regulators" (Bradsher, 2000i, p. A1).

## The New Apology

Such a difficult legal environment has changed the nature of the apology. Indeed, the problem of liability has led to one of the more interesting conclusions that make up this book: In a sense, compensation has become the new apology. That is, corporations, like Firestone, when faced with considerable evidence of wrongdoing, continue to hold to tenuous explanations that allow them to deny that they are culpable. Yet, in the same breath they offer both a "statement of concern or regret" and to pay large sums of money to settle an issue. Such liability concerns place companies in an ironic position in which they, in effect, claim that they did not do anything wrong, and yet promise never to do it again.

In this new form, the essence of the apology comes not in the actual words used to (not) apologize, but instead in the amount of money that is paid to the victims of corporate actions. This also functions as a form of proportional humiliation, whereby the amount of pain that an organization may have caused is directly tied to the sum of money that it has to pay. Benoit (1995) argued that such compensation functions as a form of bribery in which the company, in effect, pays for the problem to "go away." Although that may be one element of the process, the other dimension of compensation is that it functions as a form of "proportional humiliation" that is strikingly similar to the humbling process through which one has to go when apologizing (Courtright & Hearit, 2002; Tavuchis, 1991). Said another way, because the company has hurt victims, the payout to settle is its own form of suffering that the organization must endure. This is further proof of a change in the nature of apology, because historically the paying of restitution has not always been a part of the exchange.

Perhaps this position can be illustrated and supported best with an example. In April 2001, the attorney general of New York, Eliot Spitzer, led an investigation against Merrill Lynch, the vaunted Wall Street investment firm. The charge: Merrill Lynch had defrauded its customers—particularly individual investors, by publicly recommending that they buy certain stocks while privately, as revealed in damaging e-mails, its analysts called the stocks "dogs," "trash," and a "piece of sh_t" (N. Cohen,

2002, pp. 4–7). The purpose of such deception was to hold on to the lucrative investment banking fees generated by the issuers of these stocks, companies like pets.com, which would never turn a profit. Throughout the process, Merrill Lynch denied it had done anything wrong. Indeed, the firm finally chose to settle with the attorney general, paying a $100 million fine while not admitting to any wrongdoing (McGeehan, 2002). Cannot the willingness to settle and pay a $100 million fine be read as an admission of guilt?

Such a point brings an interesting conclusion. Due to fears of negative legal judgments, modern corporate officers offer weak statements of regret for organizational misdeeds without assuming responsibility (Hearit, 1994, 1995a). The assumption of responsibility occurs when organizations offer compensation to victims or assent to pay fines or restitution. Said another way, due to liability concerns, in the current form of contemporary apologetic speech, the acknowledgment of the wrongdoing comes not in the apology but instead in the compensation. Perhaps Attorney General Spitzer summed this up best when he said, "You don't pay a $100 million fine if you didn't do anything wrong" (McGeehan, 2002, p. A1).

## APOLOGIA AS RITUALIZED REAFFIRMATION OF PUBLIC VALUES

### The Role of Ritual

One of the primary points of this book is that apologiae are not just speeches of address to allegations of wrongdoing, but rather are a ritualistic form of communication. That is, there is a "process of correction" that individuals and organizations go through that has meaning for participants and auditors beyond just an instrumental level (Goffman, 1971, p. 100).

Drawing from the work of Rothenbuhler (1998), who defined *ritual* as "the voluntary performance of appropriately patterned behavior to symbolically effect or participate in the serious life" (p. 27), this study has found that six dimensions of ritual (discussed presently) are especially present in apologetic discourse. This is illustrated in the fact that apologiae typically are conducted in the realm of the sacred—the ceremony has a religious or priestly purpose to it, which the apologist enters into voluntarily. As such, apologiae both deliver content as well as perform the speech act of apologizing; they are cogent vehicles by which to handle offenses of the social personae. In this way, they are noninstrumental, in that they cogently accomplish complex communicative acts with meaning rooted in a complex social culture, and possess a reference to that culture.

## Relationship to "Successful" Apologia

The role of ritual has some interesting implications for what constitutes a "successful" apologia. By *successful*, I do not mean success in terms of the historic argument by rhetoricians about whether or not a speech had an "effect on an audience." Indeed, most apologia are characterized by their utter lack of success; they are a form of rhetoric that attempts to account for failure (Payne, 1989a, 1989b). To appreciate this idea of effectiveness, consider that the most famous apologia of all time—Socrates' apology for corrupting the youth of Athens—would have to be deemed a failure because he nevertheless was forced to drink the hemlock (*Plato's Apology of Socrates,* 1979).

Rather, a conceptualization of apologia as public ritual suggests a number of characteristics that constitute a successful apologia; that is, one that meets the generic expectations of the audience to whom it was directed. In particular, a successful apologia is characterized by six features. First, an effectively performed apologia gives guilt a plausible place to go. That explains why the three prototypical stances addressed in chapter 2 are so critical. Once guilt is created, it cannot just be left alone or ignored; it *has* to be propitiated. For a denial to be successful it has to be plausible that there is no offense or no guilt possessed by the social actor (and, hence, an alternative actor in which guilt can be located is likely to be required), just as for a differentiation strategy to be successful it has to be reasonable that the guilt is transferred to the place it "rightfully" belongs. Of course, to respond with an actual apology is to acknowledge the ethical offense and accept the guilt.

Second, a successful apologia is well performed. People need to look an apologist in the eye and make a critical judgment as to whether he or she "really meant it." If an apologist does not show the proper contrition or an appropriate respect for the process of discipline and correction, then an audience is less likely to be satisfied. This is why, for organizations and institutions, an apologia should be centered in the persona of a chief executive, and also why a full and complete follow-through is so critical; otherwise, there is no other easy means by which to ascertain the degree to which a company or institution "really meant it."

Third, a successful apologia must be voluntary in appearance. If it appears that the apologist chose to deliver an apology unwillingly or out of political necessity, then audiences are likely to find such an apology to be less than fitting. A voluntary apologia demonstrates that an offender has gone through an internal reflection process that has led to the conviction that what was done was wrong, or, at minimum, is worthy of an explanation. This explains why President Clinton's apology after his appearance before the grand jury was so unsatisfactory; it was evident from his performance that there was no contrition in his heart and that he apologized because his advisors had convinced him that he had a political problem.

Fourth, a successful apologia completes the drama by satisfying public expectations that the problem of guilt has been addressed and absolved. Said another way, an apologia must *conclude* the story. One cogent vehicle by which to judge the effectiveness of a defense is whether or not it has ended the escapade. A well-crafted apologia completes the guilt/forgiveness cycle and leaves the story with nowhere to go. If the apology is not full enough to provide a satisfactory end to the story, like Senator Trent Lott's for his remarks at Strom Thurmond's 100th birthday party, then it should not be given. The worst outcome an apologist can achieve is to fall into the trap of delivering a serial apologia—one right after another.

Fifth, a successful apologia demonstrates to all that the apologist adheres to the very values that said apologist is accused to have broken. Elsewhere, Hearit (1992, 1995a) demonstrated that apologiae tend to cluster around the values of honesty, responsibility, and self-control. In an effective apologia, an apologist reaffirms the nature of the social hierarchy by demonstrating adherence to those values (Burke, 1984). In this way, apologiae are a prosocial form of discourse that reaffirm faith in the existing social system.

Finally, a successful apologia is ethical. That is, it must be viewed by those who audit it that the course of action taken by the apologist constitutes ethical decision making. If the action is not seen as an ethical response, it will leave auditors less than satisfied, and subsequently it will not successfully complete the guilt/resolution cycle.

## ETHICAL ISSUES

### Ideological Motifs

The case studies presented here as well as other analyses (Hearit, 1995a) reveal the existence of a set of twin myths that inhere in apologetic speech. The first is a myth of a technological fix; that is, with technology there are always ways by which to develop complex technological solutions to those problems caused by human action. This myth provides technology with a redemptive energy; it conceptualizes technology as a resource that can be mobilized to solve social problems, not just technical ones (Brown & Crable, 1973; Marx, 1964). The logic behind a technological fix is that innovation can provide solutions to current social and technical problems, and subtly move the argumentative discussion from a public sphere to a technical one, which privileges a corporate position (Boyd, 2002; Goodnight, 1982). In the Ford versus Firestone exchange, for instance, one solution to the problem was the installation of in-car tire pressure monitoring devices. Other examples referenced in this book bear this out. In the case of the Exxon *Valdez* oil spill, Exxon officials tried to use a chemical dispersant, COREXIT 9527, to break apart the oil. Similarly, in the 1990s Domino's sought to "solve" the problem of unsafe pizza delivery with the development of high-powered ovens that could bake a pizza in 12 minutes or less, which was accompanied by the claim "the speed is in the store" (Hearit, 1995a). In this way, technology is positioned to fulfill the role of the archetypal Adam who marshals technological resources in an effort to restore the despoiled Garden to its pristine state (Brown & Crable, 1973).

A second myth present in apologetic discourse is that of managerial rationality. Meyer (1983) argued that when companies operate in a difficult and unpredictable environment, rituals that affirm organizational rationality and control become even more important. As shown in this book, the ritualistic nature of apologia, especially when coupled with carefully articulated corrective action strategies, functions to reassure key stakeholders that corporations and institutions have learned from their wrongdoing and that a reoccurrence of ethical misconduct is improbable.

This promise that an organization has "learned" from its misconduct draws on a myth of managerial rationality. The apologiae reviewed throughout this work—such as those from the American Red Cross, the Catholic Church, the Bush administration, and the U.S. Navy—reveal organizations and institutions that construct social personae in which they "reflect" in a rational manner. As a result, the organizations and institutions present evidence that they have reformed their internal structures and policies to limit any chance of future wrongdoing. Managerial rationality, according to Meyer, is rooted not in "substantive properties" but rather in "attending to ritual ones" (p. 220). Hence, organizational actions that give the impression of restructuring the corporate system of governance are not strategic business decisions but instead are political ones. Such moves by institutions are both based on and also confirm the belief that the villain can be rehabilitated, compensation can be paid, and the environment can be fixed. When these conditions are met, the curtain can be dropped on the performance, critics can judge the performance compelling, and the audience can go home (Hearit, 1995a).

Such a myth of managerial rationality is persuasive rhetorically because it suggests that corporate giants can be reformed. This painful instruction and correction comes at the hand of consumers in the form of social sanction, in which they picket, cut up their credit cards, refuse to patronize a business, or exert any other form of social sanction. The organization then acquiesces to this social judgment in order to demonstrate that it has "learned" from its wrongdoing.

## The Development of What Constitutes an Ethical Apologia

The successful use by corporations and institutions of these ideological motifs raises critical questions as to whether such organizations are able to deliver ethical apologiae. One of the critical contributions of this book is the development of an ethical approach to accompany the study of apologia in order to address this problem.

Rather than dealing with ethical communication theories designed for everyday types of situations, or attempting to apply general ethical theory to apologetic situations, this analysis has developed an ethic specific to the apologetic context, one that does not focus on the (lack of) ethics of the act that precipitated the apologia, but instead looks at the ethics of the communication exchange after an individual, organization, or institution has committed a particular offense. In particular, this study has asserted that the use of casuistry offers a great deal of insight into the ethics of apologetic speech, both in its form and content.

Specifically, in terms of the form of apologetic discourse, when an offense has been committed an ethical apologia must meet criteria of truthfulness, sincerity, timeliness, and voluntariness; address all moral claimants; and be performed in an appropriate context. As to its content, for an apologia to be ethically ideal it must fully acknowledge wrongdoing, accept responsibility, express remorse and regret, identify with injured parties, ask for forgiveness and seek reconciliation, fully disclose information, provide full explanations, articulate corrective action to be performed, and offer compensation to victims when appropriate.

The value of casuistry is that it offers a standard by which such acts can be judged. That is not to say that an act has to meet every last criteria of the paradigm case for it to be considered an ethical apologia. Indeed, this theory as it is articulated suggests that it is possible to construct an ethically ideal case (e.g., the Papal apology), an ethically acceptable case (as evidenced by Ford's apologia), and an ethically unacceptable case (the many examples in chapters 5, 6, and 7 that do not meet basic ethical benchmarks). Further research needs to be conducted to flesh out more precise determinations of what specifically constitutes an ethically ideal and ethically acceptable case.

In addition, casuistry theory does recognize the presence of complicating circumstances that affect what an organization can and should say in its apologetic speech; in this way, in assessing the ethics of communication after the bad behavior, casuistry theory does provide some ethical flexibility that might legitimately warrant departures from the idea of this variegated form of discourse. This analysis has suggested that a number of potential caveats are present, such as grave liability expenses, catastrophic financial penalties, and the nature of the relationship with injured parties. For instance, in the Wall Street scandal of 2001, in which evidence came to the fore of clear conflicts of interests between the analytic and the brokerage function of major New York financial firms, the wrongdoing was such that entire firms could have been shuttered; such a move would have resulted not just in considerable pain to the employees and company stockholders, but it also would have negatively affected the leadership of the United States in the financial services industry (Morgenson & McGeehan, 2002). The use of casuistry allows for the critic to take a complicating factor into consideration and acknowledge that such factors may indeed allow for communication that deviates from the ethical ideal.

## The Reconciliation of the Ethical and the Legal

But how does one reconcile the fear of liability and legitimate liability concerns with the desire to act ethically? Some researchers have observed or proposed, as a potential solution, a nonapology apology (Cohen, 1999; Hearit, 1994; Patel & Reinsch, 2003). In this form of discourse, an organization or institution caught in a wrong releases a statement in which it expresses sympathy or sorrow that harm has occurred but is linguistically careful not to assume responsibility or culpability. In fact, much of the program of J. R. Cohen (1999, 2002) seeks to articulate, from a legal perspective, how to apologize without assuming guilt before the law.

A more precise and ethically defensible position exists in which organizations and institutions can communicate in an ethical manner without incurring legal liability. To do so, they must separate their public discourse from their private discourse. In effect, to handle public relations concerns, an organization should demonstrate sorrow for the act and sympathy for the victims, even as it articulates corrective action strategies that it will implement to prevent future problems from reoccurring.

Subsequently, the public apologetic statement of concern should be followed up privately with a one-to-one apology, particularly in the context of a mediation environment designed to provide appropriate and just compensation to the victim (Cohen, 1999). In addition to avoiding the incurrence of general legal liability, such a stance also has the salutary effect of respecting the privacy of the victim(s). In this way, the apology counteracts the trend documented in this book and moves the preferred form of discourse from a many-to-many exchange to a many-to-one exchange, and turns a public exchange back into a private one that can then bring about reconciliation between the offender and the victim(s).

### APOLOGIA AND SOCIAL FUNCTION

This reaffirmation of social values arrives at the critical social function that apologiae perform. Burke maintained that advertisers are part of the elite of society who function in a priestly role, that of upholding and partly transcending the mysteries of class (Burke, 1984). When an organization or institution uses advertisements to assert its social legitimacy, it fulfills a priestly role through the justification of its current hierarchical position in the economic order and the legitimacy of the existing order itself.

A hierarchy is a system that guides the process of social relations; it "binds people together in a system of rights and obligations" (Brummett, 1981, p. 254). Capitalism is an economic system warranting that social relationships be based on principles of private property and capital. Within this hierarchy, "mystery" manifests itself between classes and professions and, in the process, allows for significant inequalities to exist within this economic system, even though this economic system is situated in a political system that specifies equality for all (Burke, 1984).

When an organization engages in wrongdoing, it violates the spirit of the hierarchy; the result is disorder. That is, an organization has exposed some of the mystery between social classes. In apologetic situations, the violation is quite overt (Brummett, 1981). This violation of the hierarchy results in guilt: the symbolic rupture of the identifications that allow the organization to establish claims of social legitimacy (Burke, 1984).

Through strategies of denial, scapegoating, or mortification—as explicated in chapters 5, 6, and 7—individuals, corporations, and institutions use discourse to purge themselves of guilt. As noted in chapter 2, in one sense, the *entrance* of an organization into the public confessional is more important than what the organization *says* once there; that is, the act of the confession signifies the organization's reacceptance of the current hierarchy. After an organization reaffirms its adherence to the social order and the values it was reputed to have broken, mystery and hierarchy may be restored; the apologetic discourse, then, functions to complete the order/guilt/redemption cycle. In so doing, an apologia performs a social action—it reaffirms the mystery of the hierarchy (Miller, 1984).

When an organization reaffirms its adherence to public values, it also reaffirms its acceptance of the current economic order. As Habermas (1975) noted, capitalism regularly faces crises of legitimacy (1979). Apologetic situations—such as those involving Enron, WorldCom, and Tyco—call into crisis the legitimacy of the system as a whole because they raise questions as to how an economic system can impel its participants to make choices between profit and negative social and environmental costs. In this way, corporate apologiae—attempts by organizations to redemonstrate their social legitimacy—perform a vital social function because they not only reaffirm the social legitimacy of organizations but also restore the legitimacy of capitalism as the current economic order. Burke (1984) noted as much when he wrote:

> Insofar as all complex social order will necessarily be grounded in some kind of property structure [i.e., capitalism], and insofar as all such order in its divisive aspects makes for the kind of social malaise which theologians would explain in terms of "original sin," is it possible that rituals of victimage are the "natural" means for affirming the principle of social cohesion above the principle of social division? (p. 286)

Thus, individuals, organizations, and institutions utilize apologiae as a natural way to restore their social legitimacy and acquiescence to the private property system known as *capitalism*.

# References

2 more bodies recovered from vessel hit by U.S. submarine. (2001, October 21). *The New York Times*, p. 1A.

A $100-million donor's ultimatum. (2001, February 23). *The Chronicle of Higher Education*, p. A47.

Abercrombie & Fitch. (1999, November 19). (Available from Attorney General, Consumer Protection Division, P. O. Box 30213, Lansing, MI 48909).

Abramson, J. (1998, August 18). Testing of a president: The first lady; still playing a key role on a most painful day. *The New York Times*, p. A15.

Adamson, J. (2000). *The Denny's story: How a company in crisis resurrected its good name and reputation*. New York: Wiley.

Albrecht, S. (1996). *Crisis management for self defense*. New York: AMACOM.

Ambrose, S. E. (2001). *The wild blue: Men and boys who flew B-24s over Germany 1944–45*. New York: Simon & Schuster.

Angell, M. (1996). *Science on trial: The clash of medical evidence and the law in the breast implant case*. New York: Norton.

Apple, R. W., Jr. (1999, January 22). The trial of the president: The defense—in the chamber; Clinton defense concludes by weighing admitted sins against good of the nation. *The New York Times*, p. A1.

Applebome, P. (2002, December 22). The nation; what did we just learn? *The New York Times*, p. 4-3.

Araton, H. (1999, December 26). Sports of the *Times*; John Rocker's persona and "corporate synergy." *The New York Times*, p. 8-2.

Araton, H. (2000, March 3). Sports of the *Times*; the pitcher faces toughest critics; Braves teammates. *The New York Times*, p. D1.

Arras, J. (1993). Thinking about hard cases: Lessons from Baby Johnson. *Ethically Speaking, 2*(1), 1–3.

Austin, J. L. (1979). A plea for excuses. In J. O. Urmson & G. J. Warnock (Eds.), *Philosophical papers* (pp. 123–152). Oxford, UK: Clarendon.

Banks, D. (1993). Tribal names and mascots in sports. *Journal of Sport and Social Issues, 17*(1), 5–8.

Barboza, D. (2000a, August 15). Workers question evidence in tire recall. *The New York Times*, p. C6.

Barboza, D. (2000b, September 15). Firestone workers cite lax quality control. *The New York Times*, p. C5.

Barboza, D. (2001c, May 25). Firestone's revival strategy: Be contrite and attack Ford. *The New York Times*, p. C2.

Barboza, D. (2001d, June 28). Bridgestone/Firestone to close tire plant at center of huge recall. *The New York Times*, p. C1.

Barkan, E. (2000). *The guilt of nations: Restitution and negotiating historical injustices.* New York: Norton.

Barney, R., & Black, J. (1994). Ethics and professional persuasive communications. *Public Relations Review, 20,* 233–248.

Barstow, D. (2001, November 7). In Congress, harsh words for Red Cross. *The New York Times,* pp. B1, B7.

Barstow, D., & Seelye, K. Q. (2001, October 31). Red Cross halts collections for terror victims. *The New York Times,* p. B11.

Barton, L. (1993). *Crises in organizations: Managing and communicating in the heat of chaos.* Cincinnati: South-Western.

Baskin, O. W., & Aronoff, C. E. (1988). *Public relations: The profession and the practice* (2nd ed.). Dubuque, IA: William C. Brown.

Batulis, A. P. (1976). Congress, the president, and the press. *Journalism Quarterly, 53,* 509–515.

Bauman, R. (1989). Performance. In E. Barnouw (Ed.), *International encyclopedia of communications* (Vol. 3, pp. 262–266). New York: Oxford University Press.

Beam, A. (2002, August 15). Goodwin on borrowed tome again? *Boston Globe,* p. C13.

Belkin, L. (2002, December 8). Just money. *The New York Times Magazine,* pp. 92–97, 122, 148–149.

Beniger, J. R., & Westney, D. E. (1981). Japanese and U.S. media: Graphics as a reflection of newspapers' social roles. *Journal of Communication, 31,* 14–27.

Bennet, J. (1998, September 10). Testing of a president: The president; president appeals to Democrats with pleas for their forgiveness. *The New York Times,* p. A1.

Bennet, J., & Broder, J. M. (1999, February 13). The president's acquittal: The White House; president says he is sorry and seeks reconciliation. *The New York Times,* p. A1.

Bennet, J., & Van Natta, D., Jr. (1998, August 4). Calls for Clinton to confess affair are turned aside. *The New York Times,* p. A1.

Bennett, M., & Dewberry, C. (1994). "I've said I'm sorry, haven't I?" A study of the identity implication and constraints that apologies create for their recipients. *Current Psychology, 13(1),* 10–21.

Benoit, W. L. (1995). *Accounts, excuses, and apologies: A theory of image restoration strategies.* Albany: State University of New York Press.

Benoit, W. L. (2000). Another visit to the theory of image restoration strategies. *Communication Quarterly, 48,* 40–43.

Benoit, W. L., & Brinson, S. L. (1994). AT&T: Apologies are not enough. *Communication Quarterly, 42,* 75–88.

Benoit, W. L., & Dorries, B. (1996). *Dateline NBC's* persuasive attack on Wal-Mart. *Communication Quarterly, 44,* 463–477.

Benoit, W. L., Gullifor, P., & Panici, D. A. (1991). Reagan's discourse on the Iran–Contra affair. *Communication Studies, 42,* 272–294.

Benoit, W. L., & Lindsey, J. J. (1987). Argument strategies: Antidote to Tylenol's poisoned image. *Journal of the American Forensic Association, 23,* 136–146.

Benson, J. A. (1988). Crisis revisited: An analysis of strategies used by Tylenol in the second tampering episode. *Central States Speech Journal, 39,* 49–66.

Berg, D., & Robb, S. (1992). Crisis management and the "paradigm case." In E. L. Toth & R. L. Heath (Eds.), *Rhetorical and critical approaches to public relations* (pp. 97–105). Hillsdale, NJ: Lawrence Erlbaum Associates.

Berger, P., & Luckmann, T. (1967). *The social construction of reality.* New York: Anchor.

Berke, R. L. (1998, August 14). President weighs admitting he had sexual contacts. *The New York Times,* p. A1.

Berke, R. L., & Van Natta, D., Jr. (1998, August 18). Testing of a president: The friends; one by one, the president told his closest aides the painful truth. *The New York Times,* p. A1.

Billings, R. S., Milburn, T. W., & Schaalman, M. L. (1980). A model of crisis perception: A theoretical and empirical analysis. *Administrative Science Quarterly, 25,* 300–316.

Bird, S. E., & Dardenne, R. W. (1988). Myth, chronicle, and story: Exploring the narrative qualities of news. In J. W. Carey (Ed.), *Media, myths, and narratives: Television and the press* (pp. 67–86). Newbury Park, CA: Sage.

Bitzer, L. (1968). The rhetorical situation. *Philosophy & Rhetoric, 1,* 1–14.

Black, E. (1970). The second persona. *Quarterly Journal of Speech, 56,* 109–119.

Blair, J. (2000, August 11). Tire recall brings some panic and a large need for patience. *The New York Times,* p. C1.

Blaney, J. R., & Benoit, W. L. (2001). *The Clinton scandals and the politics of image restoration.* Westport, CT: Praeger.

Blaney, J. R., Benoit, W. L., & Brazeal, L. M. (2002). Blowout! Firestone's image restoration campaign. *Public Relations Review, 28,* 379–392.

Boeyink, D. E. (1992). Casuistry: A case-based method for journalists. *Journal of Mass Media Ethics, 7*(2), 107–120.

Bok, S. (1989). *Lying: Moral choice in public and private life.* New York: Vintage.

Boorstin, D. J. (1961). *The image: A guide to pseudo-events in America.* New York: Atheneum.

Borden, S. L. (1995). Gotcha! Deciding when sources are fair game. *Journal of Mass Media Ethics, 10*(4), 223–235.

Borden, S. L. (1999). Character as a safeguard for journalists using case-based ethical reasoning. *International Journal of Applied Philosophy, 13*(1), 93–104.

Borden, S. L. (2002). Janet Cooke in hindsight: Reconsideration of a paradigmatic case in journalism ethics. *Journal of Communication Inquiry, 26*(2), 155–170.

Bostdorff, D. M., & Vibbert, S. L. (1994). Values advocacy: Enhancing organizational images, deflecting public criticism, and grounding future arguments. *Public Relations Review, 20,* 141–158.

Botan, C. (1997). Ethics in strategic communication campaigns: The case for a new approach to public relations. *Journal of Business Communication, 34,* 188–202.

Boulding, K. E. (1956). *The image.* Ann Arbor: University of Michigan Press.

Boulding, K. E. (1978). The legitimacy of the business institution. In E. E. Epstein & D. Votaw (Eds.), *Rationality, legitimacy, responsibility: Search for new directions in business and society* (pp. 83–98). Santa Monica, CA: Goodyear.

Bowen, S. A. (2004). Expansion of ethics as the tenth generic principle of public relations excellence: A Kantian theory and model for managing ethical issues. *Journal of Public Relations Research, 16*(1), 65–92.

Boyd, J. (2000). Actional legitimation: No crisis necessary. *Journal of Public Relations Research, 12,* 341–353.

Boyd, J. (2002). Public and technical interdependence: Regulatory controversy, out-law discourse, and the messy case of olestra. *Argumentation and Advocacy, 39,* 91–109.

Brabant, M. (2001, April 14). McDonald's pays over pickle. *BBC.* Retrieved February 7, 2004 from http://news.bbc.co.uk/go/em/fr/-/1/hi/world/americas/1276819.stm

Bradford, J. L., & Garrett, D. E. (1995). The effectiveness of corporate communicative responses to accusations of unethical behavior. *Journal of Business Ethics, 14,* 875–892.

Bradsher, K. (2000a, August 14). Ford says Firestone was aware of flaw in its tires by 1997. *The New York Times,* p. A1.

Bradsher, K. (2000b, August 15). Tire company is encouraged to broaden recall plans. *The New York Times,* pp. C1, C6.

Bradsher, K. (2000c, August 16). Tire deaths are linked to rollovers. *The New York Times,* pp. C1, C21.

Bradsher, K. (2000d, August 25). Ford attacks the lawyers pursuing suits over tires. *The New York Times,* p. C6.

Bradsher, K. (2000e, September 1). Firestone struggles in center of an ever-widening storm. *The New York Times,* pp. A1, C5.

Bradsher, K. (2000f, September 2). Warning issued on more tires from Firestone. *The New York Times,* p. A1.

Bradsher, K. (2000g, September 11). Documents portray tire debacle as a story of lost opportunities. *The New York Times,* p. A1.

Bradsher, K. (2000h, September 15). Ford chairman speaks out on tires for the first time. *The New York Times,* p. C5.

Bradsher, K. (2000i, September 17). Ideas and trends: Don't tread on me; a road to truth paved with fingerpointing. *The New York Times,* p. 4-1.

Bradsher, K. (2000j, September 19). Auto industry may ease safety-ratings stance. *The New York Times,* p. C16.

Bradsher, K. (2000k, September 20). More deaths attributed to faulty Firestone tires. *The New York Times,* p. C2.

Bradsher, K. (2000l, September 23). Ford raises recommended tire pressure. *The New York Times,* p. C1.

Bradsher, K. (2000m, September 29). Firestone uneasy over threatened changes. *The New York Times,* p. C6.

Bradsher, K. (2000n, September 30). A 2nd front in the inquiry into Firestone. *The New York Times,* p. C1.

Bradsher, K. (2000o, October 2). 2 Firestone studies in 1999 pointed to tire problems. *The New York Times,* p. A25.

Bradsher, K. (2000p, November 22). U.S. safety panel begins inquiry on Goodyear tires. *The New York Times,* p. C5.

Bradsher, K. (2000q, December 15). Firestone and Ford make progress on tire inquiries. *The New York Times,* p. C4.

Bradsher, K. (2000r, December 19). Firestone engineers offer a list of causes for faulty tires. *The New York Times,* pp. C1, C6.

Bradsher, K. (2001a, April 5). The media business: Advertising; 2 approaches to aftermath of tire recall. *The New York Times,* pp. C1, C7.

Bradsher, K. (2001b, May 18). Ford is said to consider seeking recalls of more tires. *The New York Times,* p. C13.

Bradsher, K. (2001c, May 19). Bridgestone disputes need for bigger Firestone recall. *The New York Times,* p. C2.

Bradsher, K. (2001d, May 22). Firestone to stop sales to Ford, saying it was used as scapegoat. *The New York Times,* pp. A1, C4.

Bradsher, K. (2001e, May 23). Ford intends to replace 13 million Firestone Wilderness tires. *The New York Times,* pp. C1, C4.

Bradsher, K. (2001f, June 1). Firestone asks U.S. to study Ford Explorer. *The New York Times,* pp. C1, C8.

Bradsher, K. (2001g, June 15). Ford has harsher words for latest recalled tires. *The New York Times,* p. C4.

Bradsher, K. (2001h, June 24). S.U.V. tire defects were known in '96 but not reported. *The New York Times,* p. 1.

Bradsher, K. (2001i, July 4). Ford wants to send drivers of sport utility vehicles back to school. *The New York Times,* p. A9.

Bradsher, K., & Wald, M. L. (2000, September 7). More indications hazards of tires were long known. *The New York Times,* pp. A1, C8.

Braves recall Rocker from minor leagues. (2000, June 14). *The New York Times,* p. D7.

Bridgestone cuts earnings forecast 81%. (2000, December 14). *The New York Times,* p. C9.

Brinson, S. L., & Benoit, W. L. (1996). Attempting to restore a public image: Dow Corning and the breast implant crisis. *Communication Quarterly, 44,* 29–41.

Brinson, S. L., & Benoit, W. L. (1999). The tarnished star: Restoring Texaco's damaged public image. *Management Communication Quarterly, 12,* 483–510.

Broder, J. M. (1998a, February 7). Testing of a president: The overview; Clinton rules out any consideration of stepping down. *The New York Times,* pp. A1, A8.

Broder, J. M. (1998b, September 3). Testing of a president: In Moscow; Clinton defends his tv admission on Lewinsky case. *The New York Times,* p. A1.

Broder, J. M. (1998c, September 5). Clinton says he is "very sorry" after senator's harsh criticism. *The New York Times,* p. A1.

Broder, J. M., & Van Natta, D., Jr. (1998, September 12). Testing of a president: The overview; Starr finds a case for impeachment in perjury, obstruction, tampering. *The New York Times,* p. A1.

Brooke, J. (2004, August 10). Four workers killed in nuclear plant accident in Japan. *The New York Times,* p. A3.

Brooks, R. L. (Ed.). (1999). *When sorry isn't enough: The controversy over apologies and reparations for human injustice.* New York: New York University Press.

Brown, G. (1991). Jerry Falwell and the PTL: The rhetoric of apologia. *Journal of Communication and Religion, 14,* 9–18.

Brown, W. R., & Crable, R. E. (1973). Industry, mass magazines, and the ecology issue. *Quarterly Journal of Speech, 59,* 259–272.

Browning, L., (2003, January 12). Class-action suits mean delays and, maybe, cash. *The New York Times,* s. 3, p. 9.

Brownstein, A. (2001, February 23). A battle over a name in the land of the Sioux. *The Chronicle of Higher Education,* pp. A46–A49.

Brummett, B. (1980). Towards a theory of silence as a political strategy. *Quarterly Journal of Speech, 66,* 289–303.

Brummett, B. (1981). Burkean scapegoating, mortification, and transcendence in presidential campaign rhetoric. *Central States Speech Journal, 32,* 254–264.

Burke, K. (1961). *Attitudes toward history.* Berkeley: University of California Press.

Burke, K. (1966). *Language as symbolic action: Essays on life, literature, method.* Berkeley: University of California Press.

Burke, K. (1969). *A grammar of motives.* Berkeley: University of California Press.

Burke, K. (1970). *The rhetoric of religion: Studies in logology.* Berkeley: University of California Press.

Burke, K. (1973). *The philosophy of literary form* (3rd ed.). Berkeley: University of California Press.

Burke, K. (1984). *Permanence and change: An anatomy of purpose* (3rd ed.). Berkeley: University of California Press.

Burkholder, T. R. (1990). Symbolic martyrdom: The ultimate apology. *Southern Communication Journal, 56,* 289–297.

Burns, J. P., & Bruner, M. S. (2000). Revisiting the theory of image restoration strategies. *Communication Quarterly, 48,* 27–39.

Burrough, B., & Helyar, J. (1990). *Barbarians at the gate.* New York: Harper & Row.

Butler, S. D. (1971). The apologia, 1971 genre. *Southern Speech Communication Journal, 37,* 281–289.

Campbell, R. (1991). *60 Minutes and the news.* Urbana: University of Illinois Press.

Canada says sorry to Indians, Inuits. (1998, January 8). *The Detroit News,* p. A4.

Charles, J., Shore, T., & Todd, K. (1979). The New York Times coverage of Equatorial and Lower Africa. *Journal of Communication, 29,* 148–155.

Chass, M. (1999, December 24). Baseball; remarks could hurt Rocker most of all. *The New York Times,* p. D1.

Chass, M. (2000a, February 1). Baseball; baseball suspends Rocker till May for comments. *The New York Times,* p. A1.

Chass, M. (2000b, March 2). Baseball; Rocker permitted to attend camp, to Selig's dismay. *The New York Times,* p. D1.

Chass, M. (2000c, March 15). Baseball; it's a security alert: "Rocker's pitching." *The New York Times,* p. D4.

Chass, M. (2000d, June 6). Baseball; Rocker demoted a day after outburst. *The New York Times,* p. D1.

Chass, M. (2000e, June 22). Baseball; Rocker's subway ride creates security headaches. *The New York Times,* p. D2.

Chass, M. (2000f, July 3). Baseball; showdown comes to a quiet finish as Rocker and Shea fans behave. *The New York Times,* p. D5.

Cheney, G. (1991). *Rhetoric in an organizational society: Managing multiple Identities.* Columbia: University of South Carolina Press.

Cheney, G. (1992). The corporate person (re)presents itself. In E. L. Toth & R. L. Heath (Eds.), *Rhetorical and critical approaches to public relations* (pp. 165–183). Hillsdale, NJ: Lawrence Erlbaum Associates.

Cheney, G., & Vibbert, S. L. (1987). Corporate discourse: Public relations and issue management. In F. Jablin, L. Putnam, K. Roberts, & L. Porter (Eds.), *Handbook of organizational communication: An interdisciplinary approach* (pp. 165–194). Newbury Park: Sage.

Childer, T. (1996). *Wings of morning.* Cambridge, MA: Perseus.

Chin, T., Naidu, S., Ringel, J., & Snipes, W. (1998). Denny's: Communication amidst a discrimination case. *Business Communication Quarterly, 61,* 180–197.

Clines, F. X., & Gerth, J. (1998, January 22). The president under fire: The overview; subpoenas sent as Clinton denies reports of an affair with aide at White House. *The New York Times,* p. A1.

Cohen, J. R. (1999, May). Advising clients to apologize. *Southern California Law Review, 72,* 1009–1069.

Cohen, J. R. (2002, Spring). Legislating apology: The pros and cons. *University of Cincinnati Law Review, 70,* 819–872.

Cohen, N. (2002, May 5). Word for word/mixed messages; swimming with stock analysts, or sell low asnd buy high … enthusiastically. *The New York Times,* p. 4-7.

Coleman, J. S. (1974). *Power and the structure of society.* New York: Norton.

Connolly, M. R. (2000). What in a name? A historical look at Native American related nicknames and symbols at three U.S. universities. *Journal of Higher Education, 71*(5), 515–547.

Coombs, W. T. (1995). Choosing the right words: The development of guidelines for the selection of the "appropriate" crisis-response strategies. *Management Communication Quarterly, 8*, 447–476.

Coombs, W. T. (1998). An analytic framework for crisis situations: Better responses from a better understanding of the situation. *Journal of Public Relations Research, 10*(3), 177–191.

Coombs, W. T. (1999). *Ongoing crisis communication.* Thousand Oaks, CA: Sage.

Coombs, W. T. (2004). Impact of past crises on current crisis communication: Insights from situational crisis communication theory. *Journal of Business Communication, 41*, 265–289.

Coombs, W. T., & Holladay, S. J. (2002). Helping crisis managers protect reputational assets: Initial tests of the situational crisis communication theory. *Management Communication Quarterly, 16*, 165–186.

Coombs, W. T., & Schmidt, L. (2002). An empirical analysis of image restoration: Texaco's racism crisis. *Journal of Public Relations Research, 12*, 163–178.

Cooper, D. A. (1992). CEO must weigh legal and public relations approaches. *Public Relations Journal, 48*, 40, 39.

Corder, M. (1999, August 26). Aussies face key tests on Aborigine issue. *Kalamazoo Gazette*, p. A3.

Courtright, J. L., & Hearit, K. M. (2002). The good organization speaking well: A paradigm case for religious institutional crisis management. *Public Relations Review, 28*, 347–360.

Cox, J. R. (1981). Argument and the "definition of the situation." *Central States Speech Journal, 32*, 197–205.

Crable, R. E. (1986). The organizational "system" of rhetoric: The influence of *Megatrends* into the twenty-first century. In L. W. Hugenberg (Ed.), *Rhetorical studies honoring James L. Golden* (pp. 57–68). Dubuque, IA: Kendall/Hunt.

Crable, R. E. (1990). "Organizational rhetoric" as the fourth great system: Theoretical, critical and pragmatic implications. *Journal of Applied Communication Research, 18*, 115–128.

Crable, R. E., & Vibbert, S. L. (1985). Managing issues and influencing public policy. *Public Relations Review, 11*, 3–16.

Crable, R. E., & Vibbert, S. L. (1986). *Public relations as communication management.* Edina, MN: Bellwether.

Crader, B. (2002, January 28). A historian and her sources. *The Weekly Standard*, pp. 12–13.

Criticism of A & F catalog spreads. (1999, December 7). *Associated Press*, n.p. Retrieved November 11, 2000 from Lexis/Nexis database.

Curry, J. (2000a, January 7). Baseball; baseball orders tests for Rocker. *The New York Times*, p. D1.

Curry, J. (2000b, January 8). Baseball; Rocker agrees to undergo testing immediately. *The New York Times*, p. D1.

Curry, J. (2000c, January 14). On baseball; Rocker is off base in ESPN interview. *The New York Times*, p. D3.

Curry, J. (2000d, March 2). Baseball; at Braves' complex, the circus is in town. *The New York Times*, p. D3.

Curry, J. (2000e, March 3). Baseball; Rocker returns, and the reaction is ... polite. *The New York Times,* p. D1.

Curtin, P. A., & Boynton, L. A. (2001). Ethics in public relations: Theory and practice. In R. L. Heath (Ed.), *Handbook of public relations* (pp. 411–421). Thousand Oaks, CA: Sage.

Cushman, J. H., Jr. (2001, February 11). Sub in collision was conducting drill, Navy says. *The New York Times,* pp. 1, 22.

Cutlip, S. M., Center, A. H., & Broom, G. M. (2002). *Effective public relations* (8th ed.). Upper Saddle River, NJ: Prentice-Hall.

Darley, J. M., & Zanna, M. P. (1982). Making moral judgments. *American Scientist, 70,* 515–521.

Daugherty, E. L. (2001). Public relations and social responsibility. In R. L. Heath (Ed.), *Handbook of public relations* (pp. 389–401). Thousand Oaks, CA: Sage.

Davidson, D. V., Knowles, B. E., & Forsythe, L. M. (1998). *Business law* (6th ed.). Cincinnati: West.

Day, K. D., Dong, Q., & Robins, C. (2001). Public relations ethics: An overview and discussion of issues for the 21st century. In R. L. Heath (Ed.), *Handbook of public relations* (pp. 403–409). Thousand Oaks, CA: Sage.

Dershowitz, A. M. (2000, February 2). Baseball's speech police. *The New York Times,* p. A21.

Deutsch, C. H. (2000, August 10). Where rubber meets the road; recall of Firestone tires is aimed at damage control. *The New York Times,* pp. C1, C4.

Dionisopoulos, G. N., & Vibbert, S. L. (1983, November). *Re-fining generic parameters: The case for organizational apologia.* Paper presented at the annual meeting of the Speech Communication Association, Washington, D.C.

Dionisopoulos, G. N., & Vibbert, S. L. (1988). CBS vs. Mobil Oil: Charges of creative bookkeeping in 1979. In H. R. Ryan (Ed.), *Oratorical encounters* (pp. 241–251). New York: Greenwood.

Douglas, M. (1982). *Natural symbols: Explorations in cosmology.* New York: Pantheon.

Dowie, M. (1977, September/October). Pinto madness. *Mother Jones.* Retrieved September 9, 2004 from http://www.motherjones.com/news/feature/1977/09/dowie.html

Dowling, J., & Pfeffer, J. (1975). Organizational legitimacy: Social values and organizational behavior. *Pacific Sociological Review, 18,* 122–136.

Downey, S. (1993). The evolution of the rhetorical genre of apologia. *Western Journal of Communication, 57,* 42–64.

Drew, C. (2001, February 17). Civilian says submarine took precautions. *The New York Times,* p. A13.

Duncan, H. D. (1968). *Symbols in society.* New York: Oxford University Press.

Edelman, M. (1988). *Constructing the political spectacle.* Chicago: University of Chicago Press.

Edgett, R. (2002). Toward an ethical framework for advocacy in public relations. *Journal of Public Relations Research, 14*(1), 1–26.

Eisenberg, E. M. (1984). Ambiguity as strategy in organizational communication. *Communication Monographs, 51,* 227–242.

Egan, T. (1989, March 28). High winds hamper oil spill cleanup off Alaska. *The New York Times,* p. A1.

*Ehime Maru* families demand court-martial. (2001, April 15). *The Daily Yomiuri,* p. 2.

Englehardt, K. J., Sallot, L. M., & Sprintston, J. K. (2004). Compassion without blame: Testing the accident decision flow chart with the crash of ValuJet flight 592. *Journal of Public Relations Research, 16*(2), 127–156.

Enright, R. D., & Fitzgibbons, R. P. (2000). *Helping clients forgive: An empirical guide for resolving anger and restoring hope*. Washington, DC: American Psychological Association.

Enright, R. D., & North, J. (Eds.). (1998). *Exploring forgiveness*. Madison: University of Wisconsin Press.

Epstein, E. E., & Votaw, D. (Eds.). (1978). *Rationality, legitimacy, responsibility: Search for new directions in business and society* (pp. 83–98). Santa Monica, CA: Goodyear.

Epstein, E. M. (1972). The historical enigma of corporate legitimacy. *California Law Review, 60*, 1701–1717.

Ermann, M. D., & Lundman, R. J. (1992). *Corporate and governmental deviance* (4th ed.). New York: Oxford University Press.

Excerpts from Senator Lieberman's talk on President's personal conduct. (1998, September 4). *The New York Times*, p. A18.

Excerpts from the apology by the Pope and Cardinals. (2000, March 13). *The New York Times*, p. A10.

Fabrikant, G. (2001, June 6). Blockbuster settles suits on late fees. *The New York Times*, p. C1.

Families OK end to search for 9 *Ehime Maru* missing. (2001, April 8). *The Daily Yomiuri*, p. 1.

Farrell, T. B., & Goodnight, G. T. (1981). Accidental rhetoric: The root metaphors of Three Mile Island. *Communication Monographs, 48*, 271–300.

Fearn-Banks, K. (1996). *Crisis communications: A casebook approach*. Mahwah, NJ: Lawrence Erlbaum Associates.

Firestone adds data in feud with Ford. (2001, May 20). *The New York Times*, p. 30.

Firestone settles suit over tire separation. (2001, August 29). *The New York Times*, p. C6.

Firestone's update on the voluntary safety recall. (2000, August 23). *The Detroit Free Press*, p. 9A.

First National Bank of Boston, et al. v. Bellotti, Attorney General of Massachusetts, 435 US 765 (1978).

Fisher, W. R. (1970). A motive view of communication. *The Quarterly Journal of Speech, 56*, 131–139.

Fitzpatrick, K. R. (1995). Ten guidelines for reducing legal risks in crisis management. *Public Relations Quarterly, 40*, 33–38.

Fitzpatrick, K. R., & Gauthier, C. C. (2001). Toward a professional responsibility theory of public relations ethics. *Journal of Mass Media Ethics, 16*(2&3), 193–212.

Fitzpatrick, K. R., & Rubin, M. S. (1995). Public relations vs. legal strategies in organizational crisis decisions. *Public Relations Review, 21*, 21–33.

Flynn, K. (2000, June 28). Baseball; Subway plans stalls for Rocker. *The New York Times*, p. D3.

Ford settles more Explorer lawsuits. (2001, October 12). *Kalamazoo Gazette*, p. A5.

Foucault, M. (1980). *The history of sexuality* (R. Hurley, Trans.). New York: Vintage.

Franks, R. (1982). *What's in a nickname? Naming the jungle of college athletics mascots*. Amarillo, TX: Ray Franks.

French, H. W. (2001a, February 14). Politics and traditions propel the search effort. *The New York Times*, p. A20.

French, H. W. (2001b, February 23). Sub accident shakes Japan's security ties with U.S. *The New York Times*, p. A3.

French, H. W. (2001c, February 28). U.S. admiral delivers apology to the Japanese in sub sinking. *The New York Times*, p. A4.

French, H. W. (2002, November 15). Japanese accept U.S. offer in ship accident. *The New York Times*, p. A1.

From statement by Admiral Fargo. (2001, April 24). *The New York Times*, p. A16.

Galbraith, J. K. (1997). *The great crash*. New York: Mariner.

Gilpin, K. N. (2001, July 19). Ford says $752 million loss is mostly from tire costs. *The New York Times*, p. C5.

Globe Staff. (2002, March 28). Goodwin: Problems due to sloppiness. *Boston Globe*, p. C18.

Go play. (2000, Summer). *A & F quarterly*. Reynoldsburg, OH: Abercrombie & Fitch.

Goffman, E. (1971). *Relations in public*. New York: Basic.

Gold, E. R. (1978). Political apologia: The ritual of self-defense. *Communication Monographs, 45*, 306–316.

Goldberg, S. B., Green, E. D., & Sander, F. E. A. (1987). Saying you're sorry. *Negotiation, 3*, 221.

Goodnight, G. T. (1982). The personal, technical, and public spheres of argument: A speculative inquiry into the art of public deliberation. *Journal of the American Forensic Association, 18*, 214–227.

Goodstein, L. (1998, September 15). Testing of a president: The counselors; Clinton selects clerics to give him guidance. *The New York Times*, p. A1.

Goodwin, D. K. (1987). *The Fitzgeralds and the Kennedys*. New York: Simon & Schuster.

Goodwin, D. K. (1994). *No ordinary time*. New York: Simon & Schuster.

Goodwin, D. K. (2002, January 27). How I caused that story. *Time*, p. 69.

Goodwin, D. K. (2003, February 17). The man in our memory. *The New York Times*, p. A21.

Granholm, J. M. (1999, November 17). *Notice of intended action*. (Available from Attorney General, Consumer Protection Division, P.O. Box 30213, Lansing, MI 48909)

Grimaldi, J. V. (2000, October 10). Firestone CEO says apology wasn't admission of fault. *The New York Times*, p. E2.

Gronbeck, B. E. (1978). The rhetoric of political corruption: Sociolinguistic, dialectical, and ceremonial processes. *Quarterly Journal of Speech, 64*, 155–172.

Gronbeck, B. E. (1999). Underestimating generic expectations: Clinton's apologies of August 17, 1998. Retrieved March 29, 2005 from http://www.acjournal.org/holdings /vol2/Iss2/editorials/gronbeck

Grossman, M. A. (2002, March 7). Historian Goodwin says reputation will sustain her. *Pioneer Press*. Retrieved May 10, 2004 from http://www.twincities.com/mld/pioneerpress/ 2815555/htm?template=contentModules/ printstory.jsp

Grove, A. S., Barrett, C. R., & Moore, G. E. (1994, December 21). To owners of Pentium processor-based computers and the pc community. *Wall Street Journal*, p. A7.

Grunig, J. E. (Ed.). (1992a). *Excellence in public relations and communication management*. Hillsdale, NJ: Lawrence Erlbaum Associates.

Grunig, J. E. (1992b). On the effects of marketing, media relations, and public relations: Images, agendas and relationships. In W. Armbrecht, H. Avenarius, & U. Zabel (Eds.), *Image Und PR: Kann Image Gegenstand Einer Public Relations-Wissenschaft Sein?* (pp. 263–295). Wiesbaden, Germany: Westdeutscher Verlag.

Grunig, J. E., & Hunt, T. (1984). *Managing public relations*. New York: Holt, Rinehart and Winston.

Habermas, J. (1975). *Legitimation crisis*. Boston: Beacon.

Habermas, J. (1979). *Communication and the evolution of society* (T. McCarthy, Trans.). Boston: Beacon.

Harrell, J., Ware, B. L., & Linkugel, W. A. (1975). Failure of apology in American politics: Nixon on Watergate. *Speech Monographs, 42,* 245–261.

Harter, L. M., Stephens, R. J., & Japp, P. M. (2000). President Clinton's apology for the Tuskegee Syphilis Experiment: A narrative of remembrance, redefinition, and reconciliation. *The Howard Journal of Communications, 11,* 19–34.

Hearit, K. M. (1992). *Organizations, apologia, and crises of social legitimacy.* Unpublished doctoral dissertation, Purdue University, West Lafayette, IN.

Hearit, K. M. (1994). Apologies and public relations crises at Chrysler, Toshiba, and Volvo. *Public Relations Review, 20,* 113–125.

Hearit, K. M. (1995a). "Mistakes were made": Organizations, apologia, and crises of social legitimacy. *Communication Studies, 46,* 1–17.

Hearit, K. M. (1995b). From "we didn't do it" to "it's not our fault": The use of apologia in public relations crises. In W. N. Elwood (Ed.), *Public relations inquiry as rhetorical criticism* (pp. 117–131). New York: Greenwood.

Hearit, K. M. (1996). The use of counter-attack in public relations crises: The case of General Motors vs. NBC. *Public Relations Review, 22,* 233–248.

Hearit, K. M. (1998). Really blue jean advertisements: The use of strategic offense and apologia by Calvin Klein. *MASC Journal, 33,* 37–57.

Hearit, K. M. (1999). Newsgroups, activist publics, and corporate apologia: The case of Intel and its Pentium chip. *Public Relations Review, 25,* 291–308.

Hearit, K. M. (2001). Corporate apologia: When an organization speaks in defense of itself. In R. L. Heath & G. M. Vasquez (Eds.), *Handbook of public relations* (pp. 595–605). Thousand Oaks, CA: Sage.

Hearit, K. M., & Brown, J. (2004). Merrill Lynch: Corporate apologia and fraud. *Public Relations Review, 30*(4), 459–466.

Hearit, K. M., & Courtright, J. L. (2003a). A social constructionist approach to crisis management: Allegations of sudden acceleration in the Audi 5000. *Communication Studies, 54,* 79–95.

Hearit, K. M., & Courtright, J. L. (2003b). A symbolic approach to crisis management: Sears defense of its auto repair policies. In D. P. Millar & R. L. Heath (Eds.), *Responding to crisis: A rhetorical approach to crisis communication* (pp. 201–213). Mahwah, NJ: Lawrence Erlbaum Associates.

Heath, R. L. (1997). *Strategic issues management: Organizations and public policy challenges.* Beverly Hills, CA: Sage.

Heath, R. L., & Nelson, R. A. (1986). *Issue management: Corporate public policy making in an information age.* Beverly Hills, CA: Sage.

Henriques, D. B., & Barstow, D. (2001, November 15). Red Cross pledges entire terror fund to Sept. 11 victims. *The New York Times,* pp. A1, B10.

Herring, H. B. (2000, March 36). Pope speaks of Holocaust during visit to Israel. *The New York Times,* p. 4-2.

Hilts, P. J. (1992, February 11). Top manufacturer of breast implant replaces its chief. *The New York Times,* p. A1.

Hofstader, R. (1964). *The paranoid style in American politics and other essays.* Chicago: University of Chicago Press.

Holmes, C. W. (1998, October 16). Pope marks 20 momentous years; historians begin debate on legacy of century's longest papal reign. *Milwaukee Journal Sentinel,* p. 1.

Honderich, T. (1988). *A theory of determinism: The mind, neuroscience and life-hopes.* Oxford, UK: Oxford University Press.

Hoover, J. D. (1989). Big boys don't cry: The values constraint in apologia. *Southern Communication Journal, 54*, 235–252.

Hopcke, R. H. (1995). *Persona: Where sacred meets profane.* Boston: Shambhala.

Hughes, J. (1997, October 10). Big jury awards rarely become reality. *Kalamazoo Gazette,* p. A6.

Huxman, S. S., & Bruce, D. B. (1995). Toward a dynamic generic framework of apologia: A case study of Dow Chemical, Vietnam, and the Napalm controversy. *Communication Studies, 46*, 57–72.

Ice, R. (1991). Corporate publics and rhetorical strategies. *Management Communication Quarterly, 4*, 341–362.

In Clinton's remarks: A focus on interdependence and forgiveness. (1998, August 29). *The New York Times,* p. A10.

Ito, T. M. (1997, October 20). Chrysler hit by record jury award. *U.S. News & World Report,* p. 59.

Jackall, R. (1988). *Moral mazes: The world of corporate managers.* New York: Oxford University Press.

Jackall, R. (1997). Moral mazes: Bureaucracy and managerial work. In P. J. Frost, V. V. Mitchell, & W. R. Nord (Eds.), *Organizational reality: Reports from the firing line* (pp. 105–122). Reading, MA: Addison-Wesley.

Jehl, D. (2001, February 12). Clues sought in sub accident; some Japanese fault rescue. *The New York Times,* pp. A1, A18.

Johannesen, R. L. (2001). *Ethics in human communication* (5th ed.). Prospect Heights, IL: Waveland.

Jonsen, A. R., & Toulmin, S. (1988). *The abuse of casuistry: A history of moral reasoning.* Berkeley: University of California Press.

Judge throws out McDonald's lawsuit. (2003, January 24). *CNN.* Retrieved September 9, 2004 from http://www.cnn.com/2003/ALLPOLITICS/01/23/cf.opinion. mcdonalds. lawsuit/

Just minutes might have sufficed to avert collision, sailor says. (2001, March 17). *The New York Times,* p. A9.

Kahn, J. P. (2002, June 1). Goodwin resigns Pulitzer board post. *Boston Globe,* p. F1.

Kahney, L. (2000, February 17). Windows: The next generation. *Wired.* Retrieved September 8, 2004 from http://www.wired.com/news/technology/ 0,1282,34381,00.html

Kane, R. (1996). *The significance of free will.* Oxford, UK: Oxford University Press.

Kaufman, J. B., Kesner, I. F., & Hazen, R. L. (1994, July–August). The myth of full disclosure: A look at organizational communication during crisis. *Business Horizons, 37*, 29–39.

Keenan, J. F., & Shannon, T. A. (Eds.). (1995). *The context of casuistry.* Washington, DC: Georgetown University Press.

Kennedy, R. (1974). *Times to remember.* Garden City, NY: Doubleday.

Kent, M. L., & Taylor, M. (2002). Toward a dialogic theory of public relations. *Public Relations Review, 28*(1), 21–37.

Kepner, T. (2000, June 23). Baseball: Mets notebook; Rocker to be fenced in when Braves visit Shea. *The New York Times,* p. D2.

Kernisky, D. A. (1997). Proactive crisis management and ethical discourse: Dow Chemical's issues management bulletins 1979–1990. *Journal of Business Ethics, 16*(8), 843–853.

Kifner, J. (2001a, April 14). Navy's Court of Inquiry submits its report on submarine collision. *The New York Times,* p. A11.

Kifner, J. (2001b, April 23). Despite sub inquiry, Navy still sees need for guests on ships. *The New York Times*, pp. A1, A12.

Kifner, J. (2001c, April 24). Captain of sub is reprimanded and will quit. *The New York Times*, pp. A1, A16.

Kilgannon, C. (2001, November 12). Red Cross offers to refund gifts for Sept. 11. *The New York Times*, p. B10.

King, C. R. (1998). *Spectacles, sports, and stereotypes: Dis/playing Chief Illiniwek. Colonial discourse, collective memories, and the exhibition of Native American cultures and histories in the contemporary United States*. New York: Garland.

King, C. R., Springwood, C. F., & Vine, D., Jr. (Eds.). (2001). *Team spirits: The Native American mascots controversy*. Lincoln: University of Nebraska Press.

King, P. H. (2002, August 4). As history repeats itself, the scholar becomes the story. *The Los Angeles Times*, p. A1.

Kirk, K. (1936). *Conscience and its problems*. London: Longman.

Kirkpatrick, D. D. (2002a, January 23). Historian says publisher quickly settled copying dispute. *The New York Times*, p. A10.

Kirkpatrick, D. D. (2002b, February 23). Historian says borrowing was wider than known. *The New York Times*, p. A10.

Kirkpatrick, D. D. (2002c, February 28). Writer leaves "NewsHour" in furor over book. *The New York Times*, p. A23.

Kirkpatrick, D. D. (2002d, March 31). Historian's fight for her reputation may be damaging it. *The New York Times*, p. 18.

Koeppel, D. (2000, March 2). Baseball; fan reaction is divided on arbitrator's decision. *The New York Times*, p. D3.

Koesten, J., & Rowland, R. C. (2004). The rhetorical of atonement. *Communication Studies, 12*(4), 341–353.

Kramer, M. R., & Olson, K. M. (2002). The strategic potential of sequencing apologia stases: President Clinton's self-defense in the Monica Lewinsky scandal. *Western Journal of Communication, 66*, 347–368.

Kruse, N. W. (1977). Motivational factors in non-denial apologia. *Central States Speech Journal, 28*, 13–23.

Kruse, N. W. (1981a). The scope of apologetic discourse: Establishing generic parameters. *Southern Speech Communication Journal, 46*, 278–291.

Kruse, N. W. (1981b). Apologia in team sport. *Quarterly Journal of Speech, 67*, 270–283.

KU revokes invitation to author. (2002, March 13). *The Topeka Capital-Journal*, n.p. Retrieved March 21, 2004 from www.cjonline.com/cgibin/printint2000.pl

Kupchella, C. E. (2000, December 21). *Statement regarding State Board of Higher Education decision*. Retrieved July 7, 2004 from http://www.und.edu/president/html/statements/122100.html

Kupchella, C. E. (2001, March). *Following is a letter from President Kupchella*. Retrieved July 7, 2004 from http://www.und.edu/president/html/statements/march2001.html

Lash, J. (1971). *Eleanor and Franklin*. New York: Norton.

Latané, B., & Darley, J. M. (1970). *The unresponsive bystander: Why doesn't he help?* New York: Appleton-Century-Crofts.

Lazare, A. (1995, January–February). "Go ahead, say you're sorry." *Psychology Today, 28*, 40–42.

Leach, E. R. (1968). Ritual. In *International encyclopedia of the social sciences* (Vol. 13, pp. 520–526). New York: Macmillan.

Lee, F. R. (2003, October 4). Are more people cheating? Despite ample accounts of dishonesty, a moral decline is hard to calculate. *The New York Times,* p. B7.

Leeper, K. A. (1996). Public relations ethics and communitarianism: A preliminary investigation. *Public Relations Review, 22*(2), 163–179.

Leeper, R. V. (1996). Moral objectivity, Jurgen Habermas's discourse ethics, and public relations. *Public Relations Review, 22*(2), 133–150.

Leites, E. (Ed.). (1988). *Conscience and casuistry in early modern Europe.* Cambridge, UK: Cambridge University Press.

Lessiter, M. (1989). *The college names of the games: The stories behind the nicknames of 293 college sports teams.* Lincolnwood, IL: NTC/Contemporary.

Lessl, T. M. (1989). The priestly voice. *The Quarterly Journal of Speech, 75,* 183–197.

Levy, T. L. (1986). *Organizational rhetoric: Multinational corporations legitimation in Brazil, France, and the United States.* Unpublished doctoral dissertation, University of Maryland, College Park.

Lieberman, J. (1981). *The litigious society.* New York: Basic.

Lindsey, F. D. (1985). Leviticus. In J. F. Walvoord & R. B. Zuck (Eds.), *The Bible knowledge commentary: Old Testament* (pp. 163–214). Wheaton, IL: Victor.

Ling, D. A. (1972). A pentadic analysis of senator Edward Kennedy's address to the people of Massachusetts July 25, 1969. *Central States Speech Journal, 21,* 81–86.

Lipsyte, R. (2000, January 16). Backtalk; the vanity of human wishes, once again on display. *The New York Times,* p. 8-13.

Liptak, A. (2002a, August 15). Court has dubious record as a class-action leader. *The New York Times,* p. A14.

Liptak, A. (2002b, August 26). Debate grows on jury's role in injury cases. *The New York Times,* p. A1.

Liptak, A. (2002c, November 17). Playing the angles in class-action lawsuits. *The New York Times,* p. 3-11.

Look at sunken ship halted to repair robot. (2001, February 19). *The New York Times,* p. A10.

Lyall, S. (1997, June 22). The "McLibel" verdict; her majesty's court has ruled: McDonald's burgers are not poison. *The New York Times,* p. 4-7.

Making it right. (2001, April 6). *USA Today,* p. 11A.

Marcus, A. A., & Goodman, R. S. (1991). Victims and shareholders: The dilemmas of presenting corporate policy during a crisis. *Academy of Management Journal, 34,* 281–305.

Marquis, C. (2001, February 9). 9 are missing off Pearl Harbor after U.S. submarine collides with Japanese vessel. *The New York Times,* p. A16.

Marx, L. (1964). *The machine in the garden.* New York: Oxford University Press.

Mayer, C. E., & Swoboda, F. (2000, September 7). "I come … to apologize"; Firestone CEO hears coverup allegations on hill." *The New York Times,* p. A1.

McFadden, R. D. (1986, February 18). Maker of Tylenol discontinuing all over-counter drug capsules. *The New York Times,* p. A1.

McGeehan, P. (2002, May 22). $100 million fine for Merrill Lynch. *The New York Times,* p. A1.

McGinniss, J. (1993). *The last brother.* New York: Simon & Schuster.

McGraw, D. (1996, January 8). Tipping the scales of justice. *U.S. News & World Report,* pp. 39–40.

McKinley, J. C., Jr. (2000, January 9). Ideas & trends; weighing therapy for a narrow mind. *The New York Times,* p. 4-5.

McTaggart, L. (1983). *Kathleen Kennedy: Her life and times*. New York: Bantam Dell.

McTaggart, L. (2002, March 16). Fame can't excuse a plagiarist. *The New York Times,* p. A15.

Mehegan, D. (2002a, March 2). Goodwin to speak publicly on plagiarism controversy. *Boston Globe,* p. F3.

Mehegan, D. (2002b, March 5). Goodwin withdraws from Pulitzer judging. *Boston Globe,* p. E4.

Mehegan, D. (2002c, March 8). Goodwin defends her role as a historian. *Boston Globe,* p. A3.

Mehegan, D. (2002d, March 12). Crimson to Goodwin: Quit Harvard board. *Boston Globe,* p. E6.

Mehegan, D. (2002e, March 24). When words collide; as the plagiarism charges settle in, historians say Doris Kearns Goodwin remains a serious author—but that doesn't mean they excuse her methods. *Boston Globe,* p. E1.

Meyer, J. W. (1983). Organizational factors affecting legalization in education. In J. W. Meyer & W. R. Scott (Eds.), *Organizational Environments: Ritual and Rationality* (pp. 219–221). Beverly Hills: Sage.

Middleton, K. R., & Chamberlin, B. F. (1988). *The law of public communication*. New York: Longman.

Miller, C. R. (1984). Genre as social action. *Quarterly Journal of Speech, 70,* 151–167.

Miller, R. B. (1996). *Casuistry and modern ethics: A poetics of practical reasoning*. Chicago: University of Chicago Press.

Millon, D. (2001). The ambiguous significance of corporate personhood [Electronic version]. *Stanford Agora, 2*(1), 39–58.

Minow, M. (1998). *Between vengeance and forgiveness: Facing history after genocide and mass violence*. Boston: Beacon.

Mitchell, A. (1998, December 12). Testing of a president: The vote; panel, on party lines, votes impeachment; Clinton voices remorse, invites censure. *The New York Times,* p. A1.

Mitchell, A. (1999, February 13). The president's acquittal: The overview; Clinton acquitted decisively: no majority for either charge. *The New York Times,* p. A1.

Mitroff, I. I., & Kilmann, R. H. (1984). Corporate tragedies: Teaching companies to cope with evil. *New Management, 1,* 48–53.

Mogi, C. (2001, April 24). Japanese government satisfied with sub verdict; victims' families bitter. *The Associated Press,* n.p. Retrieved November 6, 2001 from Lexis/Nexis database.

Morgenson, G., & Justice, G. (2005, February 20). Taking care of business, his way. *The New York Times,* p. 3-1.

Morgenson, G. &, McGeehan, P. (2002, December 20). Corporate conduct: The overview; Wall Street firms are ready to pay $1 billion in fines. *The New York Times,* p. A1.

Mother files complaint against Abercrombie & Fitch. (1999, December 2). *Associated Press,* n.p. Retrieved November 11, 2000 from Lexis/Nexis database.

Moulton, H. K. (1978). *The analytical Greek lexicon revised/edited by Harold K. Moulton*. Grand Rapids, MI: Zondervan.

Murray, E., & Shohen, S. (1992, February). Lessons from the Tylenol tragedy on surviving a corporate crisis. *Medical Marketing & Media, 27*(2), 14–15, 18–19.

Myers, S. L. (2001a, February 18). Navy to convene a public inquiry on sub accident. *The New York Times,* pp. 1, 25.

Myers, S. L. (2001b, March 3). Submarine conducted only a brief surface check, board says. *The New York Times*, p. A8.

Myers, S. L. (2001c, March 6). Errors by submarine crew led to sinking, court is told. *The New York Times*, p. A10.

Myers, S. L. (2001d, March 7). Orders on sub raised doubts, officer says. *The New York Times*, p. A17.

Myers, S. L. (2001e, March 8). Defense lawyer challenges idea that sub crew rushed. *The New York Times*, p. A14.

Myers, S. L. (2001f, March 9). Admiral says sub captain did not act criminally. *The New York Times*, p. A10.

Myers, S. L. (2001g, March 10). Investigator faults periscope search by captain of submarine. *The New York Times*, p. A6.

Myers, S. L. (2001h, March 12). Sub's crew may have hesitated to question a trusted captain. *The New York Times*, p. A10.

Myers, S. L. (2001i, March 13). Admiral says cruise just for sake of civilians violated policy. *The New York Times*, p. A17.

Myers, S. L. (2001j, March 15). Captain of trawler testifies on collision with submarine. *The New York Times*, p. A18.

Myers, S. L. (2001k, April 20). Officials say captain of sub won't be tried. *The New York Times*, p. A1.

Myers, S. L., & Dao, J. (2001, March 4). Sub's only mission on day of incident was civilian tour. *The New York Times*, pp. 1, 24.

Namenwirth, J. Z., Miller, R. L., & Weber, R. P. (1981). Organizations have opinions: A redefinition of publics. *Public Opinion Quarterly, 45*, 463–476.

Nathan, S. (2000, August 1). Safety groups want SUVs recalled because of tire concerns. *USA Today*, p. 1B.

Naughty or nice. (1999, Christmas). *A & F Quarterly*. Reynoldsburg, OH: Abercrombie & Fitch.

Navy divers find first body on Japanese trawler sunk by sub. (2001, October 18). *The New York Times*, p. A18.

Navy stonewalling. (2001, February 17). *The New York Times*, p. A16.

Navy to raise *Ehime Maru* from depths. (2001, July 22). *The New York Times*, p. 23.

New clues from the *Greeneville*. (2001, February, 23). *The New York Times*, p. A18.

Noddings, N. (1984). *Caring, a feminine approach to ethics & moral education*. Berkeley: University of California Press.

Notz, J. R. (1997). Prearrest silence as evidence of guilt: What you don't say shouldn't be used against you. *The University of Chicago Law Review, 64*, 1009–1037.

Nuessel, F. (1994). Objectionable sports team designations. *Names: A Journal of Onomastics, 42*, 101–119.

Olney, B. (2000, January 13). Baseball; Rocker speaks out, professing no evil intent. *The New York Times*, p. D2.

Oppel, R. A., Jr. (2001a, August 22). Texas jurors deliberate in first tire lawsuit since big recall. *The New York Times*, p. C3.

Oppel, R. A., Jr. (2001b, August 25). Bridgestone agrees to pay $7.5 million in Explorer crash. *The New York Times*, p. C1.

Orr, C. J. (1978). How shall we say: "Reality is socially constructed through communication?" *Central States Speech Journal, 29*, 263–274.

Panel says replacement tires may have higher failure rates. (2001, June 19). *The New York Times*, p. C4.

Papal apology. (1998, April 8). Answering for the past. *The Newshour*. Retrieved October 28, 2004 from http://www.pbs.org/newshour/bb/religion/jan-june98/vatican_4–8.html

Partridge, E. (1958). *Origins: A short etymological dictionary of modern English*. New York: Macmillan.

Patel, A., & Reinsch, L. (2003). Companies can apologize: Corporate apologies and legal liability. *Business Communication Quarterly, 66*, 17–26.

Payne, A. D. (1989a). *Coping with failure: The therapeutic uses of rhetoric*. Columbia: University of South Carolina Press.

Payne, A. D. (1989b). *The wizard of oz*: Therapeutic rhetoric in a contemporary media ritual. *Quarterly Journal of Speech, 75*, 25–39.

Pearlman, J. (1999, December 23). At full blast. *Sports Illustrated*, pp. 61–62, 64.

Perelman, C., & Olbrechts-Tyteca, L. (1969). *The new rhetoric*. (J. Wilkinson & P. Weaver, Trans.). Notre Dame, IN: University of Notre Dame Press.

Perera, S. B. (1986). *The scapegoat complex: Toward a mythology of shadow and guilt*. Toronto: Inner City.

Perrow, C. (1984). *Normal accidents*. New York: Basic.

Petrucci, C. J. (2002). Research evidence: What we know about apology. *Behavioral Science and the Law, 20*, 337–362.

Phillips, K. R. (Ed.). (2004). *Framing public memory*. Tuscaloosa: University of Alabama Press.

Pickler, N. (1999a, November 18). Granholm orders Abercrombie to stop selling catalog to minors. *The Associated Press*, n.p. Retrieved November 11, 2000 from Lexis/Nexis database.

Pickler, N. (1999b, November 19). Abercrombie & Fitch agrees to card young catalog buyers. *The Associated Press*, n.p. Retrieved November 11, 2000 from Lexis/Nexis database.

Pines, W. L. (1985). How to handle a PR crisis: Five dos and five don'ts. *Public Relations Quarterly, 30*(2), 16–19.

*Plato's apology of Socrates* (T. G. West, Trans.). (1979). Ithaca, NY: Cornell University Press.

Pope repeats an apology. (1999, September 2). *The New York Times*, p. A8.

Pope to apologize for sins committed by Roman Catholics. (2000, March 7). *CNN*. Retrieved October 28, 2004 from http://archives.cnn.com/2000/WORLD/europe/03/07/vatican.pardon.02/

Poussaint, A. F. (2000, January 9). What a Rorschach can't gauge. *The New York Times*, p. 4-19.

Pratt, C. B. (1994). Applying classical ethical theories to ethical decision making in public relations: Perrier's product recall. *Management Communication Quarterly, 8*, 70–94.

Purloined letters. (2002, February 27). *USA Today*, p. A12.

Purnick, J. (2002, February 21). For Red Cross, a new round of complaints. *The New York Times*, p. B1.

Rawson, R., & Thomsen, S. (1998). Purifying a tainted corporate image: Odwalla's response to an E. coli poisoning. *Public Relations Quarterly, 43*, 35–46.

Recall of 4 million Explorers is sought. (2001, June 4). *The New York Times*, p. C2.

Reed, D. (2003, April 22). AA transport union to vote again; Carty apologizes about undisclosed perks. *USA Today*. Retrieved September 9, 2004 from http://www.usatoday.com/travel/news/2003/2003-04-22-american-update.htm

Rocker blasts New York, drawing ire. (1999, December 23). *The New York Times*, p. D2.

Rosenfield, L. W. (1968). A case study in speech criticism: The Nixon–Truman analog. *Speech Monographs, 35*, 435–450.

Ross, W. D. (1930). *The right and the good.* New York: Oxford University Press.

Rothenbuhler, E. W. (1998). *Ritual communication: From everyday conversation to mediated ceremony.* Thousand Oaks, CA: Sage.

Rowland, R. C., & Jerome, A. M. (2004). On organizational apologia: A reconceptualization. *Communication Theory, 14,* 191–211.

Rueckert, W. (1982). *Kenneth Burke and the drama of human relations* (2nd ed.). Berkeley: University of California Press.

Ryan, H. R. (1982). Kategoria and apologia: On their rhetorical criticism as a speech set. *Quarterly Journal of Speech, 68,* 254–261.

Sack, K. (1998, August 18). Testing of a president: The reaction; president's explanation apparently fails to quiet the Republicans or fire up the Democrats. *The New York Times,* p. A16.

Sandman, P. M. (1993). *Responding to community outrage: Strategies for effective risk communication.* Fairfax, VA: American Industrial Hygiene Association.

Saulny, S. (2002, February 1). Red Cross announces plans for rest of disaster funds. *The New York Times,* p. B3.

Scher, S. J., & Darley, J. M. (1997). How effective are the things people say to apologize? Effects of the realization of the apology speech act. *Journal of the Psycholinguistic Research, 26,* 127–140.

Schiappa, E. (2003). *Defining reality.* Carbondale: Southern Illinois University Press.

Schlesinger, A., Jr., Brinkley, D., Dallek, R., & Halberstam, D. (2003, October 25). A historian's integrity [Letter to the editor]. *The New York Times,* p. A18.

Schultz, P. D., & Seeger, M. W. (1991). Corporate centered apologia: Iacocca in defense of Chrysler. *Speaker and Gavel, 28,* 50–60.

Sciolino, E. (2001a, February 22). Sailor says sub tracked ship but guests were distraction. *The New York Times,* pp. A1, A22.

Sciolino, E. (2001b, February 26). Sub's commander expresses regret to victims' families. *The New York Times,* p. A10.

Sciolino, E. (2001c, March 1). Sub commander apologizes more directly to families. *The New York Times,* p. A12.

Sciolino, E. (2001d, April 15). Navy panel urges no court-martial for sub's skipper. *The New York Times,* pp. 1, 18.

Scott, M. H., & Lyman, S. M. (1968). Accounts. *American Sociological Review, 33,* 46–52.

Searls, H. (1969). *The lost prince: Young Joe, the forgotten Kennedy.* New York: World.

Seeger, M. W., Sellnow, T. L., & Ulmer, R. R. (1998). Communication, organization, and crisis. In B. R. Burleson (Ed.), *Communication yearbook, 21* (pp. 231–275). Thousand Oaks, CA: Sage.

Seeger, M. W., Sellnow, T. L., & Ulmer, R. R. (2003). *Communication and organizational crisis.* Westport, CT: Praeger.

Seelye, K. Q. (1998, August 3). Lawmakers call for explanation in Lewinsky case. *The New York Times,* p. A1.

Seelye, K. Q., & Henriques, D. B. (2001, October 27). Red Cross president quits, saying that the board left her no other choice. *The New York Times,* p. B9.

Seglin, J. (2002, December 15). Wanted: More civility, not civil suits. *The New York Times,* p. 3-4.

Seib, P., & Fitzpatrick, K. R. (1995). *Public relations ethics.* Fort Worth, TX: Harcourt Brace.

Sellnow, T. L. (1993). Scientific argument in organizational crisis communication: The case of Exxon. *Argumentation & Advocacy, 30*(1), 28–43.

Sellnow, T., & Seeger, M. W. (1989). Crisis messages: Wall Street and the Reagan administration after black Monday. *Speaker and Gavel, 26,* 9–18.

Sellnow, T. L., & Seeger, M. (2001). Exploring the boundaries of crisis communication: The case of the 1997 Red River Valley flood. *Communication Studies, 52*(2), 154–169.

Sen, F., & Egelhoff, W. (1991). Six years and counting: Learning from crisis management at Bhopal. *Public Relations Review, 17*(1), 69–84.

Sennett, R. (1980). *Authority.* New York: Vintage.

Shepard, C. (1992, February 16). Perks, privileges and power in the nonprofit world. *The Washington Post,* p. A1.

Silverstone, R. (1988). Television myth and culture. In J. W. Carey (Ed.), *Media, myths, and narratives: Television and the press* (pp. 20–47). Newbury Park, CA: Sage.

Simons, H. W. (2000). A dilemma-centered analysis of Clinton's August 17th apologia: Implications for rhetorical theory and method. *The Quarterly Journal of Speech, 86,* 438–453.

Simpson, J. A., & Weiner, E. S. C. (1989).*The Oxford English dictionary.* New York: Oxford University Press.

Sims, C. (2000a, August, 10). A takeover with problems for Japanese tire maker. *The New York Times,* p. C4.

Sims, C. (2000b, August 11). Bridgestone to register record charge. *The New York Times,* p. C2.

Sims, C. (2001, April 25). Japanese outraged at commander's fate. *The New York Times,* p. A16.

Small, W. J. (1991). Exxon Valdez: How to spend billions and still get a black eye. *Public Relations Review, 17,* 9–25.

Smoker's award cut to $28 million. (2002, December 19). *The New York Times,* p. A30.

Snyder, C. R., Higgins, R. L., & Stucky, R. J. (1983). *Excuses: Masquerades in search of grace.* New York: Wiley.

Spindel, C. (2000). *Dancing at halftime: Sports and the controversy over American Indian mascots.* New York: New York University Press.

Sproule, J. M. (1988). The new managerial rhetoric and the old criticism. *Quarterly Journal of Speech, 74,* 468–486.

St. Cloud State asks North Dakota to leave "Fighting Sioux" nickname at home. (2001, October 22). *Associated Press,* n.p. Retrieved June 25, 2002 from Lexis/Nexis database.

Stanley, A. (2000a, March 2). Vatican outline issued on apology for historical failings. *The New York Times,* p. A10.

Stanley, A. (2000b, March 13). Pope asks forgiveness for errors of the church over 2,000 years. *The New York Times,* pp. 1, 10.

Steinfels, P. (2000, March 18). Reflecting on a papal apology with few precedents in view of an abiding tension. *The New York Times,* p. B6.

Sterngold, J. (2001a, March 20). Sailor admits not reporting Japanese boat. *The New York Times,* pp. A1, A17.

Sterngold, J. (2001b, March 21). Captain of sub accepts blame, and spreads it. *The New York Times,* pp. A1, A15.

Sterngold, J. (2001c, October 13). Navy's recovery effort begins for trawler sunk in accident. *The New York Times,* p. A8.

Sterngold, J., & Myers, S. L. (2001, February 14). Civilians in sub sat at 2 controls when ships hit. *The New York Times,* pp. A1, A20.

Stodghill, R. (1990, April 11). Judge fines Chrysler on mail fraud. *Detroit Free Press*, pp. 1A, 17A.

Stone, C. D. (1975). *Where the law ends: Social control of corporate behavior*. New York: Harper & Row.

Stout, D. (2000, December 7). 29 more U.S. deaths linked to Firestone tires. *The New York Times*, p. C7.

Strom, S. (2001, February 18). Sub incident erodes trust in Japan chief and the U.S. *The New York Times*, p. 15.

Sturges, D. L. (1994). Communicating through crisis: A strategy for organizational survival. *Management Communication Quarterly, 7*, 297–316 .

Submarine commander to limit his account. (2001, February 20). *The New York Times*, p. A19.

Sugimoto, N. (1999). *Japanese apology across disciplines*. Hauppauge, NY: Nova.

Sullivan, J. (2001, October 5). Engelstad proud of new arena, Fighting Sioux tradition. *Associated Press*, n.p. Retrieved June 25, 2002 from Lexis/Nexis database.

Tabris, M. D. (1984). Crisis management. In B. Cantor & C. Burger (Eds.), *Experts in action: Inside public relations* (pp. 64–67). White Plains, NY: Longman.

Takaku, S. (2001). The effects of apology and perspective taking on interpersonal forgiveness: A dissonance-attribution model of interpersonal forgiveness. *Journal of Social Psychology, 141(4)*, 494–508.

Taking the Greeneville case to trial. (2001, March 22). *The New York Times*, p. A26.

Tanikawa, M. (2000, September 12). Bridgestone president admits tire quality-control problems. *The New York Times*, p. C12.

Tanikawa, M. (2001a, January 12). Chief of Bridgestone says he will resign. *The New York Times*, p. W1.

Tanikawa, M. (2001b, June 2). Bridgestone split from Ford is seen as most un-Japanese. *The New York Times*, p. C2.

Tannen, D. (1996, July 21). I'm sorry, I won't apologize. *The New York Times Magazine*. Retrieved November 10, 2004 from http://www.georgetown.edu/faculty/tannend/nyt072196.htm

Tannen, D. (1998, August 23). Apologies: What it means to say "sorry." *Washington Post*. Retrieved November 10, 2004 from http://www.georgetown.edu/faculty/tannend/post082398.htm

Tavuchis, N. (1991). *Mea culpa: A sociology of apology and reconciliation*. Stanford, CA: Stanford University Press.

Teammate of Rocker doesn't buy explanation. (2000, January 16). *The New York Times*, p. 8-11.

Testing of a president: In his own words. (1998a, August 18). *The New York Times*, p. A12.

Testing of a president; President Clinton's address at the National Prayer Breakfast. (1998b, September 12). *The New York Times*, p. A12.

Text of letter to Ford from Bridgestone. (2001, May 22). *The New York Times*, p. C4.

Thackaberry, J. (1996, April). *Redefinition of complex corporate crime through apologia: A case study of E. F. Hutton & Co*. Paper presented to the Central States Communication Association, St. Paul, MN.

Thackaberry, J. A. (2004). Discursive opening and closing in organizational self-study: Culture as trap and tool in wildland firefighting safety. *Management Communication Quarterly, 17*, 319–359.

Thayer, J. H. (1889). *A Greek–English lexicon of the New Testament, being Grimm's Wilke's Clavis Novi Testamenti, tr., rev., and enl. by Joseph Henry Thayer*. New York: American Book Company.

The apology. (2000, June 30). *The Atlanta Journal and Constitution*, p. 1D.

The Crimson Staff. (2002, March 11). The consequence of plagiarism. Harvard Crimson. Retrieved May 10, 2004 from http://thecrimson.com/printerfriendly.aspx?ref=180483

The difficult case of John Rocker. (2000, February 5). *The New York Times*, p. A14.

The *Forbes* 500s. (2003, March 28). *Forbes*. Retrieved August 27, 2004 from http://www.forbes.com/2003/03/26/500sland.html

The Holy Bible [New International Version]. (1973/1984). Grand Rapids, MI: Zondervan.

The president under fire; Clinton's comments denying an affair. (1998a, January 27). *The New York Times*, p. A14.

The president under fire; excerpts from interview with Mrs. Clinton on NBC. (1998b, January 28). *The New York Times*, p. A22.

The president under fire; excerpts from statements by White House and president on accusations. (1998c, January 22). *The New York Times*, p. A24.

Torpey, J. (Ed.). (2003). *Politics and the past: On repairing historical injustices*. Lanham, MD: Rowman & Littlefield.

Trustees of Dartmouth College v. Woodward, 17 U.S. (4 Wheat.) 518, 636-37 (1819).

Turner, V. (1982). *From ritual to theater: The human seriousness of play*. New York: PAJ Publications.

Turner supports Rocker. (2000, January 21). *The New York Times*, p. D4.

Tyler, L. (1997). Liability means never being able to say you're sorry: Corporate guilt, legal constraints, and defensiveness in corporate communication. *Management Communication Quarterly, 11,* 51–73.

Ulmer, R. R., & Sellnow, T. L. (2000). Consistent questions of ambiguity in organizational crisis communication: Jack in the Box as a case study. *Journal of Business Ethics, 25,* 143–155.

UND Senate Resolution. (2001, January 11). *The University of North Dakota*. Retrieved July 7, 2004 from http://www.und.edu/org/bridges/index2.html

van Es, R., & Meijlink, T. L. (2000). The dialogic turn of public relations ethics. *Journal of Business Ethics, 27,* 69–77.

Van Natta, D., Jr. & Bennet, J. (1998, August 7). Lewinsky said to detail Clinton affair. *The New York Times*, p. A1.

Vanderford, H. (1996). What's in a name? Heritage or hatred: The school mascot controversy. *Journal of Law and Education, 25,* 381–388.

Vanderford, M. L., & Smith, D. H. (1996). *The silicone breast implant story: Communication and uncertainty*. Mahwah, NJ: Lawrence Erlbaum Associates.

Vecsey, G. (1999, December 24). Sports of the Times; Ted should just fire the bigot. *The New York Times*, p. D1.

Vecsey, G. (2000, June 5). Sports of the Times; Majority of Braves wants Rocker gone. *The New York Times*, p. D1.

Vibbert, C. B. (1990). Freedom of speech and corporations: Supreme Court strategies of the extension of the First Amendment. *Communication, 12,* 19–34.

Vibbert, S. L., & Bostdorff, D. M. (1992). Issue management and the "lawsuit crisis." In C. Conrad (Ed.), *The ethical nexus: Communication, values, and organizational decisions* (pp. 103–120). Norwood, NJ: Ablex.

Waddle speaks, offers apology. (2001, March 9). *Asahi News Service*, p. 1.

Wagatsuma, H., & Rosett, A. (1986). The implications of apology: Law and culture in Japan and the United States. *Law & Society Review, 20*(4), 461–497.

Wald, M. L. (2000a, September 21). Ford tested Firestone tires on pickup, not on Explorer. *The New York Times*, p. C12.

Wald, M. L. (2000b, September 22). In testimony, Firestone puts onus on Ford. *The New York Times*, p. C1.

Wald, M. L. (2000c, October 11). House passes bill on tire and car defects. *The New York Times*, p. C2.

Wald, M. L. (2000d, October 12). Bill on auto-defect reporting passes Congress. *The New York Times*, p. C21.

Wald, M. L. (2000e, October 20). Safety; checking tire pressure from the driver's seat. *The New York Times*, p. F1.

Wald, M. L. (2001, June 20). House hearings on Ford and Firestone clarify little. *The New York Times*, p. C4.

Wald, M. L., & Bradsher, K. (2000, September 6). Questions on tire-defect data arise as hearings draw near. *The New York Times*, p. C1.

Wallace, B. (1998, January 19). The politics of apology. *Maclean's, 111*(3), 33.

Wal-Mart Litigation Project. (n.d.). *Tracking litigation against the world's largest retailer.* Retrieved January 14, 2004 from http://www.wal-martlitigation.com

Ware, B. L., & Linkugel, W. A. (1973). They spoke in defense of themselves: On the generic criticism of apologia. *Quarterly Journal of Speech, 59*, 273–283.

Weick, K. (1988). Enacted sensemaking in a crisis situation. *Journal of Management Studies, 25*, 305–317.

Weiner, B., Graham, S., Peter, O., & Zmuidnas, M. (1991). Public confession and forgiveness. *Journal of Personality, 59*(2), 281–312.

Wells, M. (2000, March 20). Anticlimax. *Forbes*, p. 58.

Whyte, W. H., Jr. (1956). *The organizational man.* Garden City, NY: Doubleday.

Wiesenthal, S. (1998). *The sunflower: On the possibilities and limits of forgiveness.* New York: Schocken.

Wild & willing. (2000, Spring). *A & F Quarterly.* Reynoldsburg, OH: Abercrombie & Fitch.

Williams, C. (1997). Intel's Pentium chip crisis: An ethical analysis. *IEEE Transactions on Professional Communication, 40*, 13–19.

Williams, D. E., & Treadaway, G. (1992). Exxon and the Valdez accident: A failure in crisis communication. Communication Studies, 43, 56–64.

Williams, S. L., & Moffitt, M. A. (1997). Corporate image as an impression formation process: Prioritizing personal, organizational, and environmental audience factors. *Journal of Public Relations Research, 9*(4), 237–258.

Willing, R. (2001, August 13). Lawsuits a volume business at Wal-Mart. *USA Today*. Retrieved January 14, 2004 from http://www.nfsi.org/walmart/Lawsuits%20a%20volume%20business%20at%20Wal-Mart.htm

Winerip, M. (2001, January 9). Ford and Firestone settle suit over Explorer crash. *The New York Times*, pp. C1, C11.

Worthington, E. L. (Ed). (1998). *Dimensions of forgiveness: Psychological research and theological perspectives.* Chicago: Templeton Foundation Press.

Yamaguchi, M. (2002, December 15). Waddle's Japan visit no cause for fanfare. *Honolulu Star-Bulletin.* Retrieved October 28, 2004 from http://starbulletin.com/2002/12/15/news/story5.html

Yardley, J. (2002, March 4). In search of the appropriate euphemism. *Washington Post*, p. C2.

Your safety is our top priority. (2000, September 3). *The New York Times*, p. 21.

Zald, M. N. (1978). On the social control of industries. *Social Forces, 57*, 79–102.

# Author Index

# Subject Index